Taxcafe.co.uk Tax Guides

How to Avoid Tax on Foreign Property

By Carl Bayley BSc ACA

Important Legal Notices:

Taxcafe®
TAX GUIDE – "How to Avoid Tax on Foreign Property"

Published by:
Taxcafe UK Limited
214 High St
Kirkcaldy KY1 1JT
United Kingdom
Tel: (01592) 560081

First Edition   January 2008

ISBN 1 904608 66 3

Disclaimer
Before reading or relying on the content of this Tax Guide, please read
carefully the disclaimer on the last page which applies. If you have
queries then please contact the publisher at team@taxcafe.co.uk.

About the Author

Carl Bayley is the author of a series of tax guides designed specifically for the layman. Carl's particular speciality is his ability to take the weird, complex and inexplicable world of taxation and set it out in the kind of clear, straightforward language that taxpayers themselves can understand. As he often says himself, "my job is to translate 'tax' into English".

Carl enjoys his role as a tax author, as he explains: "Writing these guides gives me the opportunity to use the skills and knowledge learned over more than twenty years in the tax profession for the benefit of a wider audience. The most satisfying part of my success as an author is the chance to give the average person the same standard of advice as the 'big guys' at a price which everyone can afford."

Carl takes the same approach when speaking on taxation, a role he frequently undertakes with great enthusiasm, including his highly acclaimed series of seminars at the London Homebuyer and Property Investor Shows and his annual 'Budget Breakfast' for the Institute of Chartered Accountants.

In addition to being a recognised author and speaker on the subject, Carl has often spoken on property taxation on radio and television. Most recently, he was featured on BBC Radio 2's Jeremy Vine Show.

Carl began his career as a Chartered Accountant in 1983 with one of the 'Big 4' accountancy firms. After qualifying as a double prize-winner, he immediately began specialising in taxation.

After honing his skills with several major international firms, Carl began the new millennium by launching his own tax and accounting practice, Bayley Miller Limited, through which he provides advice on a wide variety of taxation issues, especially property taxation, Inheritance Tax planning and tax planning for small and medium-sized businesses.

Carl is a member of the governing Council of the Institute of Chartered Accountants in England and Wales and a former Chairman of the Institute Members in Scotland group. He has co-organised the annual Peebles Tax Conference for the last six years.

When he isn't working, Carl takes on the equally taxing challenges of hill walking and writing poetry and fiction. Carl lives in Scotland with his partner Isabel and has four children.

Dedication

For the Past,

Firstly, I dedicate this book to the memory of those I have loved and lost:

First of all, to my beloved mother Diana – what would you think if you could see me now? The memory of your love warms me still. Thank you for making it all possible;

To my dear grandfather, Arthur - your wise words still come back to guide me; and to my loving grandmothers, Doris and Winifred;

Between you, you left me with nothing I could spend, but everything I need.

Also to my beloved friend and companion, Dawson, who waited so patiently for me to come home every night and who left me in the middle of our last walk together. Thank you for all those happy miles; I still miss you son.

For the Present,

Above all, I must dedicate this book to the person who stands, like a shining beacon, at the centre of every part of my life: Isabel, my 'life support system', whose unflinching support has seen me through the best and the worst. Whether anyone will ever call me a 'great man' I do not know, but I do know that I have a great woman behind me.

Without her help, support and encouragement, this book, and the others I have written, could never have been.

For the Future,

Finally, I also dedicate this book to four very special young people: Michelle, Louise, James and Robert.

I am so very proud of every one of you and I can only hope that I, in turn, will also be able to leave each of you with everything that you need.

Thanks

First and foremost, I must say an enormous thank you to Isabel: for all her help researching everything from obscure points of tax legislation to popular girls' names in Asia; for reading countless drafts; for making sure I stop to eat and sleep; for putting up with me when I'm under pressure and, most of all, for keeping me company into the 'wee small hours' on many a long and otherwise lonely night. I simply cannot ever thank her enough for everything that she does for me, but I intend to spend the rest of my life trying!

The next biggest thanks have to go to my good friend, colleague and 'comrade-in-arms', Nick, who believed in me long before I did. Thanks for keeping the faith mate.

Thanks to the rest of the Taxcafe team for their help in making these books far more successful than I could ever have dreamed.

I would like to thank my old friend and mentor, Peter Rayney, for his inspiration and for showing me that tax and humour can mix.

Thanks to the following for their help with my foreign property tax research:

> Everywhere: Isabel (of course!)
> Nearly Everywhere: Nick & the team
> Dubai: Michelle & Dean
> Spain: Rosemary & John

And last, but far from least, thanks to Ann for keeping us right!

C.B., Roxburghshire, January 2008

Contents

Contents (Cont ...)

Contents (Cont ...)

Contents (Cont ...)

Contents (Cont ...)

Contents (Cont ...)

Contents (Cont ...)

Introduction

By the author

It is now almost six years since I wrote the first edition of '*How To Avoid Property Tax*' in response to the huge demand for advice on all aspects of property taxation.

In the period since that time, the demand for property tax advice has continued to grow, both in volume and sophistication. Property investors are ever more eager to understand the tax environment in which they operate for themselves, rather than simply rely on accountants and lawyers to tell them what to do.

The investments themselves are growing more sophisticated too. The last few years have seen thousands of investors branching out into different types of property, different investment structures and, of course, different geographical markets.

One thing which has been most notable, in particular, in the last few years is the huge surge in property investments abroad by UK residents.

These more recent investors are not the first group to set their sights on overseas property however.

A 'place in the sun' has long been the ambition of many UK residents fed up with too many cold grey winters and short wet summers. As we see a general increase in disposable income in the UK, more and more people are realising this dream and claiming their own stake in the sunshine – their own 'home from home' abroad.

In this book, I aim to bring together all of the taxation issues facing both the foreign property investor and the overseas holiday home owner, including the tax issues arising here in the UK and those arising in the country where the property is located. In the course of examining these various taxation matters, we will additionally come across many legal and practical aspects of foreign property ownership and I will cover these also where appropriate.

Many of the issues which we will explore are the same for both investors and holiday home owners. After all, most holiday home owners see their overseas property as a long-term capital investment and many look to rental income to offset their running costs or even turn a small profit. The two groups inevitably tend to blur into one another and, in this guide, we will cater for the entire spectrum from the investor with no personal interest in their new Bulgarian apartment block to the proud new owner of a dream second home in the South of France.

This guide can easily be viewed as falling into three main parts.

In Chapters 1 to 11 we will be looking at the UK taxation consequences of buying property abroad. The principles outlined in this part of the guide are relevant to any UK resident owning foreign property and will hold equally true whether you buy a house in Aachen or a flat in Zyyi. Wherever your foreign property may be, it is important to understand how you will be treated back here in the UK and this first part of the guide therefore provides invaluable information for all foreign property investors and holiday home owners.

In Chapters 12 to 14 we look at some of the general principles of property taxation and law which you are likely to encounter abroad. Whilst every country's tax and legal system is unique, there are also many similarities and general concepts which are adopted by many countries. This part of the guide serves as a useful overview of foreign property taxation and its impact on a UK resident investor, as well as an introduction to what follows in the third section when we focus on some specific countries.

Within this second part of the guide we will also take a look at the European Union's effect on property taxation within its borders. One of the EU's long-term goals is the harmonisation of taxation regimes across Europe and, whilst our friends in Brussels are still a long way from achieving this seemingly impossible feat (a fact which many will no doubt applaud), there is already some degree of commonality amongst the 27 member states, especially when it comes to VAT.

Finally, in Chapters 15 to 21 we look at the taxation and legal systems applying to property in seven of the most popular destination countries for UK investors and holiday home buyers. Each chapter includes a detailed description of that country's legal and tax system as it relates to property and, in particular, to UK residents owning property in that country. This last part of the guide also includes advice on the best way to structure property investments in the relevant country and on the interaction between the local tax system and our own. Common pitfalls and popular tax-saving measures are pointed out where they arise.

Whilst this guide includes seven chapters describing the local property tax systems in some selected popular overseas destination countries, it is worth remembering that the major tax burden for most UK residents purchasing overseas property will be their UK tax liabilities.

Hence, even if your chosen destination country is not one of the popular locations included in the final part of this guide, it will still remain vitally important for you to obtain a good grasp of the UK taxation principles covered in Chapters 1 to 11.

In fact, by combining the UK tax aspects covered in the first part of the guide with the general principles covered in Chapters 12 to 14, I believe that every overseas property investor and foreign holiday home owner should benefit from this guide whether their chosen destination country is included or not.

Throughout the entire guide there are plenty of **'Tax Tips'** to help you minimise or delay your tax bills, as well as **'Wealth Warnings'** designed to keep you away from some of the more treacherous pitfalls awaiting the unwary taxpayer and **'Practical Pointers'** which will make the whole process of meeting your obligations as a taxpayer, both here and abroad, as painless as possible.

Taken as a whole, this guide will provide you with an invaluable insight into all of the taxation implications of buying, letting or selling property abroad. Whether you are an investor seeking out the rewards of exciting new property markets, or just looking for your own little piece of paradise, my ambition in this guide is to provide the tool which you need to enable you to enjoy as much benefit from your foreign property investment as legally possible.

Finally, I would just like to thank you for buying this guide and wish you every success with your overseas property.

Chapter 1

Background

1.1 DOUBLE TROUBLE

A popular national radio show recently ran a segment on the top ten most common taxation myths. Way up there on the list was the myth that foreign property is not liable to UK tax.

Not only is this completely false, but HM Revenue and Customs are, in fact, currently engaged in a 'witch hunt' to track down UK taxpayers with undeclared income or gains from foreign property.

The truth, unfortunately, is that most UK residents remain liable to UK taxation on all worldwide income and capital gains, no matter where they arise. This is just as true of foreign rental income, and capital gains arising on sales of foreign property, as it is of anything else.

Foreign property owned by most UK taxpayers also generally remains subject to UK Inheritance Tax.

Sadly, to add insult to injury, the fact that foreign property owned by UK residents is taxable in the UK does not generally make any difference to the owners' local tax liabilities in the country in which the property is situated.

In other words, a UK resident owning foreign property faces 'double trouble' – tax in both the local country and in the UK.

The fact that foreign tax must often also be paid makes no difference to the general requirement to account for UK tax on foreign property. Whilst, as we shall see in the chapters which follow, the taxpayer is often able to claim double tax relief, they are nevertheless still left with the administrative nightmare of dealing with two different tax regimes (sometimes even three – see Section 7.8) and the additional costs which this inevitably entails.

Hence, in order to plan for the tax consequences of any foreign property purchase, it is absolutely vital to understand the UK property tax regime as it applies to foreign property, the local tax regime of the country in which the property is situated and, perhaps most importantly, the way in which the two regimes interact with each other. The essential aim of this guide is to enable you to achieve this level of understanding.

1.2 WHERE DO UK RESIDENTS LIKE TO BUY PROPERTY?

In the course of compiling this guide, we did some research to establish the most popular destination countries for UK residents buying property abroad.

We found the results interesting and we thought that our readers would find them interesting too.

The table below shows the results of our findings, based on various surveys of property investors.

Rank	Country	Rank	Country
1	France	11	Dubai
2	Spain	12	Canada
3	Bulgaria	13	New Zealand
4	Florida/USA	14	South Africa
5	Italy	15	Germany
6	Ireland	16	Greece
7	Cyprus	17	Romania
8	Portugal	18	Morocco
9	Australia	19	Croatia
10	Turkey	20	India

Space does not permit us to include all 20 of these most popular destination countries in this guide, but in Appendix A we have included a quick reference guide.

1.3 USING THIS GUIDE

As we have already seen, a UK resident owning property abroad will need to deal with the taxation regime both in the UK and in the country where the property is located.

Readers who are both resident and domiciled in the UK should consult Chapters 1 to 7 to see how their foreign property will be treated for UK tax purposes.

Those who are UK resident but not UK domiciled are subject to different UK taxation rules and these are explained in Chapter 8.

The tax concepts of residence and domicile are first explained in Section 1.4 below. These issues are explored further in Chapter 9 which is devoted to the issue of changing your residence or domicile through emigration.

All readers should also benefit from reading Chapters 12 and 13 which set out some guiding principles which are likely to be encountered in the taxation regimes of most developed countries. Chapter 14 also deals with some matters relevant to all countries within the EU (see Appendix C).

By this stage, you will already be armed with a detailed knowledge of your tax position in the UK and some understanding of the basic principles of international taxation.

If the country in which your property is located, or which interests you as a possible location for a future property purchase, is included in Chapters 15 to 21, you can then select the relevant chapter for a detailed explanation of how the taxation authorities abroad will treat you and your foreign property. If your chosen destination country is not included in this edition, you will already have gained a good grasp of the main principles to watch out for from Chapters 1 to 14.

1.4   RESIDENCE & DOMICILE

The tax concepts of residence and domicile can sometimes be fairly complex and space does not permit a full examination of them. Both are extremely important, however, when we come to consider overseas property tax issues and a brief discussion of these concepts is therefore warranted.

The only way to determine your residence or domicile for certain is to examine your own personal circumstances in detail. Broadly, though, in most cases:

- You are resident in the country in which you live.
- You are domiciled in the country where you were born or where your nationality lies.

Your residence can change from year to year throughout your life. Few people will ever change their domicile and, those that do, can usually do so only once.

Whilst residence and domicile can become quite complex, for many people the situation is quite straightforward and, generally speaking, if you have British parents and have lived in the UK all of your life, then you are almost certainly UK resident and domiciled.

For those who are not so easily pigeon-holed, HM Revenue and Customs' own guidelines state that a person will usually be regarded as UK resident if:

- They spend more than 182 days here in any one UK tax year, or
- They spend more than 90 days per year in the UK on average.

The above criteria are given as rough guidelines only, however, and just because someone spends less time than this in the UK does not guarantee that they are non-UK resident. We will come back to this topic again in more detail in Chapter 9 when we look at the idea of emigrating to avoid UK tax.

More complex issues relating to domicile will also be covered in Chapter 8.

1.5 SCOPE OF THIS GUIDE

The aim of this guide is to cover the UK and overseas tax implications for UK residents investing in property abroad.

Residence in the UK for tax purposes is explained in Section 1.4 above. This guide is intended for the use of UK residents only. (Those non-UK residents who remain UK domiciled may, however, gain some benefit from the sections covering Inheritance Tax and its foreign counterparts).

For tax purposes, the UK does not include the Channel Islands or the Isle of Man, but comprises only England, Scotland, Wales and Northern Ireland.

The foreign tax rates given in the last seven chapters of this guide are the latest available at the time when the relevant chapter or section was written.

Whilst every reasonable effort is made to ensure that the information contained in this guide is up to date, it must be appreciated that tax law throughout the world is constantly changing and tax rates included in this guide may have been superseded by new legislation or government announcements.

The reader must also bear in mind the general nature of this guide. Individual circumstances vary and the tax implications of an individual's actions will vary with them. For this reason, it is always vital to get professional advice before undertaking any tax planning or other transactions which may have tax implications. In particular, when purchasing property abroad, it is also vital to seek local professional advice in the territory concerned. Neither the author nor Taxcafe UK Ltd can accept any responsibility for any loss which may arise as a consequence of any action taken, or any decision to refrain from action taken, as a result of reading this guide.

1.6   A WORD ABOUT THE EXAMPLES

This guide is illustrated throughout by a number of examples.

Unless specifically stated to the contrary, all persons described in the examples in this guide are UK resident, ordinarily resident and domiciled for tax purposes. (Even if their names may suggest otherwise!)

The examples given in the first 14 chapters of the guide will sometimes include foreign tax liabilities. These foreign taxes are included purely for the purposes of illustration and are not meant to be indicative of the general rates of taxation applying in those countries. Some of the countries used in these examples are also fictional.

UK tax rates used in the examples in this guide are partly based on estimated tax bands and allowances. Details of the estimates used are given in Appendix B.

All persons described in the examples in this guide are entirely fictional characters created specifically for the purposes of this guide. Any similarities to actual persons, living or dead, or to fictional characters created by any other author, are entirely coincidental.

Chapter 2

UK Tax on Foreign Property

2.1 NO ESCAPE?

In this chapter we will review the basic principles of UK taxation applying to any UK resident taxpayer holding overseas property.

As explained in Section 1.1, the UK continues to tax UK resident and domiciled taxpayers on all income and capital gains derived from property situated anywhere in the world.

Whilst it likes to be as all-encompassing as possible, however, the UK tax regime is also pretty xenophobic. Foreign rental income, for example, is caught, but is regarded as being completely different in character to any UK property rental income. This rather artificial distinction has some major consequences for anyone with both foreign and UK property and we will return to this issue in Chapter 3.

As far as non-UK residents are concerned, the UK generally only taxes them on income from UK property. Hence, as already stated, this guide is not aimed at non-UK residents although, for those considering non-resident status in the future, we will be looking at the benefits of emigration in Chapter 9.

One very important general point to note is that the UK tax system usually operates in sterling. This gives rise to some additional challenges for UK residents investing in foreign property and we will examine these, as well as other foreign exchange issues, in Chapter 6.

2.2 HOW IS OVERSEAS PROPERTY TAXED IN THE UK?

Under the UK tax regime, all property may be regarded as either:

   a) An investment, or
   b) Trading stock.

This distinction is unaltered by the property's location and applies equally to any foreign property held by UK residents.

Generally speaking, any property which is held long-term will usually be regarded as an investment. This will include properties held for the owner's own personal use – their main home, holiday homes and properties bought for the use of family or friends. It will also include properties which the owner uses as a long-term asset in their own business.

Rental properties will usually be regarded as investments and again this remains equally true wherever they may be located.

Properties which are held for short periods only and which are developed or held purely for onward re-sale at a profit will be regarded as trading stock.

The distinction between investment properties and properties held as trading stock is crucial to their UK taxation treatment. Whilst the vast majority of foreign property held by UK residents will be classed as investment property, it nevertheless remains important to understand this distinction and the consequences which arise whenever a property becomes trading stock.

Gains arising on investment properties are dealt with under the UK Capital Gains Tax regime. This is generally good news as a great many reliefs apply to reduce the tax payable. We will look at UK Capital Gains Tax on foreign property in Chapter 5.

Gains arising on properties held as trading stock are regarded as trading profits and may be subject to both Income Tax and National Insurance in the UK. Furthermore, where foreign properties are held as trading stock, they will be regarded as forming part of a UK trade if the owner controls the business from the UK. We will look at how the UK taxes property trading income in Chapter 4.

Rental income from foreign property received by UK resident individuals is subject to a special tax regime, which we will cover in Chapter 3. All foreign rental income is strictly subject to this regime although, occasionally, small amounts of incidental rental income received from properties held as trading stock may be included within trading profits instead.

It is also important to realise that where foreign property is held via some form of 'Special Purpose Vehicle', rather than by an individual directly, this may change the character of any income or capital gains received. The tax implications of this are covered in Chapters 10 and 11.

Foreign income or gains received by an individual who is UK resident, but either not UK ordinarily resident or not UK domiciled, may be subject to the 'remittance basis' of taxation. This is covered in Chapter 8.

All types of income or gains derived from foreign property, whether directly or indirectly, may be subject to foreign taxation and may thus benefit from double tax relief. We will look at double tax relief in Chapter 7.

2.3   OTHER UK TAXES ON FOREIGN PROPERTY

In the previous section, we considered how the UK taxes income and capital gains derived from foreign property. What about other UK taxes?

The other major UK tax which will also generally apply to foreign property held by UK taxpayers is Inheritance Tax. We will look at Inheritance Tax on overseas property in Section 5.12.

It is also worth noting that foreign property income will be taken into account in determining a UK resident taxpayer's entitlement to Tax Credits. This can create an additional tax cost of up to 37% (39% from 6th April 2008).

Corporation Tax will of course apply where a UK company is used to own foreign property and we will look at this in further detail in Chapter 10.

Other UK taxes, however, do not generally apply to foreign property.

Stamp Duty Land Tax only applies to land and buildings located in the UK, although UK Stamp Duty at 0.5% would remain payable on a purchase of shares in a UK company which holds foreign property.

As far as VAT is concerned, any foreign property is generally subject to the local VAT regime (if any) in the country in which it is located and is outside the scope of UK VAT.

In summary, therefore, the only UK taxes which will generally apply to foreign property are Income Tax, Capital Gains Tax, Inheritance Tax and Corporation Tax where a company is used (with the occasional instance of National Insurance and the need to consider any implications for Tax Credit entitlement).

2.4 OVERSEAS HOLIDAY HOMES

At this stage, it is probably worth providing a quick summary of the UK tax position on overseas holiday homes. In this context, an 'overseas holiday home' means an overseas residential property held directly by a UK resident taxpayer, purely for their own personal use. Such a property is:

- Not subject to any Income Tax charge unless rented out at a profit, but
- Is subject to UK Capital Gains Tax on sale, and
- Will usually be subject to Inheritance Tax on the owner's death.

Personal use includes use by the owner's immediate family and any other rent free occupation by their wider family, friends, etc.

In general, any contributions towards running costs received from family and friends using the property will not give rise to taxable income for UK tax purposes where these do not produce a profit. The Income Tax position on occasional rental income from an overseas holiday home is considered in more detail in Section 3.4.

The Capital Gains Tax position on an overseas holiday home is considered further in Chapter 5.

Overseas property held by non-UK domiciled taxpayers may not be subject to Inheritance Tax, although for most UK resident taxpayers it usually will be. This topic is examined in further detail in Chapter 8.

The treatment of an overseas holiday home held through a company is covered in Section 10.3.

2.5   BASIC PRINCIPLES OF UK INCOME TAX

The UK tax year runs from 6th April each year to the following 5th April. The year ending 5th April 2009 is referred to as '2008/9' and the tax return for this year is known as the '2009 Return'.

Under the self-assessment system, the taxpayer must complete and submit a tax return following each tax year. From 2008, paper tax returns will have to be submitted by 31st October, although the current 31st January deadline will remain for those who file their returns electronically.

The taxpayer must also calculate the amount of tax he or she is due to pay, although Revenue & Customs will do the calculation for you if the return reaches them by 30th September following the tax year (frankly, however, I would not recommend relying on Revenue and Customs' calculation).

The Income Tax due under the self-assessment system is basically the taxpayer's total tax liability for the year less any amounts already deducted at source or under PAYE and less any applicable tax credits (but **not** Child Tax Credits or Working Tax Credits – despite their names, these are not part of the Income Tax system).

All Income Tax due under the self-assessment system, regardless of the source of the income or rate of tax applying, is payable as follows:

- A first instalment or 'payment on account' is due on 31st January during the tax year.
- A second payment on account is due on 31st July following the tax year.
- A balancing payment or, in some cases, a repayment, is due on 31st January following the tax year.

Each payment on account is usually equal to half of the previous tax year's self-assessment tax liability. However, payments on account need not be made when the previous year's self-assessment liability was either:

a) No more than £500, or

b) Less than 20% of the taxpayer's total tax liability for the year.

The £500 threshold referred to above will be increased to £1,000 in respect of payments on account due on or after 31st January 2010.

Taxpayers receiving foreign property income and who are also in employment, or in receipt of a private pension, may alternatively apply to have self-assessment tax liabilities not exceeding £2,000 collected through their PAYE codes for the following tax year. This produces a considerable cashflow advantage, where relevant.

The Self-Assessment 'Double Whammy'

The system of payments on account under self-assessment, as described above, causes major cashflow problems whenever a taxpayer first receives a new source of income or experiences a significant increase in an existing source of income.

Effectively, one and a half years' worth of tax on the new source, or the increase, falls due on 31st January following the tax year. Six months later, another half years' worth of tax becomes payable, meaning that two years' worth of tax must be paid within a six month period.

This is often the cause of major cashflow problems and it is imperative that anyone receiving foreign rental income for the first time, or experiencing a significant increase in that income, makes appropriate provision for the tax arising.

Example

In April 2008, William buys an apartment block in a popular Black Sea resort. In the 2008/9 UK tax year, this property yields rental profits of £20,000. Due to a local incentive scheme, William pays no foreign tax on these profits (please don't ask me about this incentive scheme, I have just made it up in order to simplify this example).

William is a higher rate taxpayer and, prior to 2008/9, all of his income was received under the PAYE system. Hence, on 31st January 2010, William has to pay additional Income Tax under the self-assessment system for the first time. On that date, he will have to pay a total of

£12,000, made up of £8,000 tax due for 2008/9 (£20,000 x 40%) and his first payment on account for 2009/10 of £4,000 (half of £8,000).

Furthermore, William will also have to make a second payment on account of £4,000 in respect of 2009/10 on 31st July 2010. By this point, William has had to pay UK Income Tax equivalent to 80% of his first year's profits!

What If Income Reduces?

Applications to reduce payments on account may be made when there are reasonable grounds to believe that the following year's self-assessment tax liability will be at a lower level.

Reduced payments on account may then be made based on the estimated tax liability for the following year. If, however, it later transpires that the actual liability for the following year is greater than the reduced payments on account made by the taxpayer, interest will be charged on the difference.

Income Tax Rates on Foreign Property Income

The UK Income Tax rates and main allowances for 2006/7 to 2008/9 are set out in Appendix B (some estimates have been used for 2008/9, as indicated in the appendix). Foreign property income is classed as part of the 'non-savings' or 'other' element of a taxpayer's income and will therefore be taxed at just two rates, 20% and 40%, from 6th April 2008.

The same Income Tax rates will apply to any overseas property trading profits but these will additionally be subject to Class 4 National Insurance, which is also collected through the self-assessment system, as described above.

2.6 NEW FOREIGN PROPERTY INCOME

Strictly speaking, whenever a UK taxpayer begins to receive income from a new source, they should advise Revenue & Customs of this new source by 5th October following the UK tax year in which it first arises.

'New source' refers to the commencement of a property business, rather than a new property within an existing property business.

However, when someone with an existing UK property business begins to rent out their first property overseas, this **does** amount to a new source as far as the UK tax regime is concerned.

Oddly enough though, all foreign rental property is regarded as a single source of income for UK tax purposes.

Commencing a property development trade when you already have a property investment business, or vice versa, will also constitute a new source of income for UK tax purposes. However, a UK-based property developer undertaking a development overseas is likely, in most cases, to still be carrying on a single business (as far as the UK is concerned anyway).

In practice, as far as overseas rental income is concerned, as long as the tax return includes the new source of income, and is completed and submitted on time, no penalties will arise.

The commencement of a property trade, however, also gives rise to further, and more immediate, reporting requirements, as detailed in Section 4.5.

2.7   UNREMITTABLE INCOME AND GAINS

As explained in Section 1.1, most UK residents are liable for UK tax on all worldwide income and capital gains as they arise, whether they remit the proceeds back to the UK or not.

There is an exception, however, where it is not actually possible to remit funds back to the UK. This may occur, for example, due to exchange control restrictions imposed by a foreign government.

In such a case, the UK taxpayer may claim to defer any UK tax liability until such time as it becomes possible to remit the relevant funds back to the UK.

2.8   DEALING WITH REVENUE & CUSTOMS

Your 'Tax Office' is the Revenue & Customs office that sends you
your tax return or, if you are not yet in the self-assessment system,
the office which your employer deals with. Failing either of these,
it will be the local Revenue & Customs office for the area where
you live and can be found in the telephone directory under
'Revenue & Customs' or 'Inland Revenue'.

Details of Revenue and Customs contact numbers can be found
under the 'Contact Us' pages at:

www.hmrc.gov.uk/local/individuals/index

Note, however, that 0845 numbers do not work if calling from
abroad, in which case the best contact number to use is +44 161
931 9070.

Chapter 3

UK Tax on Overseas Rental Income

3.1 OIL AND WATER

Overseas rental income received by a UK resident is regarded as an entirely different type of income to any UK rental income which they receive. Like oil and water, they do not mix.

All overseas rental income received by the same taxpayer is, however, for UK tax purposes, regarded as coming from the same source. In other words, all of a UK resident's overseas letting income is regarded, for UK tax purposes, as constituting a single business.

The most important consequences of these rather arbitrary UK tax rules arise when we begin to consider relief for rental losses and we will take a look at these in detail in Section 3.9.

The further practical impact for investors holding both UK and overseas rental property is that it becomes necessary to divide all items of income and expenditure between their UK property business and their overseas property business. Rental income, as well as most direct expenditure, can of course be allocated fairly easily.

In the case of overheads (e.g. office costs), however, some form of proportional allocation will often be required. Any such allocation must be made on a reasonable basis but it is nevertheless worth bearing in mind the rules for loss relief set out in Section 3.9.

3.2 ACCOUNTS AND TAX RETURNS

Like UK rental income, overseas rental income must be accounted for on a 'tax year' basis for UK Income Tax purposes. In other words, accounts must be prepared for each year ended 5th April during which the taxpayer receives any overseas rental income.

Overseas rental income should be detailed on pages F4 and F5 of the UK tax return. These pages form part of the 'Foreign

Supplement' (see Appendix D).

Where foreign tax has also been suffered on the same income, it should be included on page F3 in support of the taxpayer's claim for double tax relief.

Whilst all foreign rental properties are regarded as constituting a single business for UK tax purposes, taxpayers are nevertheless required to separate out the income from each foreign country when calculating their double tax relief claim. The purpose of this is explained further in Section 7.3.

3.3 TYPES OF FOREIGN RENTAL INCOME

Apart from the geographical separation required for double tax relief purposes, there is no further distinction between different types of foreign rental income. Residential property and commercial property are treated the same.

Most crucially, there are no special rules for foreign furnished holiday lettings. As explained in the Taxcafe.co.uk guide *How to Avoid Property Tax*, qualifying furnished holiday lettings located in the UK are subject to a special, and highly beneficial, tax regime. Sadly, this regime does not extend to overseas property.

There is an argument that, under European law, furnished holiday lettings located in any EU country should be eligible for the same relief as equivalent properties located in the UK. Sadly, however, no-one has yet been brave enough to go to Court with this argument. For the time being therefore, foreign rental property cannot qualify as furnished holiday lettings for UK tax purposes.

Amongst other things, this means that capital allowances are not available on furniture and equipment purchased for use in a furnished holiday letting property abroad. The wear and tear allowance or the 'replacements basis' are available, however, and these are explained in Section 3.5.

3.4 OCCASIONAL RENTAL INCOME

Many readers, I know, tend to view Revenue and Customs as some sort of alien monsters. In many ways, however, I have to tell you, they actually behave just like any other human beings.

One such aspect of Revenue and Customs' behaviour is their tendency to want to 'have their cake and eat it', just like many other people. This is seldom evidenced better than by their attitude to occasional rental income from foreign property. If such income produces a profit, Revenue and Customs will want to tax it, whereas if an overall loss arises, they will deny that any business exists.

The correct position, technically, is that all foreign rental income should be accounted for on a business basis. However, where such income is made up of contributions towards running costs made by family and friends, an overall loss is likely to arise. **Losses arising on such non-arm's length rentals may only be set off against a future profit from the rental of the same property to the same tenant.**

In many cases, therefore, whilst a rental loss does technically arise, it is of no practical use. Where the only rental activity for a property is of this non-arm's length nature and consistently produces a loss then, in practice, it is not worth anyone's time to account for it and Revenue and Customs are not likely to be interested in the property. (Sufficient records should nevertheless be retained to demonstrate that rental losses do consistently occur, just in case of a future Revenue and Customs enquiry.)

Wealth Warning

It is fair to say that Revenue and Customs are not likely to be interested in occasional income from family and friends where an overall loss consistently arises (but I repeat that evidence of this consistent loss must be retained).

Some other countries, however, have different property tax systems, based on a percentage of gross rental income rather than net rental profit. Where a property is located in such a country, foreign tax liabilities may arise even on small contributions received from family and friends.

Arm's Length Rentals

I have used this term once or twice – what does it mean?

In tax terminology, an 'arm's length' transaction occurs whenever a normal, open market price is charged for that transaction. Where the parties to the transaction have a personal relationship (e.g. father and son), there is a presumption (albeit a rebuttable one) that the transaction is not arm's length. Conversely, where there is no personal relationship between the parties, it would be highly unusual for the transaction not to be an arm's length one.

An arm's length rental therefore occurs when the normal market rent is charged. Where there is no personal relationship between the tenant and the owner, it would generally be assumed that an arm's length rental exists (even if, perhaps, the owner were charging a little less than the normal full market rent due to inexperience, lack of knowledge or just plain apathy).

Where a rental is 'arm's length', we sometimes also refer to it as being on 'commercial' terms or being a 'commercial rental'. (Do not confuse this with a rental of a commercial property. What is meant here is that the rental is being carried out commercially, as a business.)

Where a property is rented out on 'arm's length terms', even on an occasional basis, a rental business will exist. Any profit from such a business, no matter how small, is taxable, but any loss arising is available for set off against other foreign property rental income, as explained in Section 3.9.

At this stage, it is worth us looking at an example to illustrate some of the points covered so far. The example will also allow us to examine a few other issues which frequently occur when a property is used both privately and also for occasional 'arm's length' rentals. I will highlight some of the **key principles** as they emerge.

Example

Charles owns a villa on the Mediterranean, Maison Blique, which he uses himself for two months each year. He also lets his son Oliver use it for a month each year with no charge.

Charles' brother-in-law Dick Hens uses the villa for a month each year and pays £2,600 towards the running costs.

Charles' uncle Ebeneezer also borrows the villa for a month each year. He pays just £500 towards the running costs.

In December, Charles likes to keep the property available for the family to use, although it is rare that anyone ever does.

For the rest of the year, the property is advertised for rent at £5,000 per month. The market rate would be around £6,000, but Charles is not too bothered about this, as it is not ideally suited to the rental market and he would rather see it occupied as much as possible.

In the summer of 2008, Charles rents the property to a small lady called Nell for three months and everything works out fine, so it is with great expectations that he accepts a booking from Mr Dodger who sends Charles a cheque for £5,000 to rent the property for the month of October 2008.

Unfortunately, Mr Dodger's cheque bounces and he seems to disappear without trace. Worse still, when Charles next visits Maison Blique, he discovers two broken windows, which cost £2,500 to repair.

The property's annual running costs for the year ended 5th April 2009 amount to £30,000 (excluding the cost of repairing the windows broken by Mr Dodger and advertising costs of £1,000).

Charles' accountant, Jacob, is now faced with the task of working out the rental profit or loss on Maison Blique for the year ended 5th April 2009.

The first problem is the allocation of the property's annual running costs. There are a number of ways of viewing this.

As we know, the property was only rented out on 'arm's length terms' for four months. Revenue and Customs might therefore attempt to argue that just four twelfths of the annual running costs should be allocated to this rental income.

On the other hand, the property was only used for a total of nine months during the year and there is therefore a case for saying that four ninths of the annual running costs should be allocated to the 'arm's length' rental income.

However, Jacob decides to adopt the more usual, and often (as in this case) more beneficial, 'availability' method.

Looking at when Maison Blique was __available__ for arms' length rentals, Jacob establishes that this amounts to a total of six months during the year. This therefore enables him to claim six twelfths of the annual running costs against the arm's length rental income.

Key Principle 1

Where a property has both private use (and/or non-commercial rentals) and commercial, open market rentals, there is no single solution to the allocation of annual running costs and a number of different methods may possibly be employed.

The most usual, and generally the best, method, however, is to consider when the property is available for open market rentals. This will very often be a much more beneficial method than just looking at actual use.

This 'availability' approach will generally be justified where a property is available and advertised for rental on a genuinely commercial basis for part of the year. Naturally, the greatest benefit is obtained by maximising the period of commercial availability.

Tax Tip

In practice, it will always be beneficial to maximise the period for which the property is available for arm's length commercial rental. This, in turn, will maximise the allowable deduction for annual running costs.

Wealth Warning

However, unless the owner can demonstrate that the property was genuinely available for commercial rental, Revenue and Customs will tend to view any periods when the property was vacant as private use. This would severely restrict the level of running costs which the owner is able to deduct against any rents received.

One way to demonstrate the property's availability for rental is to enter an agreement with a letting agent under which the owner is unable to use the property during the agreed letting periods.

In the end, the allocation method used to deal with annual running costs, whilst chosen to benefit the taxpayer as much as possible, must nevertheless be reasonable considering all of the relevant factors. The reasoning behind the allocation method used should be documented for future reference and to justify the position taken in the event of a future Revenue and Customs enquiry.

Once chosen, an allocation method should be applied consistently until the facts of the case undergo some material alteration.

Where these principles are adhered to, Revenue and Customs will generally be prepared to accept the allocation method used. If, however, an allocation is made without due consideration being given to some material fact, Revenue and Customs will substitute their own, doubtlessly far less beneficial, method if and when any enquiry occurs.

Example Continued

Jacob allocates six twelfths of the £30,000 annual running costs to Charles' commercial rental business for Maison Blique. This gives a deduction of £15,000. The accounts for Charles' rental business therefore look like this:

	£	£
Rent Receivable		*20,000*
Less:		
Running Costs	*15,000*	
Bad Debt	*5,000*	
Repairs	*2,500*	
Advertising	*1,000*	

		23,500

Rental Loss		*(3,500)*
		=====

(For the sake of illustration, we are assuming that Charles does not claim the wear and tear allowance (see Section 3.5) and the cost of any qualifying replacements fall within the running costs of £15,000.)

Jacob's assistant Bob asks if these losses really arise from genuinely commercial rentals given that Charles only charged £5,000 per month instead of the market rate of £6,000. Jacob responds by saying that although the price charged was a little less than the market rate, the rents to little Nell and the rather artful Mr Dodger were nevertheless made entirely at 'arm's length' as Charles had no other connection with these tenants.

Charles' rental loss of £3,500 therefore arises from commercial rentals and is available to set off against any other foreign rental income which Charles has for 2008/9.

Bob also asks why Charles is able to claim the full cost of the window repairs instead of just six twelfths. Jacob explains that the window repairs arose entirely because of a period of arm's length rental and are therefore allowable in full, just like the advertising costs.

"But 'ow can it be arm's lengf Mr Marley, when the swine never paid?" asks Bob. "Well Bob", responds Jacob, "Charles took Mr Dodger's booking in good faith and it therefore remains arm's length. Charles may have been naïve but it is still a genuinely commercial rental. Now you run off home to your family and we'll deal with the rest of Charles' rental accounts tomorrow." "Cor, fanks Mr Marley" says Bob, dashing for the door.

Key Principles 2 to 4

A rental will usually remain arm's length, even if a lower than market rate rent is charged, when there is no other connection between the owner and the tenant.

Costs specific to a period of arm's length rental are deductible in full against that rental income.

Where the owner has acted in good faith, non-payment does not alter the nature of the rental; it remains 'arm's length'. (The situation would be quite different if Dick Hens did not pay Charles, as this was never arm's length in any case.)

Example Continued

The next morning, Bob continues work on Charles' accounts and produces the following results for the 'non-commercial' rentals of Maison Blique:

	Oliver £	Dick £	Ebeneezer £
Rent received	0	2,600	500
Running costs (one twelfth per month)	2,500	2,500	2,500
	-------	-------	-------
Profit/(Loss)	(2,500)	100	(2,000)
	====	====	====

"No Bob", exclaims Jacob, "there's no need to do accounts for Oliver's use of the property. He's Charles' son and that really just constitutes personal use."

"OK boss" says Bob, feeling a little chastised. "But is it worf doin' any of 'em anyway?"

"Well, that's a good question Bob" replies Jacob. "We don't do accounts where a property is used totally rent free by an immediate family member like Oliver, because that's really just like Charles using the place himself. And with a case like Ebeneezer, the contribution is so small that there is no possibility of a profit ever arising. This just leaves us with losses carried forward which we can probably never use, as we'd need a profit from a rental to Ebeneezer to use them against and I can't see **that** ever happening."

Jacob chuckles to himself after his last point and then carries on. "As you can see though Bob, the rental to Dick has actually produced a small profit and, technically, that represents taxable rental income."

"You mus' be kiddin' Mr Marley! I mean, Dick's just paid a bit too much 'asn't he, Charles never meant to make a profit."

"Well you're right Bob, there was certainly no profit motive here and we certainly might have been better off if we'd just ignored the non-commercial rentals altogether. Now that we know there's a profit though, I'm afraid we'll have to include this rental in Charles' accounts."

"Well wot about the loss from Ebeneezer then? Can't we set that off 'gainst the profit from Dick Hens boss?" "Mmmm, good point Bob", muses Jacob, "you might have something there."

Key Principles 5 to 7

Use of the property totally rent free by family and friends is simply regarded as extra private use by the owner.

Where some small contribution to running costs is received then, in practical terms, this can probably be regarded in the same vein. Whilst a technical loss arises, its use is so restricted as to render it almost impossible to use. To all intents and purposes, therefore, this may again be regarded as further private use and the small cost contribution can be ignored.

Where a larger contribution to costs is received, the position may alter as a profit might actually begin to arise. Strictly speaking, such a profit becomes taxable. However, in practice, it is generally not unreasonable to combine the results of all 'non-arm's length' rentals of the same property. If this produces an overall loss then the income can effectively again be ignored.

The Profit Motive

It is worth noting that Charles' motives are very important here. When he rented Maison Blique to Mr Dodger, he intended to make a profit. He actually made a loss and this was therefore allowable against other foreign rental profits generally.

Conversely, when Charles allowed Dick Hens to use the property, he actually made a small profit, even though he had no intention of doing so. Strictly this is taxable, even though a loss arising under the same circumstances could not be relieved. This, of course, perfectly illustrates my opening comment about Revenue and Customs wanting to have their cake and eat it!

In practice, though, Bob's idea of combining the non-commercial rentals can usually be adopted and would usually be accepted provided that there was no intention on Charles' part to profit from his friends and relatives.

Furthermore, as Jacob implied to Bob, the really practical approach is to not even bother producing accounts for these non-commercial rental periods. Where, again, there is no intention to profit from these rentals and it can be demonstrated that an overall loss does indeed consistently arise, this approach will usually be accepted.

It is also worth remembering that, in a case like Charles' small profit on his rental to Dick, any previous losses from his rentals to Dick would be available for offset. This adds further strength to the practical stance that the preparation of accounts in such a case is not really worthwhile.

Where it gets really tricky is where there is an intermediate level of rental, sufficient to produce a profit, but considerably lower than the market rate. Where this is done in a non-arm's length situation, the result is the worst of both worlds: any profit is taxable, but any loss can only be set off against future profits on the rental of the same property to the same tenant.

In our example, this intermediate position might arise if Charles rented Maison Blique to Dick Hens for, say, £4,000 per month. Normally this would produce a taxable profit of £1,500. (Charles would then set off part of his commercial foreign rental losses, thus avoiding any actual tax bill, but reducing the losses available for use elsewhere.)

If, however, it was Dick whose cheque bounced instead of Mr Dodger's, Charles would be unable to use the loss arising of £2,500 unless he rented the property to Dick again.

Renting Out a Foreign Main Residence

The same principles as outlined above continue to apply when a foreign property qualifies as the UK resident owner's principal private residence for UK Capital Gains Tax purposes (see Section 5.6).

Sadly, rent-a-room relief is not currently available against rental income from a foreign property. (Another one for the European Courts perhaps?)

3.5 DEDUCTIBLE EXPENDITURE

In Section 3.4 we covered the principles surrounding what proportion of foreign property expenses were likely to be deductible from foreign rental income. What we now need to consider is the question of what types of expenditure may be eligible for deduction.

The items which may be deducted from foreign rental income for UK Income Tax purposes are really much the same as for a UK rental property. The main categories of deductible expenditure to consider include:

- Interest and other finance costs
- Repairs and maintenance
- Heating and lighting costs, if borne by the landlord
- Insurance costs
- Letting agent's fees
- Advertising for tenants
- Accountancy fees
- Legal and professional fees
- The cost of cleaners, gardeners, etc, where relevant
- Ground rent, service charges, etc.
- Bad debts
- Pre-trading expenditure
- Local taxes
- Travel and subsistence
- Landlord's administrative expenditure

The basic principles governing when an expense may be deducted against rental income are exactly the same as for UK rental property and are covered in depth in the Taxcafe.co.uk guide *How to Avoid Property Tax*.

Some of the key points to remember from these basic principles are:

Professional fees and other costs relating to the purchase or sale of a property are not deductible for UK Income Tax purposes. These costs do, however, feature as part of the Capital Gains Tax calculation on the property's sale (see Chapter 5).

Capital improvements may not be deducted for Income Tax purposes but are deducted from the capital gain on the property's sale instead.

Landlord's administrative expenditure may include items such as office costs, motor expenses, courses, conferences, books and publications. The over-riding principle is that the expense must have been incurred wholly and exclusively for the purposes of the foreign rental business.

Working from home: a proportion of the landlord's own household costs may be claimed where the foreign rental business is run from an office in their own home. This 'office' might in practice be their study, den, spare bedroom or dining room.

Wear and tear allowance: a deduction equal to 10% of gross rents receivable from furnished lettings is available for UK Income Tax purposes. Gross rents must be adjusted for the purposes of this calculation if the landlord bears any costs which a tenant would normally bear (e.g. heating and lighting or local municipal taxes on occupiers) or provides additional services (such as cleaning or gardening).

This allowance is given on the same terms whether the property is located in the UK or overseas but is only available for furnished lettings.

The purpose of the 'wear and tear allowance' is to provide a deduction for the cost of furnishing the property. As an alternative, the landlord may instead claim the 'replacements basis'; i.e. the cost of replacing furniture, soft furnishings, etc.

The cost of the original furniture and furnishings may not be claimed however.

It will be noted from the above list that many of the costs of running a foreign rental business are actually incurred in the UK. This is perfectly acceptable, as long as the cost is incurred wholly and exclusively for the purposes of the foreign rental business, it remains deductible, wherever it is incurred, at home or abroad.

Whilst most of the principles governing the deductibility of expenditure are the same as for a UK rental business, in the next few sections we will look in further depth at some of the issues which are more particular to foreign property.

3.6 TRAVEL AND SUBSISTENCE

Travel and subsistence costs probably represent the most significant difference between the expenses incurred in a UK rental business and a foreign rental business being run by a UK resident taxpayer.

This is also where the 'wholly and exclusively' rule comes into play the most.

Leaving that to one side for the moment, however, travel and subsistence costs may be allowable when incurred in connection with:

- Searching for foreign property in which to invest.
- Visiting property to carry out, supervise or arrange repairs and maintenance work.
- Making visits to rental agents or professional advisers.
- Inspecting tenanted property.
- Visiting the area to advertise or promote the rental business.

Where foreign property is purely rental property with no private use, the situation is fairly clear-cut, with any travel and subsistence costs incurred for any of the above purposes being fully allowable.

Example

Robert buys an apartment in Turkey as a buy to let investment. Before he can let the property, however, it needs extensive redecoration and a few minor repairs.

Robert decides to carry out the work himself, so he flies out to Turkey. At first, Robert cannot stay at the apartment, as there is no water, so he books into a local hotel for a week.

Later, however, once the plumbing problems have been resolved, Robert is able to move into the apartment while he carries out the rest of the work.

Once work is completed, Robert is able to rent out the apartment.

A year later, Robert has to return to the apartment to carry out some small repairs. As there are now tenants residing in the property, Robert has to book into the local hotel again.

Robert is delighted, however, when his accountants in the UK, Burns & Co., advise him that he is able to claim all of his travel costs to and from Turkey, the cost of his accommodation at the local hotel during both of his visits and the cost of all his meals during his stays in Turkey, as well as during his journeys there and back.

(Incidentally, on another tack, Robert can also claim all of the property's running costs during the period that he was preparing it for his first rental. These and the other costs which he incurred during this period constitute 'pre-trading expenditure' – see Section 3.8.)

Robert's situation was pretty straightforward because his Turkish property was purely an investment and he had no other interest in it.

What if Robert took a day off from his maintenance work at the apartment and did some sightseeing?

Strictly, this alters the nature of Robert's visit to Turkey, as an element of private use is now involved. The most extreme view is that this means his visit to Turkey was not wholly and exclusively for business purposes and he therefore cannot claim **any** of his travel and subsistence costs!

Fortunately, in practice, this extreme stance would not generally be considered appropriate for such a minor element of private use. A simple disallowance of any costs Robert incurred during his day of sightseeing would usually be the appropriate approach here.

Let's take it a step further. What if Robert's wife joined him for a week's holiday at the apartment in the middle of his time preparing it for rental?

Again, a total disallowance seems a little excessive as the main reason for Robert's trip remains business. None of his wife's travel and subsistence costs could be claimed in this case though.

As far as Robert's own costs are concerned, a disallowance of the costs arising during his wife's visit would usually be sufficient. Revenue and Customs might also insist on a partial disallowance of his travel costs, although this would probably depend on the overall length of his visit and on whether his wife's visit was planned from the outset or was something which the couple decided upon later.

What if Robert's wife also joined him for a holiday during his second visit to the property the following year?

If Robert spent all his waking hours working on the property, his own travel, accommodation and subsistence costs would remain fully allowable. His wife's travel and subsistence costs would, of course, again be disallowable.

However, if Robert only worked on the property during the daytime and spent the evenings with his wife, we are again faced with some private element to his expenditure. Robert's accountants would then need to work out a suitable proportion of his travel and subsistence costs to claim – probably somewhere between 50% and 75% in a case like this.

What if Robert's whole family spent a week in Turkey and Robert himself just popped around to the apartment for an hour one afternoon to check everything was OK?

In this case, Robert would only be able to claim a small proportion of the cost of his trip to Turkey, maybe 10% perhaps (and none of the costs relating to the rest of his family).

We could go on indefinitely with these 'what if' scenarios, so I think I'd better call a halt there and summarise the principles involved.

Summary of Travel and Subsistence Principles (So Far)

Where a trip is made entirely for business purposes, all travel, subsistence, and, where relevant, accommodation costs may be claimed in full.

Where there is a minor and incidental personal element to the trip, only the additional costs arising which are specific to that personal element need to be disallowed.

A more significant private element to the trip will mean that a proportion of all the costs of the trip will need to be disallowed.

Where the trip is predominantly made for private purposes, but some business element is nevertheless still present, a small proportion of the costs of the trip may usually be claimed.

Wealth Warning

Be reasonable! If you claim only a reasonable proportion of your travel and subsistence costs and can justify your reasoning, most Revenue and Customs Inspectors will accept your claim.

If, however, you take a quite unrealistic stance, you will be headed for a nasty bill for back tax, interest and penalties!

Visiting Holiday Homes

The most ridiculous of all claims for travel and subsistence costs relate to properties which are, in reality, the owner's holiday homes.

When we came to Robert's second visit in our last 'what if', he had the saving grace that the property was occupied by tenants and he was therefore unable to make any personal use of it. Hence, it was still reasonable for him to claim a small proportion of the cost of his trip to Turkey.

However, where a property is vacant for part of the time, any visits by the owner, during which he or she stays in the property, will almost always be tainted by personal use. Nevertheless, the principle remains that if the visit is made wholly for business purposes, all travel and subsistence costs remain fully allowable.

As soon as a spouse, partner or other family member joins the owner at the property, however, the personal use element really begins to look like the predominant reason for the visit.

Usually, therefore, I would not advocate claiming any of the costs associated with such a visit. There are exceptions though.

Example

Three sisters, Charlotte, Emily and Anne, each own an alpine chalet. Each chalet is closed during the winter but rented out during the spring and summer. Each sister also uses their chalet as a holiday home for part of the year.

In April each year, Charlotte travels to her chalet to prepare it for the first rental of the year. She stays as long as it takes to get the property ready and then flies straight home again. She does not return until August when she spends a month on holiday at the chalet. The cost of Charlotte's visit in April is fully allowable against her rental income.

Emily travels to her chalet in May. She takes her husband and her children with her and they spend a month on holiday there. During this time, Emily and her husband spend at most one day preparing the chalet for the summer rentals (a local 'man' does most of the maintenance work for them). The cost of Emily's visit to her chalet cannot be claimed as the main purpose of her visit is personal.

Anne visits her chalet for two weeks at the end of March. She spends the first week getting the chalet ready for the rental season, although she also visits some of her local friends during this week. Anne's husband joins her for the second week. If there is any maintenance work to be done, he will spend part of the week sorting it out, but usually he and Anne spend most of the week sightseeing.

Anne and her husband usually return to the chalet for another two weeks in September or October for a short holiday, at the end of which they prepare the chalet for the winter.

Anne's case is the most difficult one to decide. Both of her visits, in March and in early autumn, are for mixed purposes. Anne will need to claim a reasonable proportion of her travel and subsistence costs. In a case like this, I might suggest claiming around 50% to 75% of the cost of Anne's visit in March, around 25% to 50% of the costs of her husband's visit in March and a much smaller proportion of the cost of their visit in the autumn.

In many cases, of course, the investor's spouse or partner will also be actively involved in the property and will often be a co-owner.

This in itself does not mean that any visit to the property by the couple will automatically become a business trip. The role that each person carries out during the visit will still need to be examined on a case by case basis, just as in our example above. An appropriate proportion of each person's travel and subsistence costs should then be claimed.

3.7 LOCAL TAXES

Some local taxes may be claimed as an expense against foreign rental income. This is not to be confused with double tax relief, which works in an entirely different (and generally more beneficial) way, as we shall see in Chapter 7.

As a general rule, all foreign taxes are treated for UK tax purposes as if they were the UK equivalent. This is equally true whether the foreign tax is raised at a national, regional or local level. It is the nature of the tax which matters, not its geographical scope. For example, a UK taxpayer owning a rental property in many US States will pay both State and Federal US Income Taxes. Both of these taxes may be claimed for either double tax relief purposes or as an expense (see further below).

Hence, foreign taxes which are incurred on the purchase of a property are treated as part of the cost of that property and can only be claimed for Capital Gains Tax purposes on its eventual disposal.

Foreign taxes which appear to be equivalent to Income Tax, Capital Gains Tax or Inheritance Tax may be claimed for double tax relief purposes as a deduction against the corresponding UK tax. We will cover this in more detail in Chapter 7.

Foreign taxes which are similar to Council Tax or Rates, i.e. an annual charge on the ownership or occupation of property, may be claimed as an expense when incurred on a foreign rental property.

Foreign VAT and other purchase taxes which are incurred on allowable business expenses and which cannot be recovered (as will usually be the case) may be claimed as part of those expenses.

Any irrecoverable foreign VAT or other purchase taxes incurred on the purchase of a property or on acquisition costs (legal fees, etc) is deemed to form part of the cost of the property for Capital Gains Tax purposes and therefore cannot be claimed as an Income Tax deduction. Similarly, any such VAT or purchase taxes incurred on disposal costs are again deemed to form part of those costs and are thus not allowable for UK Income Tax purposes.

Where foreign VAT or purchase tax can be recovered, only the net expense should be claimed for UK tax purposes. This may sometimes be the case where property is let as holiday accommodation for example (see Section 14.3).

Difficulties arise where the foreign tax does not appear to have any UK equivalent. Such taxes are ineligible for double tax relief so our only option is to see if they can be claimed as a business expense.

If the tax may be regarded as a property tax or business tax then it ought to be allowable as a business expense.

Some foreign taxes might, however, be regarded as a personal tax (like our failed attempt at a Poll Tax, or Community Charge to give it its official name). In this case, no deduction will be available for the tax. Some countries impose a Wealth Tax which will generally fall into this category.

Foreign Income Tax as an Expense

Foreign taxes similar to Income Tax may sometimes also be claimed as an expense when this is more beneficial than claiming double tax relief. This might occur, for example, when there is no UK tax liability for a year or when the UK Income Tax liability is much smaller than its foreign equivalent.

Example

Jane owns a flat on Rue D'Austen in Paris which she occasionally rents out. In the UK, she is a higher rate taxpayer.

In 2008/9 her French Income Tax liability on the flat is £3,000. For UK Income Tax purposes, however, she has a rental loss on the flat of £2,000.

Clearly, Jane should choose to claim her French tax as a deduction for UK Income Tax purposes since she is not eligible for any double tax relief for the same tax.

This will increase Jane's rental loss on the flat to £5,000. If she has rental profits on other foreign property she will be able to utilise this loss immediately. If not, she can carry the loss forward to be offset against any future foreign rental profits.

Either way, by claiming her French tax as an expense, Jane could save up to £1,200 in UK Income Tax (£3,000 @ 40%).

The next year, in 2009/10, Jane again incurs a French Income Tax liability of £3,000 on her Paris flat. This time, however, her rental profits on the flat for UK tax purposes amount to £1,000, giving her a UK Income Tax liability of £400 on the same income.

Jane could claim double tax relief for her French tax on the flat, thus eliminating any UK Income Tax on this income. This will save her £400.

Alternatively, she could again claim the French tax as an expense for UK Income Tax purposes. This eliminates her rental profits (for UK tax purposes) and produces a rental loss (for UK tax purposes) of £2,000. This loss, in turn, may be set off against Jane's other foreign rental income, now or in the future, thus producing further additional savings of up to £800 (£2,000 @ 40%).

Claiming her French tax as an expense in 2009/10 therefore gives Jane a potential total UK tax saving of up to £1,200 once again (£400 + £800).

Once again, it is clear that Jane is better off treating her French tax as an expense rather than claiming double tax relief.

In 2010/11, Jane's French tax bill increases to £4,000. For UK tax purposes, she has a rental profit of £5,000, giving her a UK tax bill of £2,000.

This time, Jane is better off to claim double tax relief for her French tax, as this eliminates her UK tax bill altogether. If she were to claim the French tax as an expense for UK Income Tax purposes, she would still be left with a rental profit of £1,000 and a UK tax bill of £400. This would have saved her just £1,600, whereas her double tax relief claim saves her £2,000.

Tax Tip

Where foreign tax exceeds the rental profits computed for UK Income Tax purposes, it is better to claim it as an expense.

In all other cases, it is preferable to claim double tax relief where available.

3.8 PRE-TRADING EXPENDITURE

Where a cost would normally be allowed under general principles, relief is not denied simply because it is incurred before the first foreign rental takes place. Relief is, however, effectively deferred until that first foreign rental takes place.

As usual, the expenditure must be incurred wholly and exclusively for business purposes. It must also be incurred no more than seven years before the foreign rental business commences and must form part of that same business. It does not necessarily, however, need to be incurred in the same country! (As long as it is not part of a UK rental business.)

Example

In 2003, Winston decided that he wanted to invest in some foreign property. He spent several months looking at possible investments in Spain but eventually became disillusioned with the idea and gave up looking.

Between 2004 and 2007 Winston made a few attempts to start a UK buy to let business but without success.

In April 2008, Winston hears that there are some great opportunities for investments in the Baltic States. He renews his search and spends the rest of the 2008/9 tax year searching Estonia, Latvia and Lithuania for a suitable property incurring various costs totalling £8,000.

Eventually, however, in May 2009, Winston decides to buy an old converted church on a hill just outside Kaliningrad. Kaliningrad just happens to lie in an area between Lithuania and Poland which still belongs to Russia.

Despite this, in 2009/10 Winston is able to claim the £8,000 of costs incurred the previous year against his first rental income from his Russian property as these were incurred as part of the same business.

"What about the costs he incurred in Spain in 2003?" I hear you ask. Sadly, although these were incurred within the requisite seven year period, these do not form part of the same business.

This is not because Winston was looking at a different country at that time; it is because he abandoned his search for **foreign** property for several years and hence this earlier attempt at a foreign rental business actually lapsed. His search for UK property during the intervening period cannot be regarded as part of the same business under the 'oil and water' principle explained in Section 3.1.

Tax Tip

To get relief for your 'pre-trading' expenses you must keep up the search for **foreign** rental property, even if you decide to move on to a different country.

Second and Subsequent Foreign Rentals

The pre-trading expenditure principles outlined above apply to expenditure incurred before a taxpayer rents out their first foreign property.

Once a foreign rental business exists, however, all eligible expenditure may be claimed as it arises.

Again, it is not necessary for UK Income Tax purposes for the expenditure to be incurred in connection with property in the same country, as long as it is not related to UK property.

Example

After letting out his Russian property, Winston decides to resume his search for a Spanish investment property. During 2010/11, he incurs costs of £5,000 on this search, still without finding a suitable property.

Winston can claim these costs against the rental income from his Russian property during 2010/11. For UK Income Tax purposes, these costs are regarded as being part of the same business and there is no need for Winston to wait until he has Spanish rental income. (He still cannot claim relief for the costs which he incurred in 2003 however.)

3.9 FOREIGN RENTAL LOSSES

Any loss arising on an arm's length rental of foreign property is, for UK Income Tax purposes, automatically set off against any foreign rental profits arising in the same UK tax year. No claim is necessary, nor is it even possible to disapply this automatic set off if, for any reason, it is not beneficial.

Where a taxpayer has overall net losses from arm's length rentals of foreign property in any UK tax year, the excess loss is carried forward and may be set off against future foreign rental profits.

Example

Arthur has two foreign rental properties: Conan House in the South of Ireland, and Chateau D'Oyle in Luxembourg. Both are let out on strictly arm's length terms.

In 2008/9, Arthur has rental profits of £4,000 on his Irish house, but incurs a loss of £5,500 on the Chateau in Luxembourg.

The loss on Chateau D'Oyle is automatically set off against Arthur's profits from Conan House and the excess loss of £1,500 is carried forward.

In 2009/10, Arthur has rental profits of £5,000 from Conan House and £100 from Chateau D'Oyle. His brought forward foreign rental loss of £1,500 can be set off against his combined foreign rental profits of £5,100 leaving £3,600 of taxable income.

Note that there is absolutely no problem with the fact that the losses brought forward arose on a property in one country but were mostly relieved against profits from a property in a different country.

It is also worth noting in the above example that, if Arthur had no other income in 2008/9, he would have preferred not to set the Luxembourg property loss against his Irish property profit since the latter would, in any case, be covered by his personal allowance. Sadly, this is not possible as the set off is automatic, meaning that £4,000 of rental losses would effectively be wasted in such a case.

Non-Arm's Length Rentals

Whilst an arm's length foreign rental loss may be set off against a non-arm's length rental profit, the converse is not true. As we saw in Section 3.4, a non-arm's length rental loss may not be set off against other rental profits but may only be carried forward to set off against any future profit on the rental of the same property to the same tenant.

Example

In May 2010, Arthur inherits a third foreign property, Moriarty Towers, an old stately home in Ruritania. His uncle Sherlock has lived there for many years and Arthur lets him stay on for an annual rent of £10,000, much less than the market rent which the property would otherwise command.

For the tax year 2010/11, Arthur makes a rental profit of £8,000 on Conan House and rental losses of £2,000 and £700 on Chateau D'Oyle and Moriarty Towers respectively.

The loss arising on Chateau D'Oyle is again automatically set off against the profit on Conan House, leaving Arthur with net taxable foreign rental profits of £6,000. Arthur's loss on his non-arm's length rental of Moriarty Towers can only be carried forward.

In 2011/12, Arthur makes a profit of £1,500 on Conan House, a loss of £3,000 on Chateau D'Oyle and a profit of £1,000 on Moriarty Towers. Fortunately, his accountants are sharp enough to realise that this leaves him with a rental loss of £1,200 to carry forward.

£1,200? Surely it's £500 isn't it?

No. The loss brought forward on Moriarty Towers can be set off against the profit on the rental of the same property to the same tenant, leaving a net rental profit of just £300 on this property. £300 of the loss on Chateau D'Oyle is then set off against this profit, £1,500 is set off against the Conan House profit and the remaining £1,200 is carried forward.

Furthermore, the whole of the loss carried forward now relates to arm's length rentals and may be set off against any future foreign rental profit.

This example demonstrates the benefit of ensuring that a non-arm's length loss is used in priority to other foreign rental losses whenever it is possible to do so.

What Else Can Foreign Rental Losses be Set Against?

Nothing!

Most importantly, they cannot be set against UK rental profits or capital gains on any property.

It is questionable whether the UK's rule denying relief for foreign rental losses against UK rental profits (and vice versa) is legal under European Law (see Chapter 14) but, as yet, no-one has taken a case on this to the European Court.

A similar rule which applies in Germany has recently been challenged successfully in the European Court of Justice, however, so it is possible that we may see a favourable change to the UK's rules on foreign rental losses in the foreseeable future.

How Long Can Foreign Rental Losses be Carried Forward?

Indefinitely! With one major proviso:

Foreign rental losses from arm's length rentals may be carried forward as long as the owner continues to have a foreign rental business.

It does not matter if the owner no longer owns the property which gave rise to the losses. It does not even matter if the owner no longer owns any property in the same country. It is, however, imperative that the owner continues to hold some foreign rental property let out on arms' length terms.

Chapter 4

Trading With Foreign Property

4.1 WHAT IS A FOREIGN PROPERTY TRADE?

Trades involving foreign property include the following:

Property Development

Where foreign property is built, renovated or developed for onward sale at a profit, this constitutes a trade of property development.

Property Dealing

Where foreign property is purchased and held for a short period only with the objective of selling the property on at a profit, this constitutes a trade of property dealing.

For example, the purchase of properties 'off plan' with the objective of selling them at a profit immediately on completion will usually be regarded as property dealing.

Hotels and Guest Houses

Normally, a foreign property owner provides only limited services to their tenants – cleaning, gardening and routine maintenance perhaps. The provision of services at this level does not alter the property's status as an investment property nor the treatment of the rental income received which remains as set out in Chapter 3.

Where, however, the level of services goes further and includes the provision of meals, the point may eventually be reached where the business may be regarded as a trade. Effectively, at this point, the property is being run as a guest house or hotel.

4.2 HOW ARE FOREIGN PROPERTY TRADING PROFITS TAXED IN THE UK?

Unlike rental property businesses, there is no distinction between a foreign property trade which is run from the UK by a UK resident and its UK equivalent. For example, a UK property developer might develop properties both at home and abroad as part of the same trade.

Indeed, where the trade is run from the UK, it is regarded as being a UK trade, notwithstanding the fact that some or all of its trading activities are carried on abroad.

Hence, where a UK property trade is merely expanded to also include foreign property, this is regarded merely as an extension of the existing trade for UK tax purposes and no new business has commenced.

A UK resident taxpayer carrying on any form of trade involving foreign property remains liable to UK Income Tax on their trading profits. As explained in Section 2.5, foreign property trading profits form part of a taxpayer's 'non-savings' or 'other' income and are taxed at the rates set out in Appendix B, i.e. 20% and 40% from 6th April 2008.

A UK resident with any trading profits, UK or foreign, is also liable for both Class 2 and Class 4 National Insurance. The rates applying are again shown in Appendix B.

The profits derived from sales of foreign property held for onward sale as part of a property development or property dealing trade are treated as trading profits and not capital gains.

Other foreign property held for trading purposes, however, such as a hotel, guest house or the owner's own office premises, continues to be subject to Capital Gains Tax on sale.

Where foreign tax is also suffered on foreign property trading profits, double tax relief continues to be available in the usual way, as set out in Chapter 7. The alternative of claiming foreign Income Tax as a trading expense also continues to be available and follows similar principles to those set out in Section 3.7.

In the rare instance that a foreign property trade owned by a UK resident is actually run from a base abroad, it will be regarded as a foreign trade. Where the owner is UK resident and UK domiciled, this will make little difference to the treatment of any profits, other than to mean that the trade must be reported on a different page of the tax return.

Any losses from a foreign trade are, however subject to different, and rather restrictive, rules, as we shall see in Section 4.6.

Whilst a taxpayer may have trading activities in both the UK and abroad as part of the same trade, it is also possible to have two separate trades.

This is particularly likely to be the case where the UK and foreign trading activities are of a different type. For example, a UK property developer who opens a hotel in Croatia would have both a UK trade and a Croatian trade (or possibly two UK trades if he or she somehow managed to run the hotel from the UK).

4.3 TAX RETURNS

The results of trading activities carried on abroad by UK resident taxpayers should be entered on pages SE1 to SE4 of the tax return, which form the 'Self-Employment Supplement'. This is unaltered by whether the trade is considered a UK trade or a foreign trade.

Where the trade is carried on in partnership, a separate partnership tax return will be required and each partner will also need to enter their share of the profits on the 'Partnership Supplement' of their own tax return rather than the self-employment pages.

In all cases, any claim for double tax relief for foreign tax suffered on the trade should be entered on page F3 within the 'Foreign Supplement'.

Details of how to obtain any of the necessary supplementary pages of the tax return are given in Appendix D.

4.4 DEDUCTIONS FOR FOREIGN PROPERTY TRADES

The deductions allowable for UK Income Tax purposes against a trade involving foreign property generally follow exactly the same principles as those outlined in the Taxcafe.co.uk guide *How to Avoid Property Tax*. Any additional issues which arise, or are of greater prominence, due to the property's location abroad have already been covered in Chapters 2 and 3 and the principles involved remain much the same.

4.5 COMMENCING A NEW PROPERTY TRADE

Whenever a UK resident first commences trading, whether alone or in partnership, they must register as self-employed within three months of the end of the calendar month in which trading commences. Failure to do so incurs a penalty of £100.

Registration will trigger the collection of Class 2 National Insurance back-dated to the date that trading commenced (see Appendix B for current National Insurance rates). Taxpayers already paying Class 2 National Insurance on some other trade do not need to register again. These requirements remain exactly the same when a UK resident commences a trade involving foreign property.

4.6 TRADING LOSSES

Where a UK resident is carrying on a UK trade involving foreign property, there is considerably greater scope to claim relief for any trading losses arising than for foreign rental losses. Remember, the issue of whether a UK trade exists is determined by where the trade is run from and not by the location of the trading property.

UK trading losses may be set off against any other income or capital gains of the same or previous UK tax year or may be carried forward to be set off against future profits from the same trade.

Relief for foreign trading losses, however, is severely restricted. Such losses may only be set off against profits from other foreign trades carried on by the same taxpayer or certain foreign pension and employment income.

Chapter 5

Capital Taxes on Foreign Property

5.1 THE TERRIBLE TWINS

There are two major UK capital taxes which, in most cases, for a
UK resident and UK domiciled taxpayer, apply to foreign property
in very much the same way as they apply to UK property: Capital
Gains Tax and Inheritance Tax.

For the majority of this chapter, we will focus on UK Capital Gains
Tax on foreign property with particular emphasis on overseas
holiday homes where there are some very interesting tax planning
opportunities.

Then, in Section 5.12, we will turn to the subject of Inheritance
Tax on foreign property held by UK domiciled taxpayers.

5.2 ALL CHANGE?

On 9th October 2007, Alistair Darling, the Chancellor of the
Exchequer, announced proposals for a major reform to the UK
Capital Gains Tax system to take effect from 6th April 2008.

The major elements of these proposals are:

- A new flat rate of Capital Gains Tax, 18%.
- The abolition of taper relief.
- The abolition of indexation relief.

Indexation relief currently applies to property held by individuals
which was acquired before April 1998.

The abolition of taper relief is rather more significant and we will
take a brief look at the impact of this in Section 5.10.

In a further announcement made on 24th January 2008, the
Chancellor also proposed to introduce a new Entrepreneurs' Relief
which will reduce the effective rate of tax on the first £1,000,000

of each individual's capital gains on qualifying business sales after 5th April 2008 to just 10%.

Sadly, this relief will not benefit many foreign property owners as it only applies to trading businesses or qualifying furnished holiday letting property in the UK.

The relief should, however, generally be available to anyone selling a property development business, including businesses engaged in developing property overseas.

The publication of draft legislation on 24th January 2008 suggests that it is now highly probable that the proposals announced in October 2007 will make it on to the statute books.

In this guide, I have therefore proceeded on the basis that the change to a new flat rate of Capital Gains Tax at 18% will become law and will apply to all capital gains arising on or after 6th April 2008.

More details of the impact of the proposed changes and the planning opportunities arising are given in the Taxcafe.co.uk guide *How to Avoid Property Tax*.

5.3   ALL OR NOTHING?

As explained in Chapter 2, UK resident and domiciled taxpayers are liable to UK Capital Gains Tax on any capital gains arising on the disposal of foreign property.

It is important to note that this liability arises whenever the taxpayer is UK resident at the time of sale of the foreign property. There is no relief or exemption to account for any earlier periods of non-UK residence during the ownership of the property.

Wealth Warning

A person returning to the UK after a long period abroad could find themselves with a large UK Capital Gains Tax bill on the sale of foreign property, even though little or none of the gain arose whilst they were UK resident.

This is the other side of the coin from the beneficial treatment of those who emigrate from the UK and are able to avoid UK Capital Gains Tax. (We will return to this topic in Chapter 9.)

Capital Gains Tax and residence is therefore very much an 'all or nothing' situation. If you're UK resident and domiciled at the time of sale, all of the gain is taxable, if you're non-UK resident at the time of sale, then none of it is taxable (subject to the temporary non-residence rules explained in Section 9.3).

New immigrants arriving in the UK for the first time will usually face a slightly different situation as they will tend to be non-UK domiciled and thus subject to different rules, as we shall see in Chapter 8. The same applies to any other non-UK domiciled taxpayers.

5.4   WHAT'S THE DIFFERENCE?

The computation of the gain on disposal of a foreign property for UK Capital Gains Tax purposes follows exactly the same principles as for a gain on a UK property. To summarise briefly:

1. The calculation begins by deducting the property's original cost from the sale proceeds received to produce the capital gain.
2. Incidental purchase costs and capital improvement expenditure are added to the property's cost (and therefore also deducted in computing the capital gain).
3. Disposal costs may be deducted from sale proceeds.
4. Where property is transferred to a connected person, such as a close family member, the sale proceeds are deemed to be a sum equal to the property's open market value.
5. Similarly, where property was acquired from a connected person, or inherited, its original purchase cost is deemed to be its open market value at that time.
6. Property held before 31st March 1982 is generally treated as if it were acquired for its open market value on that date.

7. Indexation relief applies to property purchased before April 1998 and sold before 6th April 2008. This relief works by adding an amount to the property's cost to represent the impact of general retail price inflation. The relief only covers the period between March 1982 and April 1998.
8. Properties qualifying as the owner's principal private residence at any time during their ownership are eligible for exemption as detailed in Sections 5.6 and 5.7.
9. Any remaining gain after steps 1 to 8 on a disposal taking place before 6th April 2008 is subject to taper relief as detailed in Section 5.10. For disposals on or after 6th April 2008 which are eligible for Entrepreneurs' Relief (see Section 5.2) the remaining gain is reduced by a factor of 5/9ths (e.g. a gain of £90,000 is reduced to £50,000). This will rarely apply to foreign investment property.
10. Each person is entitled to an annual exemption which exempts the first part of any capital gains remaining after steps 1 to 9. The annual exemptions applying for 2006/7 and 2007/8 and the estimated annual exemption for 2008/9 are included in Appendix B. Only one annual exemption is available to each person each tax year.
11. For disposals taking place on or after 6th April 2008, the remaining gain after steps 1 to 10 is taxed at 18%.
    For earlier disposals, the remaining gain is taxed at 10%, 20% or 40%, depending on the level of the taxpayer's income for the same tax year. The Income Tax bands given in Appendix B are used first against the taxpayer's income for the year. Any remaining unused part of the Starting Rate or Basic Rate Income Tax bands can then be used to tax the gain at 10% and 20% respectively. Any excess gain remaining is then taxed at 40%.
12. Transfers of a property to the transferor's spouse or civil partner are exempt from Capital Gains Tax. The transferee is then treated as if they had acquired the property at the same time, and for the same price, as the transferor.

All of the above is explained in considerably greater depth in the Taxcafe.co.uk guide *How to Avoid Property Tax*.

There are, however, one or two quirks which tend to create some key differences between gains on UK property and gains on foreign property. One of the most significant is undoubtedly the impact of foreign exchange differences, exacerbated by the fact that UK Capital Gains Tax calculations must generally be carried out in sterling. We will look at this subject in detail in Chapter 6.

5.5   THE BASIC CALCULATION

Before we get on to some of the complexities of UK Capital Gains Tax on foreign property, let's just look at a basic example to illustrate the main principles.

Example

In January 1999, Ian bought a holiday home in Jamaica for £100,000 including purchase costs.

In June 2003, Ian spent £50,000 on an extension to the property.

In May 2008, Ian sold his Jamaican house. His sale proceeds after deducting disposal costs amounted to £250,000. Ian has no other capital gains during 2008/9.

Ian's Capital Gains Tax calculation is as follows:

	£	£
Sale proceeds		*250,000*
Less:		
Cost	*100,000*	
Improvement expenditure	*50,000*	

		150,000

Capital gain		*100,000*
Less:		
Annual Exemption (see Appendix B)		*9,500*

Taxable gain		*90,500*
		======
Capital Gains Tax payable at 18%:		*£16,290*

5.6 FOREIGN PROPERTY AS A MAIN RESIDENCE

An individual's only or main residence, also known as their principal private residence, is exempt from UK Capital Gains Tax.

If the property is the taxpayer's principal private residence throughout their ownership, it will be fully exempt. If it is their principal private residence for only part of their ownership there will be a partial exemption.

Partial exemption is calculated on a time apportionment basis. The exempt proportion of the capital gain is determined by taking:

i) The number of days for which the property was the owner's principal private residence.
PLUS

ii) The number of days during the last three years of ownership not already included within (i).
DIVIDED BY

iii) The total number of days for which the property was owned.

Any periods of ownership prior to 31st March 1982 are excluded from (i) and (iii) but this does not preclude the period at (ii) from being included, even when the entire principal private residence period fell before that date.

Foreign Main Residences

The principal private residence exemption, as described above, applies to the taxpayer's main residence, wherever that residence may be located. It does not apply exclusively to UK property.

In other words, a foreign property can be a UK resident taxpayer's main residence for UK Capital Gains Tax purposes.

Furthermore, as explained in Section 5.1, liability to UK Capital Gains Tax arises when the taxpayer is UK resident at the time of sale of a property. Hence, a foreign property may often have been used as the taxpayer's main residence at an earlier time, when they were non-UK resident, and thus be eligible for partial exemption at the time of sale.

Example

On 30th April 2000 Robert decided that he'd had enough of the UK and decided to move to Tahiti where he bought a new home, Arreless, for £130,000. Robert lived in Arreless for two years but, to his immense surprise, eventually grew homesick. In the end, Robert decided to move back to the UK and returned here on 30th April 2002.

On 30th April 2008, Robert sold Arreless for £250,000. He made no other capital gains during 2008/9.

Robert is eligible for principal private residence relief for the two years that he lived in Arreless plus the last three years of his ownership, making a total of five years out of the eight years that he owned the property.

Robert's Capital Gains Tax liability is therefore computed as follows:

	£
Sale proceeds	250,000
Less:	
Cost	130,000

	120,000
Less:	
Principal private residence relief	
(five years out of eight*) £120,000 x 5/8 =	75,000

Capital gain	45,000
Less:	
Annual Exemption	9,500

Taxable gain	35,500
	======
Capital Gains Tax payable at 18%:	£6,390

* - For the sake of illustration, I have used years here. In practice, the calculation should be based on days.

Current Foreign Main Residences

In addition to the possibility of a foreign property being a former main residence, there are also a number of ways in which a UK resident might have a foreign property which is their current main residence, such as:

- A UK resident person who owns a home abroad but does not own a home in the UK (including an unmarried person whose common-law partner owns their UK home).
- A UK resident person who travels a lot and resides more often in a home in another country than anywhere else.
- A UK resident whose spouse or registered civil partner lives abroad.
- A UK resident person with a foreign holiday home which they elect to treat as their main residence.

The first two scenarios above are simply a question of fact. The third arises due to the rule that married couples and civil partners may only have one main residence between them as a couple. The fourth scenario, however, gives rise to some very interesting planning opportunities.

Before we look at those planning opportunities though, we need to take a quick look at another very important Capital Gains Tax relief – private letting relief.

5.7   PRIVATE LETTING RELIEF

Where any property which qualifies as the owner's principal private residence at any time during their ownership is also, at some time, let out as private residential accommodation, the owner is entitled to a further relief, known as private letting relief.

Private letting relief is given as the lowest of three values:

i)   The amount of principal private residence relief to which the owner is entitled on the same property,

ii)   The amount of capital gain arising during the letting period (time apportionment again applies), and

iii)   £40,000.

The £40,000 limit applies on a 'per person' basis, so joint owners may be able to claim up to £80,000 between them.

To see this relief in action, let's return to our example from the previous section.

Example Revisited

After returning to the UK, Robert rented Arreless out as private accommodation until he sold the property on 30th April 2008.

Robert's Capital Gains Tax liability is now as follows:

	£
Sale proceeds	*250,000*
Less:	
Cost	*130,000*

	120,000
Less:	
Principal private residence relief	
(five years out of eight) £120,000 x 5/8 =	*75,000*
Private Letting Relief (Maximum)	*40,000*

Capital gain	*5,000*
Less:	
Annual Exemption (restricted)	*5,000*

Taxable gain	*NIL*
	======
Capital Gains Tax payable:	*NIL*

As we can see, the additional relief which Robert is able to claim because he rented the property out has enabled him to eliminate any Capital Gains Tax liability.

This outcome is quite common when a former main residence has also been rented out. Indeed, where the total capital gain is under £80,000 per person, complete exemption will often be available in accordance with the following law:

Bayley's Principal Private Residence Relief Law

The general rule is that a gain of up to £80,000 per person is covered until at least two times (N + 3) years after you first bought the property. 'N' is the number of years that it was your own main residence, not counting the last three years of ownership.

5.8 SAVING CAPITAL GAINS TAX ON FOREIGN HOLIDAY HOMES

As we saw in the previous section, the combination of principal private residence relief and private letting relief leads to an enormous reduction in the amount of taxable capital gain on the sale of a former main residence.

This brings us back to the possibility that a foreign property might be regarded as its owner's main residence. As we saw in Section 5.6, there are many cases when this will arise simply as a consequence of the owner's own personal circumstances.

What is more interesting, however, is the fact that, where a person has more than one private residence, it is possible to elect which one is to be treated as their main residence for Capital Gains Tax purposes. Such an election is equally valid when made in respect of an overseas holiday home.

Before we go any further, it is worth pausing to consider what we mean when we refer to a property as a taxpayer's residence. A property cannot be a **_main_** residence unless it qualifies as **_a_** private residence of that individual taxpayer, married couple or registered civil partnership. (For married couples and registered civil partners, all of the principles regarding residences must be applied to the couple as a unit.)

A residence is a dwelling in which the owner habitually lives. To 'live' in a property means to adopt it as the place where you are based and where you sleep, shelter and have your home. Whilst it needs to be habitual, however, your occupation of the property might still be occasional and short.

Example

Dylan owns a small villa in the Algarve but lives and works in Cardiff. Dylan bought the villa as a holiday home, but he only manages to visit it about two or three times each year, when he will typically stay for a long weekend.

Despite the rarity of Dylan's visits to the villa, it nevertheless qualifies as his private residence.

Some actual physical occupation of the property (including overnight stays) is necessary before it can be a residence. Dylan's situation is probably just about the minimum level of occupation which could qualify.

Some other use of a property at other times, when not occupied as the taxpayer's private residence, does not necessarily prevent it from qualifying as a residence. If such a property were to be treated as your main residence though, there would be a proportionate reduction in the amount of principal private residence relief available.

Hence, as we can see, there will be many instances in which a foreign property might be regarded as the owner's private residence. If a property qualifies as a private residence then it is possible to elect for it to be treated as a main residence and thus to benefit from the substantial reliefs which we have seen in the previous sections.

Wealth Warning

As we shall see below, a property may become a main residence, by election, for a very short period of time.

To achieve this, it is however essential that the property is the owner's private residence, as described above, for an appreciable period. In practice, I would recommend at least two years, although there is no statutory rule on this.

Main Residence Elections

When someone acquires a second (or subsequent) private residence they may, at any time within two years of the date that the new property first becomes available to them as a residence, elect which of their properties is to be regarded as their main residence for the purpose of the principal private residence exemption.

The election must be made in writing, addressed to 'Her Majesty's Inspector of Taxes' and sent to the taxpayer's tax office (see Section 2.8). An unmarried individual must sign the election personally in order for it to be effective. A married couple must both sign the election, as must both members of a registered civil partnership.

There is no particular prescribed form for the election, although the following example wording would be suitable for inclusion:

'In accordance with section 222(5) Taxation of Chargeable Gains Act 1992, [I/We] hereby nominate [Property] as [my/our] main residence with effect from [Date*].'

* - The first such election which an individual, a married couple or a registered civil partnership makes in respect of any new combination of residences will automatically be treated as coming into effect from the beginning of the period to which it relates – i.e. from the date on which they first held that new combination of residences. It is this first election for the new combination of residences to which the two-year time limit applies.

However, once an election is in place, it may subsequently be changed, by a further written notice given to the Inspector under the same procedure, at any time. Such a new election may be given retrospective effect, if desired, by up to two years.

This ability to elect which property is regarded as a main residence and then to change the nominated property at will thereafter gives rise to enormous planning opportunities.

Example

Rudyard lives in a small flat in Dover where he works. In September 2006 he also bought a house in Bruges and started spending most of his weekends there. In August 2008, Rudyard realises that his Bruges house has appreciated in value significantly since he bought it. His small flat in Dover has not increased in value quite so significantly. He therefore elects, before the expiry of the two-year time limit, that his Belgian house is his main residence.

In 2011 Rudyard sells the Bruges house at a substantial gain, which is fully exempted by the principal private residence exemption.

Note in this example that Rudyard's flat in Dover will not be counted as his main residence from September 2006 until the time of sale of his Bruges house. However, should he sell the flat, his final three years of ownership will be covered by the principal private residence exemption.

Tax Tip

As soon as Rudyard decided to sell his Bruges house, he should have submitted a new main residence election nominating the Dover flat as his main residence once more, with effect from a date two years previously. This would give an extra two years of principal private residence exemption on the flat, whilst leaving the Bruges house fully exempt as long as he sold it within one year after making the new election (i.e. within three years after the date that it was now deemed to cease to be his main residence).

What If You Don't Know Which House You're Going to Sell?

One potential drawback of making a main residence election in favour of a foreign holiday home is the loss of relief on your original home back in the UK. This could lead to a significant taxable gain arising on the sale of your UK home.

We have already seen one way to minimise the impact of this lost relief – by making a new election in favour of the original home as soon as you decide to sell the holiday home.

However, where both properties are held for a substantial period of time, there might still be a significant exposure to tax on the original UK home. In many cases, this potential tax exposure will be far greater than the potential tax saving on the foreign property.

How then can you save tax on your foreign property without exposing yourself to a big Capital Gains Tax bill on your UK home?

This problem is easily resolved by making a subsequent election in favour of the UK home shortly after the first election is made.

Example

Joanne Kathleen has a large house in Edinburgh which she bought on 1ˢᵗ June 2004 for £800,000. On 1ˢᵗ October 2007 she also paid £500,000 to buy Il Castillo Ogawarta, a small castle just outside Florence, which she uses as a winter home.

In early 2009 Joanne Kathleen visits her accountant, Harry, and explains that she is concerned about the Capital Gains Tax exposure on both of her properties, although she has no intention of selling either of them in the foreseeable future.

After pottering around amongst his textbooks for a while, Harry advises Joanne Kathleen to submit a main residence election in favour of Il Castillo Ogawarta before the two year time limit expires on 1ˢᵗ October 2009.

"But what about the house in Edinburgh?" asks Joanne Kathleen. "Ah, that's the really clever bit", replies Harry, "after a week you can submit another main residence election in favour of your Edinburgh house. You can backdate the second election by up to two years, so that it applies from 8ᵗʰ October 2007. That way you won't lose much of your principal private residence exemption."

"Mmmm, that sounds alright for the Edinburgh property, but does it actually achieve very much for my Italian place? I mean, a week's worth of exemption isn't likely to save me very much tax."

*"That's just it", responds Harry, "you won't get just a week of exemption, you'll get a week **plus** three years. Every property which ever qualifies as a main residence, even by election, is always exempt for the last three years of your ownership too."*

"Wizard Harry, that's great" beams Joanne Kathleen and Harry calls for his assistant Ron to get the paperwork ready.

A few years later, on 2nd June 2012, Joanne Kathleen sells her Edinburgh house for £2,000,000. Her Capital Gains Tax calculation looks like this:

	£
Sale proceeds	2,000,000
Less Cost	800,000

	1,200,000
Less:	
Principal private residence relief	
(2,917 days out of 2,924)	1,197,128

	2,872
	=======

Harry explains that, at worst, Joanne Kathleen might have up to £517 in Capital Gains Tax to pay, but that if she manages to avoid making any other significant capital gains during 2012/13, her annual exemption will actually cover the gain arising leaving her with no tax to pay.

Harry also advises Joanne Kathleen, who has now bought a new home in Edinburgh, to make a new main residence election at this stage, since every new combination of private residences renders any previous main residence election invalid and also opens up a new two year time limit to make a fresh election.

"Should I elect in favour of Il Castillo Ogawarta again?" asks Joanne Kathleen. "Well it's not really necessary" responds Harry, "you've already 'banked' your last three years exemption anyway, so another election in favour of the castle for a short period only wouldn't really make much difference."

"Why bother then?" Joanne Kathleen retorts. "Well it's always advisable" Harry replies, "firstly because it gives you certainty as to which property will be treated as your main residence but also, more importantly because, by making the election within the requisite two year time limit, you've always got the opportunity to change it later if it looks like being more beneficial to do so."

"Oh yes, that makes sense then. Fine, let's do it." Agrees Joanne Kathleen and Harry calls for his new assistant Hermione to sort out some new election paperwork.

On 2nd October 2013, Joanne Kathleen sells Il Castillo Ogawarta for £1,000,000 and Harry works out her Capital Gains Tax bill as follows:

	£
Sale proceeds	*1,000,000*
Less Cost	*500,000*

	500,000
Principal private residence relief	
(1,103 days out of 2,194)	*251,368*

	248,632
	========

"How did I get 1,103 days of exemption Harry?" asks Joanne Kathleen. "That's three years plus a week, remember, I told you about that when you did that main residence election back in 2009" Harry points out.

"Oh, right. Well, how much has the election saved me then?" enquires Joanne Kathleen.

"Well, as things stand, your Capital Gains Tax bill at 18% will be £44,754 at the most, possibly slightly less depending on whether you make any other capital gains this year. If you hadn't made the election, the taxable gain would have been £500,000 giving you a tax bill of up to £90,000. In all, the election has saved you over £45,000."

"Wow, Harry, you're a genius" Joanne Kathleen enthuses. "How do you do it?" "Oh, I just read the right textbooks" Harry responds modestly.

If all of this sounds too good to be true: for once, it isn't. Revenue and Customs' own manual actually states that a main residence election can be made in favour of a second home for just one week.

In practice, the choice of which property to elect as a main residence can be a difficult decision. The best choice will depend on the individual circumstances of the property owner. One thing is absolutely clear though:

Tax Tip

Whenever you acquire a second, or subsequent, private residence, always, <u>always</u>, **always**, make a main residence election within two years!

Wealth Warning

Remember that each new combination of private residences means that you need to make a new main residence election within two years of the new combination coming into being.

5.9 MIXED USE PROPERTIES

Regardless of any main residence election, a property may only be a main residence for principal private residence relief purposes if it is, in fact, the taxpayer's own private residence at that time.

Hence, a property which is being let out cannot be covered by the principal private residence exemption whilst it is being let. It may nevertheless still attract private letting relief if it qualifies as the taxpayer's main residence at some other time.

In our second example in the previous section, Joanne Kathleen had a second home in Italy which she elected to treat as her main residence for just one week. This provided her with principal private residence relief for three years plus a week.

Where, as in Joanne Kathleen's case, the property is only used privately, principal private residence relief will apply exactly as shown in that example without restriction. Full exemption will be given for the period of main residence plus the last three years of ownership.

This will generally also remain the case if the period of deemed main residence falls within a period during which there is no other use of the property and there are no major structural alterations made to the property between then and its eventual sale.

Example

Robert and Elizabeth jointly own an apartment in the Florida Keys which they bought in September 2007 as a holiday home at a cost of £200,000. For the first two years, they visit the property for a week every other month and do not use it for any other purpose. They also elect to treat the property as their main residence for this period.

From September 2009 onwards, however, Robert and Elizabeth start renting out the apartment and only use it themselves for two months each year.

In September 2017, Robert and Elizabeth sell the apartment for £520,000. Neither of them have any other capital gains in the 2017/18 tax year.

Robert and Elizabeth each have an identical Capital Gains Tax calculation which looks like this:

	£
Sale proceeds (half each)	*260,000*
Less Cost (half each)	*100,000*

	160,000
Less:	
Principal private residence relief	
(five years out of eight) 5/8 x £160,000	*100,000*
Private letting relief (maximum)	*40,000*

	20,000
Less:	
Annual exemption for 2017/18	*12,900*

Taxable capital gain	*7,100*
	======
Capital Gains Tax payable @ 18% (each):	*£1,278*

There are a number of key points to note about this example:

  i) Firstly, by making the main residence election, Robert and Elizabeth have reduced the total Capital Gains Tax on the sale of their Florida apartment from £52,956 to just £2,556 (the saving of £50,400 is 18% of the total relief obtained of £280,000).

ii)   Secondly, the letting of the apartment **after** the period covered by the election made no difference to the amount of principal private residence relief available. The couple still enjoyed full exemption both for the two years when it was their main residence by election and for the last three years of ownership.

iii)   private letting relief is available as the lowest of:

    a. The gain arising due to the period of letting (£50,000).

    b. The amount of principal private residence relief (£100,000).

    c. £40,000.

    The gain arising due to the period of letting (£50,000) is calculated as 10/12 x £60,000. This is the gain during the period not covered by principal private residence relief restricted by a factor of 10/12ths due to Robert and Elizabeth's continuing private use of the property for two months each year.

iv)   Robert and Elizabeth are each entitled to the maximum amount of private letting relief, £40,000, thus giving the couple total additional relief of £80,000.

v)   The annual exemption for 2017/18 has been estimated.

What Is Other Use?

As stated above, principal private residence relief will be restricted where there is some other use of the property during the period of main residence.

'Other use' for this purpose includes both arm's length commercial rentals and exclusive business use of any part of the property.

Occasionally lending the property to family or friends does not affect its main residence status, even if they make some small contributions to running costs. However, if the property is formally leased to a friend or family member, even at a non-arms' length rent, the owner's main residence status will be lost.

Furthermore, if someone other than the owner adopts the property as _their_ private residence then the owner's main residence status will probably be lost for the relevant period. This does not apply, however, where there is no formal lease and the owner is also able to use the property themselves during the same period with everyone effectively living as a single household.

Example

Victor owns a mountain retreat in Bavaria where he stays for two months every summer. He has elected to treat the property as his main residence for UK Capital Gains Tax purposes.

In 2008, his daughter Mary and her boyfriend Percy use the property rent free for the whole summer. Victor joins them for his usual two month stay and they all live together as a single household for this period.

Mary and Percy's use of the property will not affect Victor's principal private residence relief under these circumstances.

What Impact Does Other Use Have?

Other use of a property during the main residence period will result in a restriction in the amount of principal private residence relief available.

As we have seen, however, renting out a property as residential accommodation means that private letting relief is also available, so very often the overall effect is actually beneficial to the owner's Capital Gains Tax position.

Example

As Robert and Elizabeth (in our example earlier in this section) continued to use their apartment in Florida as a private residence on a habitual basis for two months each year, they could have continued their main residence election in favour of that property up until the time they sold it.

If they had done so, their Capital Gains Tax calculations would have been as follows:

	£
Sale proceeds (half each)	*260,000*
Less Cost (half each)	*100,000*

	160,000
Less:	
Principal private residence relief	
Full (five years out of eight) 5/8 x £160,000	*100,000*
Restricted	
(three years out of eight) 3/8 x £160,000 x 2/12	*10,000*
Private letting relief (maximum)	*40,000*

	10,000
Less:	
Annual exemption for 2017/18	*10,000*

Taxable capital gain	*NIL*
	=======
Capital Gains Tax payable:	*NIL*

As we can see, the extra period of principal private residence relief has eliminated the couple's Capital Gains Tax liabilities.

However, for a three year period, the relief is restricted to only two twelfths of the gain arising in that period due to the property's use as a rental property for ten months each year.

This is fine if the couple never sell any other private residence. However, if they do have another property, it is questionable whether it is worth sacrificing another three years' worth of principal private residence relief on that property for the sake of relieving just two twelfths of the gain arising on their Florida property in the same period.

The Last Three Years

As long as every part of a property is used as the owner's private residence at some point during the period that the property qualifies as their main residence and there are no major structural alterations to the property, full relief will remain available for the last three years of ownership.

Alterations which change the character of a property so that it is no longer the same dwelling have a greater impact on principal private residence relief, however, and can cause even the last three years' relief to be lost.

The type of alterations which have this effect are generally those which result in separate dwellings being created, such as a single villa being converted into two apartments.

5.10 TAPER RELIEF

Taper relief is available on capital gains arising on disposals of property taking place before 6th April 2008.

In calculating the taper relief available on disposal of a property before 6th April 2008, the first point to establish is whether the property qualified as a 'business asset' at any time after 5th April 1998 (or the date of purchase if later).

The question of whether a property has business asset status is vital in determining the amount of taper relief available. Properties qualifying as business assets attract a far higher level of taper relief.

What Is Business Property?

The first important point to note is that a property's location has no effect on whether or not it qualifies as a business asset.

The second important point is that renting property out does not itself constitute a trade. For rented property, the key factor for taper relief purposes is what the tenant uses the property for.

As a result, in very broad terms, the vast majority of residential property does not qualify as a business asset for taper relief purposes, whereas a large proportion of commercial property does qualify.

With effect from 6th April 2004, any property, whether located in the UK or overseas, is regarded as a business asset for taper relief purposes where it is used for the purposes of a trade carried on by a qualifying trading entity.

The trading entity does not need to be in any way connected with the owner of the property and nor does it need to be based in the UK.

Most trading entities qualify for this purpose, including sole traders, partnerships and many companies. For a company to qualify, however, it must generally be either an unquoted trading company or the property owner's employer (and, in the latter case, the property owner and their family must usually not hold more than 10% of any class of shares in the company).

In summary, therefore, almost any property you own which you either use yourself in a trading activity, or which you rent out and which your tenants use in a trade, will qualify as a business asset from 6th April 2004, regardless of where the property is located or where the trade is run from.

Naturally, this will tend to cover most commercial property although, in certain circumstances, it could also extend to residential property let to a trading entity.

The major exception arises where the tenant is a quoted company, unless you are also an officer or employee of that company, or another company in the same group, or own more than 5% of the shares in a quoted trading company.

Property Owned Before 6th April 2004

A property let to a qualifying company as described above would qualify as a business asset from 6th April 2000 onwards.

Properties used in the owner's own trade, or that of a company of which the property owner owned at least 25% (or was an employee and owned at least 5%), qualified as business assets from the introduction of taper relief in 1998.

Any other property held before 6th April 2004 would only qualify as a business asset from that date onwards.

Wealth Warning

Where a property which only qualifies as a business asset with effect from 6th April 2004 was also held before that date, it will only be partly eligible for business asset taper relief. This is given effect by time apportioning any capital gain between the qualifying and non-qualifying periods.

The same approach applies whenever any property qualified as a business asset for only part of the period of ownership.

Rates of Taper Relief

The rates of business asset taper relief on disposals taking place before 6th April 2008 are:

- Assets held less than one year: Nil
- Assets held for one year, but less than two years: 50%
- Assets held for two years or more: 75%

For all other assets, there is no taper relief unless the asset has been held for at least three years. After three years of ownership, the rate is 5%. The rate of taper relief then increases in increments of 5% for every additional complete year that the asset has been held up to a maximum rate of 40%. Periods of ownership prior to 6th April 1998 are ignored but an extra year is counted when the asset was already held before 17th March 1998.

Abolition of Taper Relief

Taper relief will cease to be available on capital gains arising on disposals taking place on or after 6th April 2008. Thereafter, the current regime is to be replaced by a single flat rate of Capital Gains Tax of 18%.

The impact of this change is examined in detail in the Taxcafe.co.uk guide *How to Avoid Property Tax*.

Broadly, however, the change will give rise to an increase in the Capital Gains Tax payable on property which would qualify as a business asset under the taper relief regime (unless Entrepreneurs' Relief applies – see Section 5.2) and a decrease in the Capital Gains Tax payable on most other properties

This is because the 75% taper relief available on business assets sold before 6th April 2008 after being held for two years or more results in a maximum effective rate of Capital Gains Tax on those assets of just 10%. The change to a flat rate of 18% therefore represents a significant tax increase and this will apply to many foreign commercial properties.

On the other hand, the effective rate of Capital Gains Tax on other assets sold before 6th April 2008 ranges between 24% and 40% for higher rate taxpayers. The change to a flat rate of 18% therefore gives rise to a tax reduction for these taxpayers and this will apply to most foreign residential property.

Basic rate taxpayers selling non-business assets before 6th April 2008 will be subject to an effective Capital Gains Tax rate of between 12% and 20% on at least part of their gain. The change to a flat rate of 18% will therefore give rise to a tax increase for these taxpayers in some cases, although the position here is somewhat complex.

In broad terms though, the changes due to take place on 6th April 2008 will generally mean a reduction in the rate of Capital Gains Tax applying to foreign residential property (with some exceptions for basic rate taxpayers) and an increase in the rate applying to foreign commercial property.

5.11 CAPITAL LOSSES ON FOREIGN PROPERTY

The good news is that there is no distinction between capital losses arising on foreign property and any other capital losses.

However, the bad news, as with all other capital losses, is that, in general, such losses may only be set off against capital gains arising in the same tax year or a later one.

Furthermore, relief is denied for 'artificial' capital losses arising after 5th December 2006 as a result of transactions which were carried out with a main purpose of creating a tax advantage. At present, it is too early to tell just how widely this new rule will be interpreted.

5.12 DEATH AND TAXES

Benjamin Franklin once said that there are only two certainties in life: death and taxes. Inheritance Tax, of course, brings these two great certainties together and it is not about to be frustrated by a few trivial details like geography!

Unlike other UK taxes, liability to Inheritance Tax is dependent on domicile rather than residence. We will look at the concept of domicile in detail in Chapter 8, where we will also examine the Inheritance Tax position of non-UK domiciled taxpayers.

For a UK domiciled taxpayer, Inheritance Tax is payable at a single rate of 40% on their entire worldwide estate, subject to certain exemptions. A UK domiciled taxpayer's worldwide estate will include any foreign property, foreign company shares or other foreign assets which they own at the time of their death. Hence, for these taxpayers, UK Inheritance Tax has a universal application and cannot be avoided simply by investing in overseas property.

Contrary to popular belief, Inheritance Tax is not just payable on death but can also arise on certain other transfers of property, money or other assets made during the owner's lifetime. Where applicable, Inheritance Tax arising on lifetime transfers is usually payable at 20%, but the rate can be retrospectively increased to up to 40% when the donor dies within seven years of making the transfer.

The three most important Inheritance Tax exemptions are the nil rate band, the spouse exemption and business property relief. Each of these three exemptions applies to foreign property in just the same way as any other asset.

The Nil Rate Band

The nil rate band, as the name suggests, provides a 'band' of assets on which the rate of Inheritance Tax payable is nil. For deaths occurring during the year ending 5th April 2009, the nil rate band is £312,000.

Widows, widowers or surviving civil partners dying on or after 9th October 2007 are also entitled to any unused proportion of their late spouse or civil partner's nil rate band. Whilst the **proportion** left unused on the first spouse or partner's death is determined according to the position at that time, the **amount** of additional exemption available is based on the value of the nil rate band at the time of the widow, widower or surviving civil partner's death.

For example, if a husband dies when the nil rate band is £300,000 and uses £60,000, or 20% of his nil rate band, his widow will be entitled to an extra 80% of a nil rate band on her death. If she dies when the nil rate band is £312,000, her total exemption will be 180% of this amount, or £561,600.

Widows, widowers and surviving civil partners dying during the year ending 5th April 2009 may therefore be entitled to a total exemption of up to £624,000.

The Spouse Exemption

Anything left to the deceased's UK domiciled spouse or civil partner is exempt from Inheritance Tax. Hence, if the deceased leaves their entire estate to their UK domiciled spouse or civil partner, they will use none of their nil rate band and the survivor will be entitled to a double nil rate band on their subsequent death.

The spouse exemption generally also applies to lifetime transfers to a UK domiciled spouse or civil partner.

A restricted form of the spouse exemption applies to transfers to a non-UK domiciled spouse or civil partner and we will return to this point in Chapter 8.

Business Property Relief

Business property relief exempts certain types of business property from Inheritance Tax. The definition of business property for this purpose is not the same as we saw in Section 5.10 for Capital Gains Tax taper relief. Generally speaking, business property relief only applies to trading assets used in the taxpayer's own trade or to shares in unquoted trading companies.

Business property relief might, for example, apply to the assets of a property development business, although it cannot apply to a property dealing trade.

Most importantly, the location of any qualifying trading assets has no impact on the availability of business property relief and the relief will apply equally to any trade carried on wholly or partly overseas.

Example

John died on 8th December 2008 leaving the following assets:

- *An apartment in New York worth £2,000,000.*
- *Several investment properties in the UK and abroad with a total value of £1,000,000.*
- *A property development business with sites under development in the UK, Spain and France and a total value of £10,000,000.*
- *A house in Liverpool worth £500,000.*
- *Various investments and savings worth £800,000.*

John leaves the Liverpool house and the investments and savings to his wife Paula and divides the rest of his estate equally between his two sons George and Richard.

The assets left to Paula are exempt under the spouse exemption.

The property development business is covered by business property relief and thus escapes Inheritance Tax.

The New York apartment and the investment properties are all subject to Inheritance Tax. As John was UK domiciled, there is no distinction between UK and overseas property, so his taxable estate has a total value of £3,000,000.

After deducting the nil rate band of £312,000, we are left with a value of £2,688,000 which is taxed at 40%, leaving John's executors with an Inheritance Tax bill of £1,075,200 to pay out of his estate.

Agricultural Property Relief

Agricultural property relief applies to agricultural land and buildings in the UK, Channel Islands and Isle of Man.

Unlike business property relief, the relief is not available on property overseas.

Hence, buying a French farmhouse will not generally enable a UK domiciled taxpayer to avoid UK Inheritance Tax.

A great deal more detail on Inheritance Tax is given in the Taxcafe.co.uk guide *'How to Avoid Inheritance Tax'*. Whilst death itself may be unavoidable, we have a whole book to tell you how to avoid Inheritance Tax!

Chapter 6

Foreign Exchange

6.1 EXPOSED!

Anyone who buys property abroad will inevitably be exposed to foreign currency exchange differences.

Movements in foreign currency exchange rates will affect both the value of foreign property investments and the owner's UK tax liabilities.

In a very real sense, investing in foreign property will generally also mean that you are investing in the relevant country's currency. Whilst the property itself may have strong foundations, your investment could be severely undermined by a weak currency!

As we will see in some of the examples which follow, making gains on your investments at a local level will not necessarily mean that you make gains in sterling terms back at home.

Whilst our main aim in this guide is to cover taxation issues relating to foreign property we will, in this chapter, also give some consideration to other aspects of foreign exchange affecting UK residents buying foreign property.

6.2 STERLING RULES OK!

The UK tax system operates in sterling. Generally speaking, therefore, all UK tax calculations must be carried out in sterling.

However, where foreign property is involved, most underlying transactions will have taken place in another currency. This means that all UK residents investing in foreign property are inevitably exposed to the vagaries of foreign exchange on both their investments and their UK tax liabilities.

As we shall see as we progress through this chapter, foreign exchange differences have their greatest impact when we come to capital transactions, such as buying or selling property and, of course, capital taxation liabilities.

Inheritance Tax is the less problematic of the two main UK capital taxes since it is simply a case of establishing the sterling equivalent of a foreign property's value at the relevant date (usually the date of the owner's death).

It is when we come to Capital Gains Tax on foreign properties, however, that major problems begin to arise.

Note that companies are subject to an entirely different tax regime on their foreign exchange differences and we will consider that regime in Chapter 10.

6.3 FOREIGN PROPERTY INCOME

As far as foreign property income is concerned, there are two alternative methods which may be used for dealing with foreign exchange: actual or average.

Under the actual method, each and every item of income and expenditure is translated into sterling at the exchange rate applying on the date that it arises or is incurred. As you can imagine, this method can become quite onerous to apply in practice!

Thankfully, instead, Revenue and Customs will accept foreign property income calculations based on the average exchange rate applying for the relevant year.

For foreign rental income, which must be accounted for on a tax year basis (year ended 5th April), the average for the corresponding year ended 31st March may be used. (E.g., for income arising in 2008/9, use the average for the year ended 31st March 2009.)

Average exchange rates for the year ended 31st March 2007 for our top 20 destination countries (see Section 1.2) are given in Appendix A.

Revenue and Customs are equally happy with the actual or average method, as long as the same method is applied consistently. (Sadly, you cannot just choose whichever method suits you best each year!)

6.4   FOREIGN CURRENCY

UK investors owning foreign property will inevitably also need to hold foreign currency. Sometimes, perhaps at the time of a property's purchase or sale for example, quite significant amounts of foreign currency will be held.

In principle, foreign currency held by a UK resident individual is regarded as a chargeable asset subject to Capital Gains Tax. Amounts held for personal use, however, such as holiday money for example, are exempt from this treatment.

The exemption for amounts held for personal use extends to foreign currency held for the purpose of buying or maintaining a private residence, such as an overseas holiday home. This is not all good news, however, as it means that no relief is available for any foreign exchange losses arising on these funds.

The foreign currency proceeds of the sale of an overseas private residence will continue to be covered by the personal use exemption as long as the funds are not held in foreign currency for an excessively long period. Holding the proceeds in foreign currency for one or two months, whilst waiting for an improved rate of exchange, for example, should not alter the 'personal use' nature of those funds.

Ultimately, however, where foreign currency is held for more than a reasonable period, the funds held will become a chargeable asset subject to UK Capital Gains Tax on disposal. Where proceeds of sale are exchanged for a *different* foreign currency this will generally mean that the personal use exemption ceases to apply, although this would not be the case where this exchange was made in order to facilitate the purchase of a new overseas private residence in a different country.

Foreign Currency Held for Business Use

Where foreign currency is held in connection with overseas property other than a private residence, it becomes a chargeable asset for UK Capital Gains Tax purposes.

The main occasions when this gives rise to UK tax consequences will be on the purchase or sale of foreign investment property. We will look at some of those consequences, and how to mitigate their impact, in Section 6.8.

The other occasions where a UK resident holding foreign property is concerned with foreign exchange differences will generally be:

i)   When funds are transferred overseas to cover the running costs of foreign property, and
ii) When rental income received in foreign currency is exchanged into sterling.

In the first instance, scenario (i) above involves the acquisition of foreign currency, rather than its disposal. Strictly speaking, however, a disposal for UK Capital Gains Tax purposes occurs whenever the foreign currency funds are used to pay the property's running costs. It may, however, be rather impractical to perform a Capital Gains Tax calculation every time you pay the local window cleaner, gardener, etc.

Furthermore, where the 'average' rate of exchange method, as described in Section 6.3 above, is being used to calculate the foreign property income, it would seem nonsensical to compute short-term exchange differences arising within the same tax year. In practice, therefore, the foreign exchange consequences arising when small amounts of foreign currency are used to pay running costs are usually ignored.

Rental income received in foreign currency also strictly becomes a chargeable asset for UK Capital Gains Tax purposes. Again, however, where the funds are only held short-term, before either being exchanged into sterling or used to pay running costs, the foreign exchange differences arising may, in practice, be ignored.

The taxpayer may, however, if they so desire, insist on following the strict basis and calculating all foreign exchange differences on foreign currency held for business purposes as they arise. This would involve a great deal of work and Revenue and Customs would expect the taxpayer to apply the same principles consistently, whether they produced a capital gain or a capital loss. (It would also probably become necessary to use an actual basis for the calculation of the foreign property income for Income Tax purposes too.)

Nevertheless, following this strict basis might perhaps sometimes be worthwhile. For example, capital losses arising from these small transactions could be accumulated over a number of years and carried forward for offset against a capital gain arising on the ultimate sale of the foreign property. This strategy would work well if the property were located in a country with a weak currency and a high rate of property price inflation.

Even in the case of a fluctuating currency, the strict basis could prove useful over time as any net capital loss arising in a tax year could be carried forward for relief against future capital gains whereas net capital gains arising would only become taxable if they exceeded the annual Capital Gains Tax exemption for the year.

Whether it's worth the effort will depend on the circumstances of each individual case, but it can readily be seen that the strict basis has a lot of tax saving potential!

Where foreign property income is accumulated in foreign currency over a number of years, the foreign currency itself will be regarded as a long-term investment and it will become necessary to calculate the Capital Gains Tax consequences on its disposal. This would apply equally whether the funds were exchanged into sterling, exchanged into another currency, or used to fund the purchase of another property. A suitable example is again included in Section 6.8.

6.5   FOREIGN CURRENCY LOANS

Foreign currency loans held by UK resident individuals represent a major anomaly within the UK tax system.

Whilst foreign currency itself (including foreign currency denominated bank accounts) represents a chargeable asset and is often subject to Capital Gains Tax, any gains or losses arising on foreign currency denominated loans held by UK resident individuals are generally simply ignored. They are what we sometimes term 'tax nothings'.

Nevertheless, borrowing in foreign currency has major ramifications for UK resident investors buying foreign property and we will return to this point in Section 6.7.

6.6   FOREIGN EXCHANGE AND CAPITAL GAINS

If anyone is still labouring under the misapprehension that tax is fair, this section is the one which is sure to open their eyes.

In Section 5.4, I set out a 12 step summary of how UK Capital Gains Tax is calculated. Every step in that calculation needs to be carried out in sterling. Furthermore, the exchange rate applying at each step is the exchange rate prevailing at the time of the relevant transaction.

In other words, sale proceeds are calculated using the exchange rate applying at the time of sale, but the purchase price to be deducted from those proceeds is calculated at the exchange rate which applied at the time of purchase.

This can lead to some very unfair results!

Example

On 1st June 2008, George buys an old farmhouse in Eastasia for 200 million orwells. The orwell is the Eastasian unit of currency and, on 1st June 2008, the exchange rate is 1,984 orwells to the pound.

On 28th May 2012, George sells the farmhouse to Napoleon, having rented the property out as holiday accommodation in the meantime. Sadly, due to a slump in the Eastasian property market, George's net sale proceeds amount to just 150 million orwells. The exchange rate on 28th May 2012 is 1,200 orwells to the pound.

George has already used his 2012/13 annual exemption on other capital gains in the year. His Capital Gains Tax calculation on disposal of the Eastasion farmhouse is therefore as follows:

	£
Sale proceeds (150m/1,200)	*125,000*
Less cost (200m/1,984)	*100,806*

	24,194
	======
Capital Gains Tax payable @ 18%:	*£4,355*
	======

So, despite losing 50 million in the local currency, George ends up with a taxable capital gain in the UK and a Capital Gains Tax bill of over £4,000.

Is This Fair?

As a professional tax adviser for over twenty years, I have long since given up on trying to see fairness or logic in the tax system.

Nevertheless, I can see some logic in this system. If George, who is UK resident after all, had originally invested funds taken from the UK in order to buy his Eastasian farmhouse and then brings his sale proceeds back to the UK after its sale, then his true economic position surely is actually a gain of £24,194?

Conversely, however, if George has close ties with Eastasia and intends to reinvest his funds within the country, then surely he really has lost 50 million in the local currency and a UK tax bill is adding insult to injury.

You can look at this situation either way, but the fact of the matter remains that the UK tax position must be calculated in sterling.

Wealth Warning

Just because a loss arises in the local currency, this does not mean that a taxable capital gain will not arise in the UK.

Borrowing in Local Currency

Things get even more complicated when a UK resident owning foreign property has borrowed in a local currency in order to finance their purchase.

Example Continued

When he bought the Eastasian farmhouse, George took out a mortgage with the Bank of Eastasia for 180 million orwells. George's deposit was therefore just 20 million orwells, which, in June 2008, was equivalent to £10,081.

When he sold the farmhouse for just 150 million orwells, George was left with negative equity of 30 million orwells, and this would cost him £25,000 to pay off.

Overall therefore, George has lost £35,081 (£10,081 + £25,000) on his Eastasian investment, but still ended up with a Capital Gains Tax bill of over £4,000!

Now that's definitely unfair!

Clearly, in this case, George would have been better off if he had borrowed in sterling. With a 90% mortgage in sterling on the Eastasian farmhouse (£90,726), George would have still had net proceeds of £34,274 on his sale. This would have given George his deposit back, enough money to pay his Capital Gains Tax bill and a final profit of £19,838 (£34,274 - £10,081 - £4,355).

However, this will not always be the case!

Example

Despite losing 50 million on his first investment, George still has faith in the long-term viability of the Eastasian property market. Hence, on 3rd January 2013, he buys an apartment block in the Eastasian city of Cire for 390 million orwells.

The exchange rate on 3rd January 2013 is 1,300 orwells to the pound so George needs £300,000 for his purchase. Having lost out by borrowing locally before, George decides to borrow in sterling and takes out a loan of £250,000 from the Bank of Jura secured on the property in Cire.

Just as George hoped, the next two years see a boom in the Eastasian property market and, on 8th December 2015, George sells the property in Cire for 750 million orwells.

Unfortunately for George, however, the so-called 'boom' is really just the result of Eastasian inflation and, by the time of his sale, the orwell has slumped to a rate of 3,750 to the pound.

George's sale therefore realises just £200,000 (750m/3,750). Hence, despite making a gain of 360 million orwells, once again, George is effectively left with negative equity, as his sale proceeds amount to £50,000 less than his borrowings.

The only small consolation for George is that he has a capital loss of £100,000 for UK Capital Gains Tax purposes, although he will need a capital gain before it is any use to him (see Section 5.11). In Eastasia, however, he has a capital gain of 360 million orwells and this is likely to be taxed by the local government.

£50,000 out of pocket and facing a huge Eastasian tax bill, George turns for help to his big brother who, luckily, has been watching over him all along and is on hand to bale him out!

6.7   HEDGING

The example in the previous section demonstrates some of the problems caused by foreign exchange movements.

In the world of big business, these problems are mitigated by a process known as 'hedging'. Hedging is a complex subject but, in essence, the principle involved is to match foreign assets and liabilities. In other words, for every foreign asset held, an equal value of liability denominated in the same currency is created.

In this way, the exposure to the risk of losses arising as a result of exchange rate movements is significantly reduced.

Naturally, of course, hedging, when carried out correctly, also limits the opportunity to profit from favourable exchange rate movements. (Back in the 1980s, one luxury car manufacturer made more money as a result of its treasury department's failure to hedge its international transactions properly than it did from selling cars.)

One might therefore take the view that hedging wastes the opportunity to profit from exchange rate movements. This, of course, is up to the individual but I would just say that the international currency market can be volatile and unpredictable. If any of us knew how exchange rates were going to move in the future, we would have no need to invest in property. (Or to write tax books!)

Without hedging then, as stated in Section 6.1, you are not only investing in property but also in the relevant country's currency. This second element to your investment may be a good deal more risky than your property investment itself.

Hedging and Capital Gains Tax

The additional problem for UK resident individuals buying property overseas is that hedging their foreign assets still leaves them exposed to an effective exchange risk on their Capital Gains Tax liability.

This arises because of two important facts which combine to create a potentially disastrous mismatch. Firstly, the UK Capital Gains Tax payable by a UK resident individual must be computed on a sterling basis and, secondly, any exchange differences arising on foreign currency loans are simply ignored.

We saw the unfortunate results of this mismatch in the first part of George's story in the previous section.

Admittedly, part of George's loss on that occasion was actually caused by his failure to hedge properly. When the value of the farmhouse fell below the level of his borrowings, George was exposed to an exchange risk on the shortfall and this ultimately contributed to his losses.

Furthermore, the fact that George lost his deposit on the farmhouse had nothing to do with exchange rate movements and arose simply because of the fall in the property's value. (Another instance where foreign property is no different to UK property!)

Nevertheless, it is undeniable that exchange rate movements were responsible for the fact that George ended up with a UK Capital Gains Tax bill despite making a substantial loss in the local currency. To cover this exposure, George would need to have made further adjustments to the level of his orwell denominated borrowings. To do this truly effectively, however, requires a very sophisticated approach to hedging transactions which only a multinational corporation with a dedicated treasury department would be able to cope with. (And look what happened to that 1980s car manufacturer anyway!)

Hedging for Individuals in Practice

Whether you consider hedging to be necessary in practice is a matter of personal choice. If you have close ties with the country in which you are investing you may consider it unnecessary.

Similarly, when investing in a property in a country with a stable economy, the risk would generally seem to be less.

However, if you wish to reduce the commercial risk of losses arising through exchange rate movements, you will need to ensure that borrowings are made in the local currency and that these are kept at a level in line with the property's value.

In this way, only the difference between the property value and the local currency borrowings is exposed to foreign currency exchange risk.

This will still leave you exposed to an exchange risk on your potential Capital Gains Tax liability, but this is going to be far less significant than your exchange risk on the investment itself, and it can always be kept under review in any case.

6.8 CAPITAL GAINS TAX ON FOREIGN CURRENCY

In Section 6.4, we considered the principles which determine whether foreign currency will itself be treated as a chargeable asset for UK Capital Gains Tax purposes.

Let us now look at the practical impact of these rules by considering a detailed example.

Example

Ronald is a property investor with properties in several different countries and always uses his annual Capital Gains Tax exemption.

In December 2008, he decides that he would like to invest in Gondor and transfers £2,000,000 into an account at the Bank of Gondor where it is converted into the local currency, the bilbo, at the rate of 111 to the pound.

After a few months looking at property in Gondor, Ronald spots a suitable property in neighbouring Rohan. On 15th March 2009, he exchanges his 222 million bilbos into the local currency of Rohan, the frodo, receiving 33 million frodos in the process. At this point, the exchange rate is 15 frodos to the pound.

On 3rd April 2009, Ronald buys the property in Rohan at a cost of 28 million frodos. The exchange rate at this point is 14 frodos to the pound.

Ronald is then shocked when Gandalf, his accountant, informs him that, despite the fact that he has not yet sold any property, he still has taxable capital gains as follows:

	£	£
15/3/2009		
222 million bilbos converted to frodos		
Proceeds (33m/15)	2,200,000	
Less Cost:	2,000,000	

Gain		200,000
3/4/2009		
28 million frodos 'sold'		
Proceeds (28m/14)	2,000,000	
Less Cost: (28m/15)	1,866,667	

Gain		133,333

Total gains for 2008/9		333,333
		======
Capital Gains Tax payable @ 18%:		£60,000
		======

For the next three years, Ronald rents out the property in Rohan. Each year he makes a surplus of one million frodos which he adds to the five million frodos which he still had on deposit after buying the property. The average exchange rates for 2009/10, 2010/11 and 2011/12 are 16, 12.5 and 11 frodos to the pound respectively.

On 4th April 2012, Ronald sells his property in Rohan for 32 million frodos. At this point the exchange rate is 10 frodos to the pound.

Ronald's Capital Gains Tax calculation on the sale of the property in Rohan is as follows:

	£
Sale proceeds (32m/10)	*3,200,000*
Less Cost, 3/4/2009 (28m/14)	*2,000,000*

Taxable gain	*1,200,000*
	=======
Capital Gains Tax payable @ 18%:	*£216,000*
	=======

Having been so successful, Ronald now sets his sights on Mordor which is just emerging as a popular new location for property investments.

On 9th April 2012, Ronald converts his entire holding of 40 million frodos into the local currency in Mordor, the sauron. At this point, the exchange rate is 11 frodos to the pound. Once again, Ronald has a chargeable disposal for Capital Gains Tax purposes on the conversion of one foreign currency into another.

	£	£
Sale proceeds (40m/11)		*3,636,364*
Less cost:		
Purchased 15/3/2009 (5m/15)	*333,333*	
Accumulated 2009/10 (1m/16)	*62,500*	
Accumulated 2010/11 (1m/12.5)	*80,000*	
Accumulated 2011/12 (1m/11)	*90,909*	
Acquired 4/4/2012 (32m/10)	*3,200,000*	

		3,766,742

Capital Loss		*(130,378)*
		=======

Ronald has no tax to pay this time but his capital loss which arises in 2012/13 cannot be carried back against the gain on disposal of his Rohan property which occurred in 2011/12.

As we have seen, Ronald's various currency transactions have caused a number of 'disposals' for Capital Gains Tax purposes and led to some significant tax liabilities. In the end, if Ronald does ultimately intend to bring all of his sale proceeds back to the UK this is, perhaps, not entirely unreasonable.

Nevertheless, we have seen two distinct problems emerge here. The earlier transactions taking place prior to Ronald's property purchase created unnecessary tax liabilities three years in advance of his property sale.

Worst still, the final conversion of his foreign currency after the sale of his property yielded a loss which could not immediately be used.

In true economic terms, Ronald began this venture with an investment of £2,000,000 in December 2008 and exited from it in April 2012 with proceeds of £3,636,364. If we take the accumulated income, totalling £233,409, out of the picture, we see that Ronald's true gain was actually £1,402,955, from which he did not truly benefit until 9th April 2012.

In fact, Ronald was actually taxed on a gain of £333,333 in 2008/9 and, in total, he was taxed on gains of £1,533,333. This is £130,378 more than he would have been taxed on if everything had been treated as a single transaction. That equates to £23,468 in extra tax!

Tax Tips

To avoid unnecessary Capital Gains Tax liabilities at the time of purchase of a foreign investment property, ensure that the purchase funds are only converted into foreign currency on the date of purchase, or as close to it as possible.

When disposing of foreign property, try to ensure that sale proceeds are converted into sterling (or any other desired currency) as quickly as possible.

Most importantly of all, to avoid the danger of a capital loss which cannot be relieved, try to ensure that sale proceeds received in a foreign currency are converted before the end of the UK tax year in which the property disposal takes place.

6.9 A BIASED VIEW?

OK, I must admit that I have been focusing on the negative aspects of foreign exchange. There will be many cases where exchange rates move in a favourable way for the investor or which actually help to reduce their overall tax liability.

However, there are a number of reasons why I feel that, in general, exchange rate movements have an overall adverse effect on most investors:

- Capital losses cannot be carried back to be matched with capital gains in an earlier tax year, even when they effectively arise from the disposal of the same underlying investment.
- Gains are effectively accelerated causing tax liabilities to arise earlier, whereas losses can often only be carried forward.
- No double tax relief is available when local tax liabilities arise on a gain in the foreign currency, but a capital loss arises in sterling terms.

6.10 TRANSACTION COSTS

In addition to foreign exchange differences, investors will also generally incur transaction costs when converting funds to or from sterling or between other currencies.

Costs incurred on the acquisition of foreign currency which is regarded as a chargeable asset for Capital Gains Tax purposes may be treated as part of the cost of that currency. Similarly, where the currency transaction is itself treated as a capital disposal, the costs may be claimed as a disposal cost for Capital Gains Tax purposes.

Where, however, the taxpayer is carrying on a trade of property development or property dealing, these transaction costs will generally be allowable deductions for UK Income Tax purposes.

For a foreign property rental business, transaction costs arising when working capital is transferred overseas or when rent received is remitted back to the UK should also generally be allowable.

Chapter 7

Double Tax Relief

7.1 BIGGEST BUT NOT BOTH

As explained in Section 1.1, UK residents investing in foreign property will generally be exposed to double taxation, i.e. tax in the country where the property is located **and** tax in the UK.

Thankfully, UK tax legislation provides a system of double taxation relief which is designed to prevent UK resident taxpayers from paying tax twice on the same income, capital gains, etc.

Foreign taxes which are based on similar principles to UK Income Tax, Capital Gains Tax or Inheritance Tax may generally be deducted from any UK liability for those taxes. If they exceed the UK tax bill, however, then no repayment is possible.

This means that the investor effectively suffers an overall tax burden equivalent to the higher of the two tax rates applying.

Example

Jack owns an apartment block in Narnia. His rental profits from the property for UK tax purposes is £10,000 and £12,000 in 2008/9 and 2009/10 respectively. He is a higher rate taxpayer in both years.

For 2008/9 Jack pays Narnian Income Tax of £3,000 on his rental profits. The following year, his Narnian tax bill is £5,000.

Jack's UK Income Tax liability on his rental profits for each of the two years is calculated as follows:

	2008/9	*2009/10*
	£	*£*
Rental profits	*10,000*	*12,000*
	=====	=====
Income Tax @ 40%:	*4,000*	*4,800*
Less:		
Double tax relief	*3,000*	*4,800 (restricted)*
	--------	--------
Income Tax payable:	*1,000*	*NIL*
	=====	=====

In the first year, we can see that Jack gets full relief for his Narnian tax. His overall tax burden for the year is therefore £4,000, i.e. £3,000 paid in Narnia plus £1,000 paid in the UK. The total tax equates to his UK tax bill before double tax relief, which, on this occasion, was the higher of the two.

In the second year, we see that Jack's double tax relief is restricted, meaning that his overall tax burden remains £5,000, i.e. his Narnian tax. On this occasion, his Narnian tax bill was the higher of the two and this is the tax which Jack ends up suffering.

There is no mechanism for Jack to claim any relief for the surplus Narnian tax of £200. It cannot be carried forward, it cannot be carried back and it cannot be set off against any other tax liability. It is simply lost.

Generally speaking, there is nothing you can do about this, but sometimes there may be ways to alleviate the problem.

Example

When calculating his Narnian tax bill for 2008/9, Jack made a claim to treat some insulation costs as a repair expense under a special relief introduced in the Narnian Finance Act 2007. This had the effect of reducing his Narnian tax bill by £750.

However, Jack now realises that he could, alternatively, claim capital allowances on the same expenditure for Narnian tax purposes.

This would increase his Narnian Income Tax to £3,750 in 2008/9, but reduce it by £250 for each of the next three years.

Jack therefore changes his claim in Narnia and this alters his UK tax position as follows:

	2008/9 £	2009/10 £
Rental profits	10,000	12,000
	=====	=====
Income Tax @ 40%:	4,000	4,800
Less:		
Double tax relief	3,750	4,750
	--------	--------
Income Tax payable:	250	50
	=====	=====

Jack's UK tax bill is now the greater of the two in both years, giving him a total tax burden in both countries for the two years of £8,800.

Before Jack altered his claim, his total tax burden for both years was £9,000. This change has therefore saved him £200 with possible further savings in the next two years.

Remarkably, Jack has achieved this saving by paying more tax in the foreign country!

Tax Tip

Once foreign tax has been reduced below the level of UK tax on the same income for any given year, any further claims should be deferred to a later year where possible as this could lead to overall tax savings at a later date.

(But see Section 7.6 regarding the deferral of foreign tax claims.)

7.2   MATCHING TAXES

Double tax relief for foreign taxes may only be claimed where the foreign tax arises on the **same** income, capital gain, etc.

For Capital Gains Tax purposes, making this 'match' will usually be fairly easy, as only a single transaction is involved. As we saw in Chapter 6, however, there are some instances where local tax arises in the foreign country but no tax arises in the UK.

Where local taxes arise on a transaction which does not give rise to UK tax, no double tax relief is available. An exemption in the UK may therefore be of limited use where a significant foreign tax bill arises.

For example, there may be no point making a main residence election in favour of a foreign holiday home (see Section 5.6) when the gain on the same property will be taxed at a high rate locally.

With the move to a flat rate of 18% Capital Gains Tax in the UK from 6th April 2008, there will be many instances where the foreign tax on a capital gain is now greater than the UK Capital Gains Tax meaning that any exemptions or reliefs in the UK are effectively worthless.

Similar problems arise with Inheritance Tax. Double tax relief is available in principle but the foreign Inheritance Tax system may be very different to ours. Where foreign tax arises on assets which are exempt in the UK, such as assets transferred to a spouse or qualifying business property (see Section 5.12), there will be no double tax relief available.

Hence, whilst double tax relief sounds great in principle, it is not always as effective as one would hope.

When it comes to income from foreign property, the difficulties with double tax relief are more practical in nature.

To explain why, here is a brief extract from a conversation which I once had with an American colleague:

"Our tax year ends on 5th April" I said. "What!" My colleague exclaimed, "That's crazy." "Yes, I know", I responded. "Well, you know how we British like to be eccentric."

And there lies the problem in a nutshell. The rest of the world tends to operate with a sensible fiscal year; very often, like all of the countries covered in Chapters 15 to 21, a calendar year ending 31st December is used.

Naturally, therefore, this creates a mismatch. Foreign tax on rental income will probably be based on a different year to the UK tax on the same income.

In practice, we generally deal with this problem by using a time apportionment approach.

Example

Laurie has a villa in Spain which he rents out. His Spanish tax liabilities are £5,000 for the year ended 31st December 2008 and £8,000 for the year ended 31st December 2009.

His double tax relief claim on this income for 2008/9 may thus be calculated as follows:

9/12 x £5,000 =	*£3,750*
3/12 x £8,000 =	*£2,000*
Total claim:	*£5,750*

As above, such calculations are, in practice, often carried out in months and Revenue and Customs will usually accept this as being reasonably accurate.

The same calculation carried out more accurately in days would be as follows:

270/366 x £5,000 =	*£3,689*
95/365 x £8,000 =	*£2,082*
Total claim:	*£5,771*

As we can see, on this occasion, this more accurate method is slightly more beneficial. Either method is acceptable as long as it is applied consistently.

7.3   MULTIPLE DOUBLE TAX RELIEF CLAIMS

As explained in the previous section, double tax relief may only be claimed against UK tax on the same income, capital gain, etc.

Where a taxpayer has property in more than one country, this leads to further practical difficulties and possibly also further restrictions in the amount of double tax relief available.

Example

Walter is a higher rate taxpayer in the UK and has two foreign rental properties; Waverly Villa in Sardinia and Smailholm Apartments in Bangkok. In 2008/9, each property yields a rental profit for UK tax purposes of £10,000. The local tax suffered differs significantly, however, with Walter paying just £1,000 in Italy but £6,000 in Thailand.

Walter's UK Income Tax calculation looks like this:

	Waverly Villa	*Smailholm Apartments*
	£	*£*
Income Tax @ 40% on £10,000:	*4,000*	*4,000*
Less:		
Double tax relief	*1,000*	*4,000(restricted)*
	3,000	*NIL*

The excess Thai tax of £2,000 is simply lost and Walter cannot set it off against his Italian rental income or, indeed, against anything else.

7.4   HOW MUCH IS THE UK TAX?

In calculating the maximum double tax relief on any foreign property income, we need to know how much UK tax is payable on the same income.

This is calculated as the additional UK tax payable as a result of receiving that foreign income. This is not always a simple matter!

Example

Len owns a shop in Berlin which he rents to Palmer & Co, a firm of funeral directors. In 2008/9, Len receives rental profits of £20,000 from the shop but is subject to German Income Tax of £8,000.

In the same tax year, Len also receives a salary of £30,000 and dividend income of £4,000 (see Section 10.10 for details of how dividend income is taxed in the UK).

His UK Income Tax liability before double tax relief is as follows:

	£	£
Salary	30,000	
Less: personal allowance	5,435	

	24,565	

Income Tax @ 20%:		4,913
Foreign rental income:	20,000	
Income Tax @ 20% on remainder		
of basic rate band: £11,135 (£35,700 - £24,565):		2,227
Income Tax @ 40% on remainder		
of rental income (£8,865):		3,546
Dividend income:	4,000	
Income Tax @ 25% thereon:		1,000

Total Income Tax due before double tax relief:		11,686
		=====

So far, so good, but how much of this tax relates to Len's German rental income? At first glance, looking at the calculation above, one could be forgiven for thinking the answer is £5,773 (£2,227 + £3,546).

This, however, is not the correct answer. For double tax relief purposes, the amount of tax arising due to the receipt of the foreign income is the total additional tax arising as a result of including that income in the taxpayer's Income Tax calculation.

Hence, in order to work out Len's double tax relief, we need to perform a hypothetical Income Tax calculation on the basis that he had not received any of his foreign rental income. This looks like this:

100

	£	£
Salary	30,000	
Less: personal allowance	5,435	

	24,565	

Income Tax @ 20%:		4,913
Dividend income:	4,000	
Income Tax thereon (see Section 10.10):		NIL

Total hypothetical Income Tax due:		4,913
		======

We can now see that the tax arising as a result of Len's receipt of foreign rental income is actually £6,773 (£11,686 - £4,913).

Len may therefore claim double tax relief of £6,773 on his German rental income rather than just the £5,773 of tax which he actually pays on that income.

The reason for this additional amount of relief is the fact that, in the hypothetical tax calculation, Len's dividend income falls wholly within the basic rate band and is thus free from UK Income Tax (as explained in Section 10.10). His German rental income pushes all of his dividend income up into the effective 25% tax rate, hence creating an additional £1,000 tax liability.

By allowing Len to claim double tax relief of £6,773, however, the position is restored to what it would have been if he had not received the foreign rental income.

Practical Pointer

The complex calculations illustrated in the above example will often be necessary when the taxpayer is not already subject to higher rate tax before receiving the foreign property income.

Where, however, the taxpayer is already a higher rate taxpayer on the basis of other income, excluding the foreign property income and also excluding any dividend income, the tax arising as a result of receiving the foreign income may simply be regarded as 40% of the taxable rental profit as computed for UK tax purposes.

Tax Tip

When there is foreign income from more than one source, the taxpayer may choose the most beneficial order in which to treat the foreign income as received for the purposes of the hypothetical calculations described above.

The most beneficial order for this purpose will be to start with the foreign income which has suffered the lowest rate of local tax and work upwards.

Example

Bram and his wife Mina jointly own two foreign rental properties, one in Transylvania and one in Geneva.

In 2008/9 Bram is a higher rate taxpayer in the UK but Mina's only other income is a salary of £35,000.

Bram and Mina's taxable rental income for 2008/9 amounts to £10,000 each from the Transylvanian property and the same from the property in Geneva.

However, each of them suffers local Income Tax of £2,500 in Transylvania and £5,500 in Switzerland.

Bram's double tax relief claim is easy to calculate. He can claim the whole £2,500 in respect of his Transylvanian tax but is restricted to 40%, or £4,000, in respect of his Swiss tax bill.

Mina's position is less straightforward, as she is only a basic rate taxpayer without her foreign rental income. We start her calculation by looking at her hypothetical situation without any foreign rental income:

	£	£
Salary	35,000	
Less: personal allowance	5,435	

	29,565	

Income Tax @ 20%:		5,913
		======

Next, we do a second hypothetical calculation where we include the Transylvanian rental income but not the income from Geneva.

	£	£
Income Tax on salary, as before:		5,913
Transylvanian rental income:	10,000	
Income Tax @ 20% on remainder		
of basic rate band: £6,135 (£35,700 - £29,565):		1,227
Income Tax @ 40% on remainder		
of rental income (£3,865):		1,546

Total hypothetical Income Tax due:		8,686
		=====

Here, it is fairly easy to see the additional tax arising, which amounts to £2,773 (£1,227 + £1,546 or £8,686 - £5,913).

This means that Mina can claim double tax relief for the full amount of the Transylvanian tax suffered, £2,500.

Finally, we do the full calculation with all of Mina's income included:

	£
Income Tax on salary, as before:	5,913
Income Tax on Transylvanian income, as before:	2,773
Income Tax on Swiss income (£10,000 @ 40%):	4,000

Total Income Tax due before double tax relief:	12,686
	=====

This means that Mina can claim double tax relief of £4,000 against her Swiss rental income. Her total double tax relief claim thus amounts to £6,500 (£2,500 + £4,000).

If we had dealt with Mina's Swiss income first, her double tax relief on that income would have been only £2,773, giving her a total double tax relief claim of just £5,273 (£2,773 + £2,500).

Hence, as we can see, the order in which foreign income is dealt with can have a significant effect on the amount of double tax relief available. Thankfully, we are completely at liberty to carry out these calculations in whichever order is most beneficial.

7.5 EQUIVALENT TAXES

If a taxpayer suffers a form of foreign tax which the UK Treasury do not recognise as being equivalent to one of our own taxes, double tax relief is not available.

This leaves the investor exposed to both countries' taxes. The effect of this could be to produce an extremely high rate of tax overall, or even an after tax loss on a pre-tax profit!

Many investors are attracted by the possibility of high returns on foreign property investments, but it is essential to bear in mind the effective total tax exposure on these investments. When comparing the rates of return on potential investments, the investor should always consider the after tax return.

Example

James is considering two possible foreign property investments. The first is on the Caribbean island of San Monique and offers a return of 17.5%. The second is in the Isthmus Republic and offers a return of just 8%.

James is a higher rate taxpayer in the UK. He also finds out that San Monique imposes a property tax at the rate of 10% on the capital value of any property owned by a non-resident. This will reduce the rate of return on James' San Monique investment to just 7.5%. After also paying UK Income Tax at 40%, his overall rate of return, after tax, will be just 4.5%.

The San Monique tax cannot be deducted from James' UK tax bill, but he can claim it as an expense, like he would for council tax (see Section 3.7). What this means, however, is that instead of getting full relief for his foreign tax, James gets relief at just 40% for it.

The Isthmus Republic charges Income Tax at 25% and this will give James an after tax return in the Republic of just 6% if he buys property there. However, this tax is fully deductible against James' UK Income Tax bill. As a result, James' overall after tax return on this investment would be 4.8%.

James will therefore be better off if he invests in the Isthmus Republic.

What this example shows is that, when investing abroad, it is vital to take foreign taxes into account. It further shows that it is important to consider not only the rate of the foreign taxes, but also the nature of those taxes. The key factor for a UK resident investor is whether the foreign tax will merely be classed as a business expense for UK tax purposes or will be fully deductible from the UK tax bill as a recognised equivalent tax.

Worse still, some foreign taxes may not even qualify as a business expense. The eligibility of foreign taxes as a business expense is covered in more detail in Section 3.7.

7.6   FOREIGN TAX CLAIMS

The UK will only allow double tax relief for foreign taxes which are properly payable and which the UK resident taxpayer cannot legitimately claim to reduce.

If a UK resident is entitled to a reduced rate of tax on income in a foreign country, they must claim this reduced rate. It is not acceptable to pay the higher rate on the basis that it will be reclaimed as double tax relief in their UK tax calculation.

Example

Adam, a higher rate taxpayer from Kirkcaldy, has invested in property in Utopia.

His rental income for Utopian tax purposes amounts to £10,000 on which he has paid Utopian Income Tax at 30%, i.e. £3,000.

Under the UK-Utopian Double Taxation Agreement, however, Adam, as a UK resident, is actually entitled to a reduced rate of Utopian tax of 10%.

Adam's double tax relief claim against his Utopian income will therefore be restricted to just £1,000.

This contrasts with the position in the example involving Jack and his Narnian tax claims in Section 7.1. That earlier case is different because it involved a claim relating to the treatment of a particular business expense and the acceleration or deferral of relief for that expense.

In calculating their double tax relief claim, a UK taxpayer is not expected to defer or avoid foreign tax as much as possible. All that is required is that they pay only the rate of tax which, as a UK resident, they are entitled to pay.

7.7 DOUBLE TAX AGREEMENTS

The UK has an extensive network of double tax treaties, or agreements, covering most countries in the world other than a few tax havens and unstable dictatorships.

The purpose of these agreements is to protect the rights of any UK resident who lives, works, or invests in a treaty partner country in taxation matters. As we saw in Section 7.6, this may sometimes include the right to a reduced rate of taxation in the treaty partner country.

Double tax agreements also protect the UK Government's right to tax UK residents on their foreign income and capital gains!

Unfortunately, when it comes to property, most double tax agreements allow the country in which the property is situated to tax a non-resident investor on income or capital gains from that property. Likewise, foreign Inheritance Tax generally continues to be payable on property in that country.

Sadly, therefore, despite the name of these treaties, UK residents investing in property overseas generally continue to be exposed to double taxation.

Nevertheless, it remains vital to be aware of the terms of the UK's double tax agreement with the country in which you are investing as this may have significant implications for your tax position.

In most cases, the double taxation agreement will only cover income and capital gains. There are a few countries with which the UK also has an agreement covering Inheritance Tax and these are listed in Section 8.9.

Appendix B also sets out which of our top 20 destination countries (see Section 1.2) have double taxation agreements with the UK.

7.8 TRIPLE TAXATION

Citizens of another country, who are resident in the UK for tax purposes, may nevertheless still have obligations and liabilities under their own country's tax system, even in respect of their business or investment activities elsewhere in the world. The USA, for example, imposes this type of obligation on its expatriate citizens (although citizenship can be revoked on payment of a suitable 'exit charge').

Where a UK resident, who is also a citizen of such a country, purchases property in a third country, they could actually be subject to tax in all three countries. Ouch!

Chapter 8

Non-UK Domiciled Taxpayers

8.1 A FABULOUS BLESSING?

Being non-UK domiciled is potentially highly beneficial for UK tax purposes. It might be regarded as the tax equivalent of being born with a silver spoon in your mouth.

It must be admitted that the proposals announced in the Pre-Budget Report on 9th October 2007 have tarnished this silver spoon somewhat but the potential for tax savings both during your lifetime and on death remain significant and I therefore still maintain that being non-UK domiciled is a fabulous blessing which no-one should ever give up lightly.

The basic position is that a UK resident but non-UK domiciled individual is entitled to claim exemption from UK Income Tax and Capital Gains Tax on income or capital gains derived from foreign property unless and until they bring the relevant funds back to the UK. (They remain subject to UK tax on UK property in the normal way.)

This is known as the 'remittance basis' and is also available to a person who is UK resident but not ordinarily resident in the UK.

Unfortunately, however, from 6th April 2008 onwards, the remittance basis will come at a heavy price.

From 2008/9 onwards, any UK resident claiming the remittance basis who has unremitted overseas income and capital gains of £1,000 or more in the tax year will lose their personal allowance and their Capital Gains Tax annual exemption.

Worse still, the Government also proposes to levy an additional annual charge of £30,000 on any person claiming the remittance basis who has been UK resident for more than seven of the last ten years. This charge will not apply, however, where an individual has less than £1,000 of unremitted overseas income and capital gains for the year.

We will take a closer look at the implications of these proposed charges and some tax planning strategies designed to mitigate their impact in Sections 8.2 to 8.4.

The second major benefit of non-domiciled status is that, subject to the 'deemed domicile' rules which we shall look at in Section 8.9, a non-UK domiciled individual is exempt from UK Inheritance Tax on all foreign assets, including foreign property. (They generally remain subject to UK Inheritance Tax on any UK property which they own, subject to the terms of any double taxation agreement.)

Property in Ireland

Individuals who are UK resident but non-UK domiciled are currently unable to claim the 'remittance basis' in respect of income or capital gains derived from property in the Republic of Ireland.

From 6th April 2008, however, property in the Republic of Ireland will be treated in the same way as all other property outside the UK.

8.2   IN OR OUT?

From 2008/9 onwards, it will be possible to 'opt out' of the remittance basis on a year by year basis in order to avoid the £30,000 charge and retain the benefit of the Income Tax personal allowance and the Capital Gains Tax annual exemption.

Opting out will apply for one year only and will not affect the individual's underlying non-UK domicile status. This means that for the next year, or any subsequent year, they may claim the remittance basis once again if this becomes more beneficial.

This will introduce a significant amount of choice for non-UK domiciled individuals resident in the UK and gives rise to some useful tax planning strategies.

The question of 'in or out', i.e. whether to opt out of the remittance basis, needs to be considered differently at various different levels of overseas income and capital gains.

Before considering this question in detail, I must make some important provisos regarding the advice set out in the remainder of this section:

i)   The income and capital gains figures set out below are based on the forecast 2008/9 tax rates set out in Appendix B.

ii)   The advice given below relates to the individual's UK tax position only and is therefore subject to the impact of any double tax relief which may be available on the overseas income and capital gains. We will consider this issue in Section 8.3.

iii) The advice given below is based on the assumption that the individual has sufficient existing resources in the UK to pay the £30,000 charge and any other additional UK tax costs arising as a result of claiming the remittance basis. If this is not the case, funds will need to be remitted back to the UK in order to pay the tax and this, in turn, will give rise to further tax costs!

The matter is further complicated by the fact that a non-UK domiciled individual can only make one overall decision, for each tax year, whether to claim the remittance basis on both their overseas income and their overseas capital gains. In practice, many people will have a mixture of both income and capital gains and will need to work out the best course of action under their own particular circumstances.

Income under £1,000

Where the overseas income and capital gains for the year totals less than £1,000, the remittance basis can be claimed without incurring any extra tax charges in the UK.

This enables a non-UK domiciled individual to accumulate up to £999 a year in tax-free overseas income, producing a saving of up to £399.60 a year. It's not much, but it's better than a poke in the eye with a sharp stick.

Income between £1,000 and £6,434

Where the total overseas income and capital gains for the year lies in this bracket, the same saving of £399.60 can be preserved by remitting all but £999 of the overseas income and gains back to the UK during the tax year.

Gains should be remitted in preference to income since these will either be covered by the annual exemption or, at worst, will be taxed at just 18%.

In fact, capital gains of up to the amount of the annual exemption could often effectively be remitted back to the UK tax free and if this reduces the total unremitted overseas income and gains for the year to less than £1,000, then that unremitted income will remain tax free also.

All of the above is technically still possible where the £30,000 charge is applicable but unless you're absolutely certain of your figures, I wouldn't tend to risk it and would suggest opting out of the remittance basis instead.

Income between £6,435 and £80,435

Where a non-UK domiciled individual has unremitted overseas income of over £6,435, but is not subject to the £30,000 charge, it will generally be worth claiming the remittance basis since the tax saved will more than compensate for the loss of the personal allowance.

The loss of the Capital Gains Tax annual exemption must also be taken into account, however, as this may create additional liabilities of up to £1,710 (£9,500 @ 18% - see Appendix B) on any capital gains on UK assets in the same year.

Income between £80,435 and £97,125

Where the non-UK domiciled individual is not subject to the £30,000 charge, they will definitely benefit from claiming the remittance basis.

Where the £30,000 charge does apply, the position will depend on the level of UK income and capital gains which the person has.

Income over £97,125

Once the overseas income reaches this level, the remittance basis will be preferable in all cases.

Capital Gains

The position on overseas capital gains is slightly different as, from 6th April 2008, these are subject to a Capital Gains Tax rate of 18% when taxable in the UK.

As indicated above, overseas capital gains of up to the amount of the annual exemption may be remitted back to the UK tax free where the investor has no UK capital gains in the same tax year.

Where a non-UK domiciled individual has overseas capital gains slightly above this amount, it may be preferable to either remit them back to the UK or to opt out of the remittance basis in order to preserve the individual's personal allowance.

However, a non-UK domiciled individual who is not subject to the £30,000 charge and has overseas capital gains in excess of £21,578 will generally be better off claiming the remittance basis.

For those who are subject to the £30,000 charge, a much larger overseas capital gain will generally be required before it is beneficial to claim the remittance basis, although this does depend on the level of unremitted overseas income which also arises in the same UK tax year.

Where a non-UK domiciled individual has an unremitted capital gain in excess of £197,744, however, the remittance basis will definitely be worth claiming.

NB: Remember that all of the above is subject to any double tax relief which may be available.

A Final Point

It is worth remembering that the remittance basis may sometimes only defer UK tax on foreign income and gains. If the funds are brought into the UK at a later date whilst the investor is still UK resident then tax will arise at that time.

Hence, it will generally only be worth claiming the remittance basis from 2008/9 onwards if the overseas income and gains are to remain offshore permanently or if the investor will cease to be UK resident before the funds are remitted to the UK.

8.3   THE IMPACT OF DOUBLE TAX RELIEF

In the previous section, we considered the best course of action for a non-UK domiciled taxpayer with overseas income or capital gains based on their prospective UK tax liability before taking account of any available double tax relief.

The availability of double tax relief will reduce the amount of UK tax arising where the taxpayer opts out of the remittance basis.

Double tax relief cannot, however, be claimed against the £30,000 charge or against any additional UK tax liabilities arising due to the loss of the personal allowance or the Capital Gains Tax annual exemption.

How does this impact on the advice given in the previous section?

To begin with, in general terms it means that even higher levels of overseas income and capital gains will be required before it is worth claiming the remittance basis when double tax relief is available.

Those with less than £1,000 of overseas income and gains in a year will, however, continue to benefit from the remittance basis.

The option to remit all but £999 of the overseas income and gains arising in a year also remains. In these cases, it will make sense to remit the amounts which have suffered the highest levels of foreign tax and thus give rise to the greatest amounts of double tax relief. (As before, however, I would not generally recommend this strategy where there is a potential £30,000 charge unless you are absolutely certain of all of your figures.)

For those with overseas income and gains over £6,435, it becomes necessary to calculate the effective UK tax charge after double tax relief which would arise by opting out of the remittance basis and compare this with the cost of losing the personal allowance and the Capital Gains Tax annual exemption plus, of course, the £30,000 charge where relevant.

For 2008/9, the cost of losing the personal allowance will be £2,174 for a higher rate taxpayer and £1,087 for most other people.

As explained in Section 8.2, the estimated cost of losing the Capital Gains Tax annual exemption in 2008/9 will be up to £1,710.

Hence, for non-UK domiciled investors who are not subject to the £30,000 charge, the cost of claiming the remittance basis in 2008/9 where they have £1,000 or more of unremitted foreign income and gains will generally be between £1,087 and £3,884.

Where the £30,000 charge does apply, the total cost of claiming the remittance basis could be up to £33,884.

Example

Orhan is UK resident but non-UK domiciled and receives £100,000 in overseas rental income each year which he does not remit to the UK. He also receives sufficient UK income to make him a higher rate taxpayer.

Orhan's £100,000 of rental income comes from the small middle-eastern state of Banya which imposes a 25% Withholding Tax on non-resident landlords. Hence, if Orhan were to opt out of the remittance basis for 2008/9, his UK Income Tax liability on this income after double tax relief would be £15,000 (i.e. 15%: 40% - 25%).

Orhan will therefore be better off claiming the remittance basis if he is not subject to the £30,000 charge as his potential UK tax liability on the Banyan income is more than the maximum potential cost of losing his personal allowance and Capital Gains Tax annual exemption.

If, however, Orhan is subject to the £30,000 charge, he will clearly be better off if he opts out of the remittance basis for 2008/9. Although he has £100,000 of unremitted overseas income, his net UK tax liability on it is much less than the £30,000 charge as a result of double tax relief.

Wealth Warning

If a non-UK domiciled taxpayer opts out of the remittance basis, they will be subject to UK tax on all overseas income and capital gains arising in the year from all sources. It is not possible to opt out only in respect of those sources with significant amounts of double tax relief available.

8.4 PLANNING UNDER THE NEW REGIME

Non-UK domiciled investors with overseas property can reduce the impact of the new regime in a number of ways.

The £30,000 charge can be avoided by ensuring that you are non-UK resident for three years out of every ten.

Those who are in their seventh year of UK residence might wish to consider realising capital gains on all of their overseas properties now before the £30,000 charge comes into force. Indeed, for those who have already been resident in the UK for more than seven years, it may make sense to do this before the new regime comes into force on 6th April 2008.

Capital gains on overseas properties can be 'realised' by selling the property to an unconnected third party or by transferring it to a trust, a company or another individual such as an unmarried partner or adult child (but not to your spouse or civil partner).

The capital gain arising at this stage will escape UK tax by claiming the remittance basis and any subsequent taxable gain will be limited to the property's future growth in value.

Wealth Warning

When realising capital gains on overseas properties for UK tax planning purposes, it is essential to take any potential foreign tax liabilities into account.

New anti-avoidance rules to be introduced with effect from 6th April 2008 may also limit the scope of this planning (but are unlikely to affect the position where a sale to an unconnected third party has taken place).

Once the £30,000 charge is in force, it may be beneficial to ensure that all, or several, of your capital gains on foreign property fall into the same UK tax year. In this way, UK Capital Gains Tax can be avoided on all of your disposals for the price of one £30,000 charge rather than several.

Example

Khaled is non-UK domiciled but has been resident in the UK for many years. He owns two properties in the Pacific territory of the Chance Islands where there is no tax on capital gains. There is, however, a 40% Withholding Tax on rental income received by non-resident landlords.

Khaled also has a large portfolio of investments in the UK and always uses his Capital Gains Tax annual exemption.

In December 2008, Khaled sells one of his Chance Islands properties and makes a capital gain of £200,000. As this will give rise to UK Capital Gains Tax of £36,000 (at 18%) it will be worth Khaled claiming the remittance basis for 2008/9 and paying the £30,000 charge.

Khaled is also anticipating selling his other Chance Islands property shortly and expects that it will also yield a capital gain of around £200,000. If he sells his second property by 5th April 2009, he can avoid UK Capital Gains Tax on this sale without incurring any further UK tax charges.

If, on the other hand, Khaled sells his second overseas property on or after 6th April 2009, he will have to pay a further £30,000 charge in order to avoid UK Capital Gains Tax (plus bear the cost of losing his personal allowance and Capital Gains Tax annual exemption for 2009/10).

An investor in Khaled's position may be able to realise the capital gain on his second property by transferring it to a connected party, as described above. At present, however, it is not clear whether the new anti-avoidance rules due to come into force on 6th April 2008 would block this form of planning.

Couples

Where a couple are both UK resident but non-UK domiciled it may make sense to transfer all or most of their overseas property and other overseas assets to one of them. In this way, UK tax can be avoided on unremitted overseas income and capital gains for the price of just one lost personal allowance, Capital Gains Tax annual exemption and £30,000 charge where applicable.

In some cases, it will also make sense for the couple's overseas property and other overseas assets to be transferred to the one who has been UK resident for fewer years (where both of them have not yet been UK resident for seven years or more).

Grossing Up and How to Avoid It

As explained in Section 8.2, additional tax liabilities will arise if the remittance basis is being claimed but the necessary funds to pay the £30,000 charge or other additional UK tax costs have to be brought into the UK.

To pay the £30,000 charge out of overseas income, it may be necessary to remit as much as £50,000 back to the UK. If the £50,000 remittance is itself fully taxable at 40% this will leave a net sum after tax of £30,000 to pay the original charge.

Similarly, to pay the additional cost of £2,174 which will arise when a higher rate taxpayer loses their personal allowance for 2008/9 may necessitate bringing up to £3,623 of overseas income back to the UK.

Where it applies, this 'grossing up' effect will considerably increase the thresholds at which it becomes worthwhile to claim the remittance basis (see Section 8.2).

The 'grossing up' effect can be avoided, however, where the investor brings the necessary funds back to the UK during a year for which they have 'opted out' of the remittance basis. In such a case, it will be important to ensure that the funds brought back to the UK are clearly made up of fully taxed income or gains arising during a year in which the remittance basis is not being claimed.

8.5   A GOOD INVESTMENT?

Prior to the introduction of the new £30,000 charge, foreign property generally represented a good investment for non-UK domiciled taxpayers. If the non-UK domiciled taxpayer planned their affairs carefully, they had the opportunity to make overseas investments free from all UK taxes.

The new charge changes this position significantly, but non-UK domiciled taxpayers can still make substantial tax savings by investing in overseas property under two scenarios:

i)   Where they have not been UK resident for more than seven of the last ten years.
ii)   Where they are investing very substantial sums.

Furthermore, non-UK domiciled taxpayers will effectively be able to limit the UK tax arising on foreign capital gains to a little over £30,000.

Hence, even despite the new charges explained in Section 8.1, by investing overseas and keeping their income and sale proceeds offshore, non-UK domiciled taxpayers may still, over a period, be able to build up a significantly greater value of investments than if they had invested in the UK.

This is best illustrated by way of an example. The example which follows is long and complex, but demonstrates many of the practical issues which will be faced by UK resident but non-UK domiciled investors holding overseas property after 5th April 2008.

Example

Lewis and Carol are twins born in Wonderland. In April 2008, they both moved to the UK and, from then on, became UK resident higher rate taxpayers. Nevertheless, they both remain non-UK domiciled.

As soon as they arrive in the UK, Lewis and Carol each purchase an investment property for £500,000. Lewis buys a property in the UK, but Carol makes her investment overseas in a country which taxes non-residents on rental income at a rate of just 10% and charges no tax on capital gains. Lewis and Carol both make rental profits before all taxes of £30,000 for each of the next seven years.

Lewis and Carol both put their after tax rental profits on deposit. Lewis uses a UK high street bank, but Carol keeps her rental profits in an offshore bank account, where she pays no tax on the interest income. Both deposit accounts pay gross interest before tax at a compound rate of 7.5%.

Carol claims the remittance basis each year and thus pays no UK Income Tax on her overseas rental and offshore interest income. She does, however, lose entitlement to her personal allowance and thus has to pay a little more tax on her UK income each year.

Seven years later, on 1st April 2015, Lewis and Carol each sell their investment property for £974,359 (this figure is arrived at by using a 10% compound rate of capital growth for seven years).

Carol keeps her property sale proceeds offshore and avoids UK Capital Gains Tax on her gain by claiming the remittance basis. She therefore retains her full proceeds of £974,359 and adds these to her deposit account balance of £237,258 to give her a total of £1,211,616.

Lewis suffers UK Capital Gains Tax at 18% on his gain of £474,359 less the 2014/15 annual exemption of (say) £11,700. This amounts to £83,279 leaving him with net proceeds after tax of £891,080 to add to his funds on deposit of £144,345 giving him a total of £1,035,425. (He has less money on deposit than Carol due to the 40% UK Income Tax he has suffered each year on his rental and interest income.)

Lewis and Carol both then reinvest all of their available funds in a new investment property. Once again, Lewis buys his property in the UK. Carol buys her new property in the same country as her first one.

Both of the new properties produce pre-tax rental profits equal to 6% of their purchase cost and experience 10% compound growth in their capital value.

In 2015/16 Carol is faced with the £30,000 charge for the first time as this is her eighth year of UK residence. Her overseas rental profits for the year are £72,697 and this is not enough to warrant paying the £30,000 charge, so she now opts out of the remittance basis and pays UK tax in full on these profits.

Carol now brings enough money back to the UK to pay her UK Income Tax liability each year but continues to keep the majority of her rental income on deposit offshore. She must also now pay UK Income Tax on her offshore interest.

As Carol has now opted out of the remittance basis, bringing funds back to the UK does not in itself generate any further tax liability as long as she is careful to bring back funds arising in a year for which she has opted out.

By 2018/19, however, Carol is receiving offshore interest of £10,262 in addition to her rental income of £72,697. This is sufficient to make it worth claiming the remittance basis once again and paying the £30,000 charge. She therefore also stops remitting any funds back to the UK.

In March 2022, Lewis and Carol both sell their investment properties. Once again, both properties have increased in value at a compound rate of 10% per annum.

Lewis paid £1,035,425 for his property in 2015 and he sells it in 2022 for £2,017,750 giving him a capital gain of £982,325. After deducting his 2021/22 annual exemption of (say) £14,700, the remainder is subject to Capital Gains Tax at 18%, giving him a tax bill of £174,173. This leaves him with net proceeds of £1,843,577 to add to his funds on deposit of £298,916, giving him a total of £2,142,494.

Since Carol is already paying the £30,000 charge and claiming the remittance basis, there is effectively no additional tax cost for her when she sells her overseas property for £2,361,097. Adding her proceeds to her funds on deposit of £475,385 therefore gives her total funds offshore of £2,836,482 at this point.

Carol has, however, suffered various additional UK tax liabilities due to the loss of her personal allowance from 2008/9 to 2014/15 and from

2018/19 to 2021/22 plus the payment of the additional £30,000 charge for the last four years.

This will have cost her total extra UK tax of around £149,000 (based on estimated future personal allowances). If we assume that this has used up funds which would otherwise be invested at similar rates of return to her offshore funds, this would have led to a total depletion in her UK assets of around £177,000 by March 2022.

Taking the depletion of Carol's UK assets into account, the overall net value of each twin's investments (investment property plus funds on deposit, less all tax liabilities) will have grown in value as follows:

	Lewis	Carol	Difference	
2008	£500,000	£500,000	£0	0%
2009	£568,000	£574,826	£6,826	1%
2010	£641,810	£656,511	£14,701	2%
2011	£721,966	£745,700	£23,733	3%
2012	£809,057	£843,094	£34,036	4%
2013	£903,728	£949,465	£45,737	5%
2014	£1,006,685	£1,065,654	£58,970	6%
2015	£1,035,425	£1,192,589	£157,164	15%
2016	£1,176,243	£1,354,781	£178,538	15%
2017	£1,329,092	£1,530,830	£201,739	15%
2018	£1,495,084	£1,722,018	£226,934	15%
2019	£1,675,436	£1,922,717	£247,281	15%
2020	£1,871,484	£2,143,357	£271,873	15%
2021	£2,084,692	£2,385,878	£301,186	14%
2022	£2,142,494	£2,659,079	£516,586	24%

As we can see, by simply investing abroad rather than in the UK and retaining her funds offshore, Carol has been able to accumulate £516,586, or 24%, more net wealth than her twin brother Lewis over a 14 year period despite the new tax charges discussed in Section 8.1.

It is in particular worth noting how Carol pulls significantly further ahead when the twins make property sales in 2015 and 2022 due to the large Capital Gains Tax bills which Lewis suffers.

Note that Lewis' position would be exactly the same if he had invested in overseas property but remitted all of his income and sale proceeds back to the UK. Carol's savings arise not only because she has invested abroad but also because she keeps her investment income and sale proceeds offshore also.

But there is still one more twist to this tale!

Sadly, in June 2022, both twins are tragically killed, poisoned by a madman who had invited them to a tea party. However, as their executor, Alice, explains to their family, it was fortunate in one sense since they were both less then three years away from being deemed to have UK domicile for Inheritance Tax purposes (see Section 8.9).

Nevertheless, although Lewis is non-UK domiciled, he is still subject to Inheritance Tax on the funds which he holds in the UK. Lewis also owned a home in the UK which was worth more than the nil rate band, so his UK investment funds of £2,142,494 are subject to Inheritance Tax at 40%, resulting in a further tax bill of £856,997 and leaving his family with just £1,285,496.

Carol, on the other hand, still held her investment funds offshore at the time of her death and these funds are therefore not subject to UK Inheritance Tax. She is therefore able to leave her family the entire sum of £2,836,482, which is almost two and a quarter times as much as Lewis' family will receive.

(The depletion in Carol's UK assets will also lead to a further Inheritance Tax saving of around £71,000.)

8.6   KEEPING FUNDS OFFSHORE

As we saw in the previous section, there are substantial potential benefits for a non-UK domiciled investor in keeping their foreign property investment income and sale proceeds offshore. Keeping funds offshore still permits you to do any of the following:

- Invest funds in the Isle of Man or Channel Islands.
- Hold funds denominated in sterling, but kept offshore.
- Spend the money whilst travelling abroad on business or on holiday.
- Move the funds to a different foreign country, but still outside the UK (watch out for any local exchange control restrictions though).
- Invest in new foreign property or other foreign assets.

Wealth Warning

When doing any of the above, you must take care that the funds never flow via the UK, including any UK bank account.

What About Existing Capital Held Offshore?

Existing capital already held offshore before a non-UK domiciled person became UK resident may be brought into the UK without generating any tax charges.

Tax Tip

Have the interest on any such existing capital paid into a separate account. The 'capital' can then be safely brought into the UK, without causing a taxable remittance of offshore income to the UK.

Taxed Income Held Overseas

Income or sales proceeds which have been taxed during a year when a non-domiciled person has opted out of the remittance basis should also be kept separate from income or sales proceeds arising during a year in which the remittance basis is claimed.

The taxed income or sales proceeds effectively become a new amount of capital which may safely be remitted to the UK without incurring any further tax charges whereas a remittance of the untaxed income or sales proceeds will give rise to new tax charges.

8.7 HOW DO YOU KNOW IF YOU'RE NON-DOMICILED?

In essence, your 'domicile' is the country which you consider to be your permanent home.

This does not necessarily equate to your country of birth, nor to the country in which you happen to be living at present. Neither does it equate to citizenship; becoming a naturalised British citizen will not necessarily cause you to acquire UK domicile.

Furthermore, 'domicile' should not be confused with residence, which is a far more transitory concept (but see Section 8.9 below regarding deemed domicile).

The nearest non-tax concept to domicile is probably nationality, but even that is not a perfect match.

Domicile of Origin

To solve the question of their domicile, each person will first need to start at the beginning, i.e. their birth.

At birth, each person acquires the domicile of the person on whom they are legally dependent at that time. That person will usually be their father, but it is their mother if their father is dead or their parents are living apart and they have a home with their mother, but not with their father. The domicile which you acquire at this point is known as your 'Domicile of Origin'.

Throughout your minority, you continue to have the same domicile as the person on whom you are legally dependent. If that person changes their domicile during this period then your domicile also changes and you acquire a 'Domicile of Dependency'.

You only become capable of having your own independent domicile when you reach the age of 16 (or, in Scotland, 14 for a boy or 12 for a girl).

Example

Farrokh was born in Zanzibar in 1946 and lived with both of his parents at that time. His father was domiciled in India and his mother was domiciled in Zanzibar. Farrokh therefore acquired an Indian Domicile of Origin.

In 1960, Farrokh's parents moved to England, taking Farrokh with them. They intended to remain in England permanently. At this point, Farrokh therefore acquired a UK Domicile of Dependency.

Re-acquiring a Domicile of Origin

If it ever becomes uncertain which country you regard as your permanent home, your domicile will revert to your Domicile of Origin. Note that, under UK law, your domicile always reverts to your Domicile of Origin under these circumstances and not any Domicile of Dependency which you may have had.

Domicile and Marriage

Marriage does not generally affect domicile. However, women other than US Nationals, who married before 1st January 1974, adopted their husband's domicile at the date of marriage as a Domicile of Dependency.

Domicile of Choice

In most cases, a person's Domicile of Origin remains their domicile for the rest of their life.

This domicile can only be changed, to a 'Domicile of Choice', through permanent emigration (and, for these purposes, I <u>mean</u> permanent).

Acquiring a new domicile for tax purposes, as a 'Domicile of Choice', can be very difficult to prove. This is both good news and bad news since it cuts both ways and Revenue & Customs have had just as much difficulty proving that a taxpayer has acquired the UK as their Domicile of Choice as taxpayers have had in proving that they have acquired a domicile somewhere else.

We will return to the idea of acquiring a new Domicile of Choice through emigration in Chapter 9.

8.8   RETAINING A FOREIGN DOMICILE

If you are lucky enough to have a non-UK Domicile of Origin, it is far, far, easier to retain this as your domicile than it is to acquire a new Domicile of Choice. As I said in Section 8.1, a non-UK domicile is a fabulous blessing and it will usually be worth doing what you can to protect it.

Having said that however, it is, as stated above, actually very difficult for Revenue & Customs to prove that a non-UK domiciled individual has acquired the UK as a new Domicile of Choice.

This is especially true if the individual themselves states that it is their intention to return to their country of origin one day. In this case, an 'intention' does not actually have to be backed up by action.

Example

Oscar was born in the Irish Republic, of Irish parents, but has lived in the UK for over 40 years, having moved here in his early twenties. Despite this, he has always stated that he intends to return 'home' before he dies.

Oscar remains domiciled in the Irish Republic.

Protecting your Domicile

So, as we can see, anyone born with a non-UK domicile is fairly safe from any attack on the grounds that they have somehow become UK domiciled.

Nevertheless, for anyone interested in investing in foreign property, retaining their non-UK domicile is so important that a 'belt and braces' approach is warranted.

It may therefore be worth buying a grave plot in the country which is your Domicile of Origin. This is accepted as a very strong indication of your intention to return to that country at some future date.

8.9 DOMICILE AND INHERITANCE TAX

The basic rule is that non-UK domiciled individuals are only subject to UK Inheritance Tax on assets situated in the UK. Hence, subject to the further comments below regarding deemed domicile, foreign property owned by a non-UK domiciled taxpayer should, in principle, escape UK Inheritance Tax.

Deemed Domicile

Unfortunately, however, a taxpayer is deemed to be UK domiciled for Inheritance Tax purposes, and taxed accordingly, if they have been resident in the UK for tax purposes for at least 17 out of the last 20 UK tax years.

Deemed domicile only applies to Inheritance Tax and does not affect the Income Tax or Capital Gains Tax position of a person who is still non-UK domiciled under the basic principles which we have already covered. For this reason, it generally remains worth retaining foreign domicile, even if you have deemed UK domicile for Inheritance Tax purposes.

> **Tax Tip**
>
> To avoid ending up with deemed UK domicile for Inheritance Tax purposes, non-UK domiciled taxpayers should try to spend four years out of every twenty abroad (or one in five, if you prefer). This does not have to be in the same country as their Domicile of Origin.

Double Tax Agreements

Most double taxation agreements do not cover Inheritance Tax. A few countries do, however, have separate double taxation agreements with the UK to cover Inheritance Tax, as follows:

- France
- Irish Republic
- India
- Italy
- Netherlands
- Pakistan
- South Africa
- Sweden
- Switzerland
- USA

If you are domiciled in one of these countries, the double taxation agreement may affect your position. In particular, some of these agreements contain provisions which over-ride the 'deemed domicile' rules.

8.10 EXCLUDED PROPERTY TRUSTS

Those who did not have a UK 'Domicile of Origin' (see Section 8.7) but who have subsequently acquired actual or deemed UK domicile, may generally exclude non-UK assets that were transferred into a trust for their benefit before they acquired UK domicile, or deemed UK domicile (and which are still held therein) from the value of their estate for UK Inheritance Tax purposes.

Property held in such trusts is known as 'excluded property'.

At present, this treatment extends to property that was transferred into the trust by the beneficiary themselves. This is believed to be under review by Revenue and Customs and could be changed in the near future.

Nevertheless, for the time being at least, there still appears to be a possibility for any person who is shortly about to become UK domiciled or deemed UK domiciled (see Section 8.9) to transfer overseas property into a trust for their own benefit before this occurs and thus prevent that property from becoming subject to UK Inheritance Tax.

An excluded property trust can also be used to shelter overseas property inherited from a non-UK domiciled person.

8.11 NON-DOMICILED SPOUSES OR CIVIL PARTNERS

The spouse exemption for Inheritance Tax, which normally has no limit (see Section 5.12) is restricted to just £55,000 in the case of transfers from a UK domiciled spouse or civil partner to a non-UK domiciled spouse or civil partner.

The unlimited exemption is restored, however, if and when the non-UK domiciled spouse acquires deemed UK domicile for UK Inheritance Tax purposes.

This provides a useful planning opportunity to shelter foreign property from UK Inheritance Tax. This can best be explained by way of an example.

Example

John is UK domiciled but his wife Yoko has Japanese domicile.

John owns a house in Barcelona worth £2,000,000 and is concerned about his potential Inheritance Tax liability of £800,000 on the property.

Yoko has been resident in the UK since 6th April 1991. In 2008/9, she therefore acquires deemed UK domicile as she will have been UK resident for 17 of the previous 20 UK tax years.

John can therefore transfer the property in Barcelona to Yoko at any time during 2008/9 and the transfer will be completely exempt from Inheritance Tax. (It is, of course, also exempt from Capital Gains Tax.)

In April 2009, Yoko moves into the house in Barcelona and ceases to be UK resident. By April 2012, she will only have been UK resident for 16 out of the last 20 years; she therefore ceases to have deemed UK domicile for Inheritance Tax purposes from 6th April 2012.

The house in Barcelona is therefore now exempt from UK Inheritance Tax.

Chapter 9

Emigration to Avoid UK Taxation

9.1 WHAT'S SO GREAT ABOUT EMIGRATION?

For UK residents owning foreign property, there are three major advantages to emigration. In order of increasing difficulty to achieve, these are:

i)   As a non-resident, they would cease to be liable for UK Income Tax on foreign property income.

ii)   They may be exempt from UK Capital Gains Tax on all property.

iii)   If they emigrate permanently and obtain a new Domicile of Choice, they will eventually be exempt from UK Inheritance Tax on foreign property.

To understand why there is an increasing hierarchy of difficulty here, we need to understand how the three key concepts of residence, ordinary residence and domicile affect a taxpayer's liability for UK taxation.

To avoid UK Income Tax on foreign property income, it is only necessary to become non-UK resident.

To avoid Capital Gains Tax, one must become both non-UK resident and also non-UK ordinarily resident. Furthermore, it is also generally insufficient to be merely 'temporarily non-resident'.

To avoid Inheritance Tax on foreign property, it is necessary to acquire a new Domicile of Choice in another country. This will almost certainly also involve becoming both non-UK resident and also non-UK ordinarily resident.

In Sections 9.2 to 9.4, we will look at the basic rules governing each of these three levels of emigration. In each case, however, the taxpayer must meet not only these basic rules but also demonstrate a genuine intention to make their home in another country and to make a break with the UK. Further practical advice on how to achieve this is included in Section 9.5.

Before that, however, I would just like to make the point that emigration alone, in itself, is only half the story.

It is essential to ensure that, by emigrating elsewhere, you do not inadvertently become liable for even greater tax liabilities in your new home country. There is no point in jumping out of the frying pan and into the fire!

9.2   HOW TO BECOME NON-RESIDENT

Let's start with the basic rules; the ones which everyone seems to know.

As we saw in Section 1.4, a taxpayer is generally treated as UK resident if:

- They spend more than 182 days in the UK in any one UK tax year, or
- They spend an average of more than 90 days per year in the UK.

At present, days of arrival and departure in and out of the UK are not counted for the purpose of these tests. From 6th April 2008, however, such days will be counted.

Now, I want you to note the way in which I have worded this very carefully. What I have set out here are some basic rules which tell you when someone **will** be treated as UK resident.

What the above rules do **not** say is that a person who does not spend this much time in the UK is not UK resident.

These basic rules are just the beginning. They are effectively just a preliminary test which a taxpayer must pass before we can even begin to consider if they might be non-UK resident.

Recent case law suggests that a much harsher view is now being taken on the question of emigration. In practice, it is not sufficient just to meet the basic rules set out above and the taxpayer's overall situation must be reviewed to determine if they can genuinely be regarded as non-UK resident.

Even the basic rules themselves are being tightened up. Until recently, visits to the UK which did not include an overnight stay were not counted when considering whether a person met the basic criteria for UK residence. Now, however, it appears that such visits may have to be counted in many cases.

With the further change to count days of arrival and departure from 6th April 2008, many people who think they are non-UK resident at the moment will need to think again!

9.3 EMIGRATING TO AVOID CAPITAL GAINS TAX

Sadly, the days when a UK taxpayer could avoid Capital Gains Tax by going on a world cruise for a year have long since been consigned to history.

In addition to the fact that achieving non-UK residence is not as easy as it used to be, anyone trying to avoid Capital Gains Tax through emigration is faced with the additional problem that they will also need to become non-UK ordinarily resident.

Furthermore, a taxpayer who is only 'temporarily non-resident' will be subject to Capital Gains Tax on any capital gains made during their absence when they return.

This is a complex field of tax planning, which really requires a separate guide on its own. However, the key points worth noting are:

- Emigration must generally be permanent, or at least long-term. The prospective emigrant will usually need to remain non-UK resident for at least five complete UK tax years.

- Disposals should be deferred until non-residence has been achieved.

- Returning prematurely to the UK, to resume permanent residence here, may result in substantial Capital Gains Tax liabilities.

When a taxpayer emigrates, they may often be regarded as non-resident immediately on the day of departure. This is not something which I would like to rely on, however, and I would always recommend that the sales giving rise to capital gains are deferred until the next tax year after the tax year of departure.

9.4 CHANGING YOUR DOMICILE

This is the big one and it is not for the faint-hearted. To change your domicile, you really have to be very serious about wanting to emigrate.

The rewards are equally serious, however, and all of the UK tax savings outlined in Section 9.1 are available to a taxpayer who successfully changes their domicile.

To acquire a new domicile as a Domicile of Choice, it is necessary to not only demonstrate an intention to adopt the new country as your permanent home, but also to follow this up by action and subsequent conduct.

If the taxpayer ever abandons their Domicile of Choice at any time in the future, their domicile automatically reverts to their Domicile of Origin.

Example

Spike is UK domiciled. However, in 2008, he decides to emigrate permanently to New Zealand and thus become New Zealand domiciled.

He declares this intention on form P85, which he lodges with the UK Revenue & Customs shortly before he departs for Wellington.

In 2009, Spike gets a terrific offer to work in California, so he leaves New Zealand to adopt California as his new permanent home.

Spike's domicile has now reverted to the UK!

Wealth Warning

If you intend to change your domicile, make sure you pick the right country first time!

Although Spike might eventually be able to establish Californian domicile, this will now be very difficult for him

133

because he has established a 'track record' of abandoning his so-called 'permanent home'.

How could he possibly now prove that he has no intention of ever returning to the UK?

9.5   A GUIDE TO EMIGRATION

There is no set procedure for successful emigration. Like many things in the tax world, each individual case will be examined on its own particular merits.

In this section, however, I have set out a few practical tips to follow. These tips are merely a guide and failing to meet one or more of them will not necessarily mean that you fail to achieve non-UK residence or domicile. However, in general terms, the more of these tips you can adhere to, the better your chances will be.

As we have seen in the previous sections, there are two levels of emigration which we need to consider: non-residence and non-domicile. Accordingly, I have therefore set out my practical tips in two levels also. (Although there is no harm in adopting some of the tips from the second level even if you are only trying to achieve non-residence.)

In broad terms, achieving non-residence requires an intention to make a break with the UK. The practical steps required therefore mainly revolve around severing your ties with the UK.

Achieving non-domicile additionally requires an intention to settle permanently in a specific new country. The practical steps required here are not only those revolving around severing your ties with the UK but also those revolving around putting down roots in your new home country.

Level 1: Establishing Non-Residence.

- Declare your intentions to Revenue & Customs on form P85 before leaving the UK (see Appendix E).

- Buy a home in your new country.

- Take your family with you (including the pets).

- Take up employment in your new country (or, alternatively, establish your own business there).

- Get on the electoral roll in your new country.

- Try to visit the UK as little as possible.

- Make sure that your former home in the UK is not available for your use. Preferably, it should be sold.

- Ensure that residential accommodation is not available to you elsewhere in the UK. If you must visit the UK, try to stay in hotels.

- Sell as many UK assets as you can (but note the advice given in Section 9.3 regarding the timing of such sales).

- Resign membership of any clubs, associations, etc, in the UK.

- Close your UK bank accounts.

- Cancel any Child Tax Credit or Child Benefit claims.

Level 2: Establishing a Domicile of Choice through permanent emigration.

- Follow the steps set out under Level 1. Remember that an even greater demonstration of your intention to make a clean break with the UK is now required.

- When completing form P85 ensure that you declare your intention to adopt your destination country as your new permanent home.

- Take whatever steps you can to establish citizenship, nationality, etc, in your new country.

- Buy a grave plot in your new country (this is given a great deal of importance by the tax authorities when looking at domicile).

- Write a Will in your new country.

- Write letters (e.g. to your solicitor) which express your intention of never returning to reside in the UK.

- DO NOT MOVE ON AGAIN TO ANOTHER COUNTRY!

9.6　EMIGRATION AND INHERITANCE TAX

A person who ceases to be UK domiciled will continue to have deemed UK domicile for Inheritance Tax purposes for three years after ceasing to be UK domiciled under general principles.

This may, however, be affected by one of the double tax treaties referred to in Section 8.9.

Generally, however, emigrating to avoid Inheritance Tax needs to be done early and carefully.

Chapter 10

Using a Company

10.1 WHY USE A COMPANY?

Many people are forced, or encouraged, to use a company to buy foreign property for a variety of reasons.

In some countries, for example, a company is used as a means to avoid the local succession laws.

In other countries, a local company is a necessary means to enable a non-resident to buy property.

In other cases, a company is used for tax planning purposes. The advantages and disadvantages of using a company to invest in property from a UK tax perspective are covered in depth in the Taxcafe.co.uk guide *'Using a Property Company to Save Tax'*.

When it comes to companies owning foreign property, we may be concerned with UK companies or foreign companies and we will take a closer look at each of these in Sections 10.4 and 10.5 respectively.

10.2 NOMINEE COMPANIES

In some cases, it may be appropriate to hold foreign property through a nominee company.

A nominee company holds property in name only. All of the benefits and responsibilities of ownership remain with the individual themselves. This is achieved through a legal agreement between the company and the individual.

Where a nominee company is used, all income and capital gains derived from property held by the company are treated as belonging to the individual for UK tax purposes.

Beware, however, that the country where the property is located may not recognise the concept of a nominee company and may continue to treat all of the income and gains derived from the property as belonging to the company and thus tax it accordingly.

This can lead to problems in some cases as the individuals are not generally entitled to any double tax relief for foreign tax paid by their nominee company, thus giving rise to an effective double tax charge.

10.3 COMPANIES HOLDING FOREIGN HOLIDAY HOMES

For the reasons set out in Section 10.1, many people buy a foreign holiday home through a company.

Where the company is used purely for this purpose alone and does not realise any profit, income or capital gains, there will be no Income Tax or Corporation Tax to pay in the UK.

There used to be a concern that holding a foreign holiday home through a company would give rise to a UK Income Tax charge on the deemed 'benefit in kind' derived by the company's owners.

Thankfully, however, in 2007 it was confirmed that the owners of a company which exists solely to hold a private residence overseas will be exempt from any benefit-in-kind Income Tax charge in the UK on their personal use of the property.

The exemption only applies, however, if the company exists solely to hold foreign property. If the company has any other activities, the benefit-in-kind charge for personal use by the company owners will continue to apply under normal principles.

The company must also be held directly by individuals. The exemption is not available, for example, where a company is held by a trust or another company.

This exemption does not apply to UK property held under similar circumstances.

Wealth Warning

It is important to remember that local taxes may still arise in the country where a foreign holiday home held by a company is located.

138

Capital Gains

The treatment of a capital gain arising on the sale of a holiday home held by a company will depend on whether or not the company is UK resident. Capital gains in UK resident companies are covered in Section 10.8 and the further issues to be considered when extracting the sale proceeds from the company are covered in Section 10.10. In both cases, the tax position is unaltered by the fact that the property was used as the company owner's holiday home.

The main residence exemption (see Section 5.6) is not available on a property held by a company. (Remember, however, that if a nominee company is used, the property is treated as belonging to the individual for UK tax purposes.)

10.4 UK COMPANIES

Any company registered in the UK is usually treated as a UK resident company for UK tax purposes.

UK resident companies are subject to UK Corporation Tax on their worldwide income and capital gains. Foreign property income and capital gains on foreign property held by a UK resident company are included as part of its worldwide income and taxed at the appropriate Corporation Tax rate as set out below.

Foreign property trading profits received by a UK resident company are computed in the same way as for an individual, as explained in Chapter 4.

A company's foreign property rental income and taxable capital gains are, however, calculated slightly differently and we will look at these in Sections 10.6 and 10.8 respectively.

Officially, there are just two rates of Corporation Tax: the 'Small Companies Rate' and the 'Main Rate'. For the year ending 31st March 2009, these are 21% and 28% respectively.

However, the Corporation Tax system does not operate in the same way as the Income Tax system. A large company, paying tax at the main rate, does not benefit at all from the Small Companies

Rate and will pay Corporation Tax at the main rate on all of its profits and gains.

The benefit of the Small Companies Rate is progressively withdrawn through a system known as marginal relief. As a result of the marginal relief system there are, in fact, actually three effective Corporation Tax rates.

The effective Corporation Tax rates applying to profits for the year ending 31st March 2009 are given below. The rates applying for the previous year are given in brackets.

UK Corporation Tax Rates
On the Company's Total Profits and Gains:

First £300,000:	21%	(20%)
From £300,000 to £1.5m:	29.75%	(32.5%)
Over £1.5m:	28%	(30%)

In practice, once the company's total profits and gains exceed £1.5m, everything is simply taxed at the main rate and the other effective rates can simply be ignored.

The £300,000 and £1.5m limits are proportionately reduced where the company prepares accounts for a period of less than a year. They will also be reduced when the company has any 'associated companies' and we will look at this concept further in Section 10.11.

Double Tax Relief

UK resident companies are entitled to double tax relief on their income and capital gains in much the same way as UK resident individuals (see Chapter 7).

Individual shareholders do not, however, obtain any double tax relief in respect of foreign tax suffered by the company.

10.5 FOREIGN COMPANIES

Subject to the terms of any applicable double taxation agreement, companies registered in another country are treated as UK resident for tax purposes if their place of central management and control is in the UK.

The place of central management and control is the place where the major decisions affecting the company are made. In larger, more formally structured companies, it will usually be the place where directors' board meetings are held.

In the case of a smaller company, however, the likelihood is that directors will make the major decisions affecting the company through less formal arrangements and, where the directors are UK resident, those decisions will generally be made in the UK.

In some cases, the company may be owned by UK resident individuals but may have foreign directors. However, if the foreign directors effectively merely implement decisions made in the UK by the UK resident shareholders, then the company will remain UK resident.

Hence, in effect, most small companies registered overseas which are owned by UK resident individuals will actually be UK resident companies. They will therefore be subject to UK Corporation Tax as set out in Section 10.4.

To prevent a foreign company owned by UK resident individuals from becoming a UK resident company will require a formal structure which is rigidly adhered to in practice. As this will generally involve some substantial professional costs, this is seldom worthwhile for most people.

Furthermore, in many cases, the UK resident owners of a non-UK resident company may be taxed personally on the income and capital gains received by that company.

In short therefore, using a foreign company to hold foreign property may have other benefits but it is not an easy way to avoid UK tax.

A foreign registered company is also likely to be subject to local tax in its country of registration.

10.6   FOREIGN RENTAL INCOME

UK resident companies are generally taxed on foreign rental income in much the same way as UK resident individuals (see Chapter 3) but with one major difference.

Interest and other finance costs incurred in connection with a UK resident company's foreign property letting business are treated as general overheads of the company rather than expenses of the letting business itself.

This provides a tremendous advantage for foreign property letting businesses run through a company when compared with the same type of business run by an individual or a partnership.

The interest and finance costs incurred in connection with the company's foreign property letting business may be set off against any other income or capital gains received by the company during the same accounting period, including UK letting income.

If we contrast this with the position for an individual or a partnership where these same costs can only be set against foreign rental income, we can readily see what an enormous advantage this provides.

Furthermore, as an alternative, the company may instead:

a) Carry the costs back for set off against any interest, non-trading foreign exchange gains (see Section 10.9) and certain other limited categories of income, received during the previous three years,

b) Carry the costs forward for set off against any non-trading income and capital gains in future periods, or

c) Surrender the costs as 'group relief' (where the company is a member of a group of companies).

Tax Tip

Option (b) above enables a property investment company to effectively 'roll up' its accumulated interest costs and set them off against the capital gains arising on the sale of its investment properties.

This presents a massive advantage over individual investors whose interest costs on overseas investments effectively become foreign rental losses which cannot be set off against capital gains.

What do we mean by 'Other Finance Costs'?

In addition to interest, other costs falling within this category include:

- Guarantee fees
- Loan arrangement fees
- Early redemption fees
- Reimbursement of lender's expenses
- Certain foreign exchange losses (see Section 10.9)

Loans and other Facilities Provided by the Company's Owner

In general terms, interest and other finance costs (as described above) may continue to be claimed for Corporation Tax purposes even when paid to one of the company's directors, shareholders, or another connected person. There are two important provisos here, however:

i)   The amount paid must not exceed a normal commercial rate.
ii)   Payment must actually be made within twelve months of the end of the company's accounting period.

The issue of loans from the owner to the company is considered in more detail in the Taxcafe.co.uk guide *Using a Property Company to Save Tax*.

Non-Commercial Lettings

Corporation Tax relief for interest and other finance costs incurred in connection with any 'non-commercial' lettings (see Section 3.4) will be restricted so that, broadly speaking, relief is only given against any income from those lettings.

Foreign Rental Losses

The treatment of interest and other finance costs as general overheads means that a company is unlikely to make foreign rental losses on genuine 'arm's length' rental businesses.

Where a company does make such a loss, however, the loss may be carried forward and set off against future overseas rental profits received by the company. No other relief is available.

As with an individual, losses from 'non-commercial' lettings may only be set off against future profits from the same letting.

10.7 FOREIGN PROPERTY TRADES

As explained in Section 10.4, a UK resident company's trading profits are generally calculated in the same way as for an individual.

However, whilst the amount of profit is the same, the rate of tax applying is different and provides the potential to make huge savings in certain circumstances (subject to the extra costs of 'profit extraction' which we will see in Section 10.10).

The main reason that savings are often made is the fact that companies do not pay National Insurance on their trading profits.

As with an individual, a UK resident company which is carrying on a trade with foreign property will be regarded as carrying on a UK trade where its activities are managed from the UK. Where trading activities of a similar nature are also being carried on in the UK, it will generally be treated as part of the same trade.

Foreign tax may also apply to trading profits derived from overseas activities. Double tax relief may be claimed but only against the UK Corporation Tax on the profits of those same activities.

Losses of a UK trade may be set off against the company's other income *and capital gains* of the same accounting period. The company is not forced to make this set-off, however, and may choose not to claim it.

For example, where the company is anticipating a higher marginal rate of Corporation Tax in the following year, it may prefer to carry its loss forward.

If the claim for set-off of trading losses within the same accounting period is made, however, the company may additionally claim to carry back any surplus loss against its total profits and capital gains in the twelve months preceding the accounting period which gave rise to the loss.

If, however, the loss-making trade was not being carried on by the company throughout the previous twelve months, the relevant period for loss set-off is the period beginning with the commencement of that trade.

10.8 CAPITAL GAINS IN COMPANIES

A UK resident company is entitled to indexation relief on its capital gains. This relief is designed to protect the company from any element of capital gain arising purely due to inflation.

Indexation relief is based on the increase in the Retail Prices Index over the period since the company purchased the property. The UK Retail Prices Index is used regardless of where the property is located.

Example

Shakespeare Limited bought a merchant's house in Venice for £100,000 in May 1990 when the Retail Price Index was 126.2. The company sells the property for £300,000 in May 2008 when the Retail Price Index is (say) 214.5.

The increase in the Retail Price Index over the company's period of ownership is 70%, calculated as follows:

214.5 – 126.2 = 88.3
88.3/126.2 = 70%

Shakespeare Limited is therefore entitled to indexation relief of £70,000 (£100,000 x 70%), thus reducing its taxable capital gain to £130,000 (£300,000 - £100,000 - £70,000).

As with individuals, a company is exempt on capital gains arising prior to 31st March 1982 and this is usually achieved by substituting a property's market value at that date in place of its original cost in the capital gains calculation.

Capital Losses

In a similar way to an individual, a company can only set capital losses off against capital gains arising in the same or future accounting periods.

Restrictions apply to capital losses arising on transactions with connected parties or arising due to 'artificial' transactions designed to avoid tax.

10.9 FOREIGN EXCHANGE DIFFERENCES

As with an individual, a UK resident company will usually be required to prepare all of its UK tax calculations in sterling. (A company whose operations are based entirely in a different country may, however, sometimes prepare its calculations in the local currency.)

A UK resident company's capital gains calculations on the disposal of foreign property are therefore usually prepared in sterling in the same way as we saw in Chapter 6 (but subject to indexation relief).

Unlike an individual, however, exchange differences arising on a UK resident company's foreign currency transactions are not treated as capital gains and losses.

Where foreign exchange differences arise in connection with foreign property trading transactions these are treated as part of the company's trading results.

All other foreign exchange differences arising in a UK resident company are treated as follows:

- Foreign exchange losses are treated as general overheads in exactly the same way as interest and finance costs relating to an overseas rental business (see Section 10.6).
- Foreign exchange gains are treated as sundry non-trading income.

10.10 PROFIT EXTRACTION

So far, we have seen quite a few advantages to using a company to hold foreign property, including lower tax rates on rental income, indexation relief on capital gains and beneficial relief for interest costs and foreign exchange losses.

This is all very well, but the after tax income and sale proceeds held in a company still belong to the company and not to you, the shareholder.

To get your hands on this money, you have three basic choices:

- Pay yourself a dividend
- Pay yourself a salary
- Wind up or sell the company

UK Dividends

Dividends paid by a UK resident company carry a tax credit of one ninth. This tax credit is set against the UK Income Tax liability arising when a shareholder receives a UK dividend but cannot be repaid where no such liability arises.

Higher rate taxpayers are subject to Income Tax at 32.5% on dividend income. Other taxpayers are subject to Income Tax at 10%.

The one ninth tax credit gives higher rate taxpayers an effective Income Tax liability of 25% on their UK dividend income and also means that most other taxpayers effectively receive dividends tax free.

Example

Dirk and Clive each receive a £900 dividend from Titanic Limited, a UK company with a portfolio of overseas investment property.

The £900 dividend carries a tax credit of one ninth, or £100, meaning that, for Income Tax purposes, Dirk and Clive are each treated as if they have received a gross dividend of £1,000.

Dirk is a higher rate taxpayer and he therefore has an Income Tax charge of £325 on his Titanic Limited dividend (£1,000 x 32.5%). After deducting the £100 tax credit, however, his actual liability is just £225 which works out at 25% of the £900 dividend which he actually received.

Clive is a basic rate taxpayer and his Income Tax charge on his Titanic Limited dividend is therefore just £100 (£1,000 x 10%). After deducting the tax credit of £100, he is left with no UK Income Tax liability.

Foreign Dividends

Dividends received from a non-UK resident company, or 'foreign dividends', are taxed at the same rates of 10% for basic rate taxpayers and 32.5% for higher rate taxpayers.

At present, foreign dividends do not carry any tax credit for UK tax purposes meaning that the effective rate of tax suffered by shareholders is higher than on UK dividends.

From 6th April 2008, however, many foreign dividends will carry a tax credit and will therefore be treated exactly the same as UK dividends.

Sadly, however, it is currently proposed that the tax credit will not be available on foreign dividends when the shareholder receiving the dividends owns 10% or more of the shares in the company paying those dividends or receives £5,000 or more in foreign dividends during the relevant tax year.

Hence, in the case of a property investor investing in foreign property through their own non-UK resident company, the tax credit will not be available and the effective Income Tax rates on any dividends they receive from that company will remain 10% for basic rate taxpayers and 32.5% for higher rate taxpayers.

Salaries

For most UK residents, any salary you pay yourself from your company will suffer Income Tax in the UK unless it is covered by your personal allowance (£5,435 for 2008/9 – but most people will have already used it up on other income). Income Tax is payable on salary income at 20% (22% until 5th April 2008) if you are a basic rate taxpayer, or 40% if you are a higher rate taxpayer.

Any salary paid in excess of the 'earnings threshold' (see Appendix B) is also subject to National Insurance. As the employee, you will generally suffer National Insurance at 11%, although this reduces to 1% where your total earnings for the year are, broadly speaking, over the 'upper earnings limit' (see Appendix B). The company will also have to pay secondary employer's National Insurance at the rate of 12.8% on all salary in excess of the 'earnings threshold'.

If you are non-UK domiciled or non-UK ordinarily resident you may be able to avoid UK tax on any salary paid wholly in respect of duties performed overseas.

The company can usually claim Corporation Tax relief for salaries and employer's National Insurance paid as long as the salaries are commercially justified by the work you do for the company.

Selling or Winding Up the Company

If you sell the company, this is a disposal for Capital Gains Tax purposes and will be treated in exactly the same way as the sale of a property as explained in Chapter 5.

If you wind up the company and pay its net assets out to yourself as shareholder, this will also be treated as a capital disposal in the same way.

From 6th April 2008, all capital disposals will be subject to Capital Gains Tax at a flat rate of 18%. Double tax relief is not available in respect of any tax already suffered by the company in either the UK or overseas and this gives rise to an effective double tax charge.

Example

As we saw in Section 10.8, Shakespeare Limited sold its Venetian property for £300,000, giving rise to a taxable capital gain of £130,000 for UK Corporation Tax purposes.

Shakespeare Limited's total income and gains for the year ending 31st March 2009 are less than £300,000 meaning that it pays UK Corporation Tax at 21% on its capital gain, i.e. £27,300.

This leaves the company with net proceeds of £272,700. Let us now suppose that the company borrowed the original £100,000 purchase cost for the Venetian property and that all of its other assets and liabilities exactly match each other. Hence, after selling all its assets and paying off all its liabilities, the company is left with the net sum of £172,700, which is the after tax profit on is Venetian property.

Anne set up Shakespeare Limited some years ago with a share capital of just £1. In order to get her net proceeds of £172,700 out of the company, she now winds it up. This gives rise to a capital gain of £172,699 on which Anne will pay Capital Gains Tax at 18%, or £31,086 (slightly less if she has not yet used her annual exemption).

This leaves Anne with net proceeds of £141,614 from Shakespeare Limited's original £200,000 gain, equivalent to an overall tax rate of just over 29%.

Note that in the above example, I have ignored the costs of winding up Shakespeare Limited. In practice, winding up a company tends to be an expensive business. A cheaper alternative is to have the company struck off, but this has some important legal consequences and professional advice is therefore essential.

The UK Capital Gains Tax position is exactly the same where a shareholder sells or winds up a foreign company. Double tax relief may be claimed for any foreign tax suffered by the shareholder on the sale or winding up but not for foreign tax paid by the company itself.

Tax Efficient Profit Extraction

In most cases, the overall result of all of the above is that the best way to extract profits whilst the company still holds foreign property is to pay yourself a salary up to the amount of the 'primary threshold' (£5,435 for 2008/9) and to take any additional payments by way of dividend.

Where your spouse, partner or other family members also work for the company, it will often also make sense to pay them a salary up to the amount of the 'primary threshold'.

All salaries should, however, be limited to an amount which can be justified commercially.

Where surplus funds are left in a company which has sold all of its foreign property and other assets, and where the company is not going to be used for some other purpose, it will generally be more tax efficient to have the company wound up or struck off so that the remaining funds can paid out to the shareholder and treated as a capital disposal taxed at 18% (after deducting the annual exemption if still available).

However, where a sale or winding up of a UK resident company is in prospect and the shareholder is a basic rate taxpayer, it will make sense to first pay a dividend sufficient to use up their remaining basic rate band as this will effectively be tax free.

A similar approach may be suitable where a foreign company is to be sold or wound up but there will usually be a tax cost of 10% for a basic rate taxpayer receiving foreign dividends and any available Capital Gains Tax annual exemption should therefore be considered first.

Anyone intending to emigrate should read Chapter 9 and wait until they are non-resident before selling or winding up their company.

More information on extracting profits from property companies tax efficiently is included in the Taxcafe.co.uk guides *Salary versus Dividends* and *Using a Property Company to Save Tax*.

10.11 ASSOCIATED COMPANIES

The Corporation Tax profit bands described in Section 10.4 must be divided up where there are any associated companies. The bands are divided equally between all of the relevant associated companies, meaning that the more companies you have, the higher your effective rates of Corporation Tax in each company are going to be.

One associated company alone could cost you up to £13,125 in extra Corporation Tax in the year ending 31st March 2009 alone.

What is an Associated Company?

An associated company is another company under the control of the same persons and <u>their</u> associates. A person's associates are other persons with whom they are 'connected'; broadly this means spouses, relatives and business partners.

Hence, in the simplest case, if you form two companies and own all of the shares in both of them, then these companies are associated with each other.

Exceptions

- A company does not need to be counted as an associated company if it is not carrying on a business. The term 'business' is defined very widely here and might include, for example, a company holding a portfolio of stock market investments. However, a company which simply had an interest-bearing bank account, and no other assets, has been held <u>not</u> to be carrying on a business for this purpose.
- A company which exists only to hold property and which is not actively seeking to rent out any property does not

usually need to be counted as an associated company. Amongst other things, this means that a company formed purely to hold a second home overseas may usually be excluded from the associated company rules.

- Companies which are controlled by relatives other than spouses and minor children do not need to be counted as associated companies unless there is a substantial commercial relationship between the companies.

Subject to the above exceptions, however, <u>any</u> associated company must be taken into account, regardless of what country it is based in, or registered in, and regardless of what kind of business it is carrying on.

The upshot of all this is that any investor who already controls a company operating in any type of business may potentially cause themselves a significant increase in their annual Corporation Tax bill if they choose to invest in overseas property through another company.

Example

Donatien has a private trading company, Marquis Limited, which makes annual profits of £200,000. As things stand, Marquis Limited's Corporation Tax bill for the year ending 31st March 2009 will be £42,000 (£200,000 at 21%).

In April 2008, however, Donatien decides to form a second company, Desade Limited, to invest in foreign property throughout Europe.

In its first year, the new company just manages to break even. However, because there are now two associated companies, the Corporation Tax profit bands must now be divided in two. Each of Donatien's companies therefore gets half of the relevant tax bands.

Marquis Limited's Corporation Tax bill is therefore now £46,375 (£150,000 @ 21% plus £50,000 @ 29.75%).

If Donatien had kept all of his business interests in just one company, its Corporation Tax liability would have remained just £42,000.

Hence, whilst Desade Limited has no tax to pay itself (as it has not yet made a profit), its mere existence has cost Marquis Limited an extra £4,375!

The moral here is that a proliferation of companies is generally a bad idea. As with everything in tax though, there are exceptions.

A nominee company (see Section 10.2) should not be regarded as having any business and hence, if managed correctly, should not impact on the Corporation Tax position of any other companies controlled by its owner.

Furthermore, as stated above, a company which exists wholly for the purpose of holding a holiday home should not need to be counted as an associated company. Care must be exercised, however, as almost any form of business activity will bring the associated company rules into operation.

10.12 COMPANIES AND INHERITANCE TAX

Companies do not generally pay Inheritance Tax themselves. Inheritance Tax is, however, generally payable on the death of a shareholder, based on the value of the shares they own.

Shares in property development companies will usually be eligible for business property relief (see Section 5.12). The relief is not affected if some or all of the company's developments take place overseas.

Shares in property investment companies, however, are usually fully subject to Inheritance Tax. Again, this is unaffected by the location of the properties held by the company.

Chapter 11

Special Purpose Vehicles

11.1 WHAT IS AN 'SPV'?

I used to think that an 'SPV' was something which Captain Scarlet drove.

Nowadays, however, 'SPV' generally stands for 'Special Purpose Vehicle', a fancy term, which in the context of foreign property, simply means any type of legal structure used for holding property other than direct ownership by an individual.

Apart from simple direct ownership of foreign property by an individual, other structures through which a foreign property might be owned include:

- Joint ownership by two or more individuals.
- Partnerships (both 'traditional' and Limited Liability Partnerships).
- Trusts.
- Companies (UK or foreign).
- Syndicates.

Companies have already been covered in detail in Chapter 10.

The UK tax consequences of joint ownership of foreign property or ownership through a partnership are generally not hugely different to those for individual owners which we have examined in previous chapters.

That leaves us with trusts, which we shall look at in Section 11.2, and syndicates.

A syndicate is a very broad term which may encompass any other form of Special Purpose Vehicle. These may sometimes involve Unit Trusts which are often more like a stock market investment than owning property.

11.2 TRUSTS

Trusts come in many different forms. In essence, however, a trust is an arrangement under which a person (the trustee) holds property on behalf of one or more beneficiaries. The person putting assets or funds into the trust is known as the 'settlor'.

A UK trust is subject to UK Income Tax and Capital Gains Tax on income and capital gains from foreign property along broadly similar lines to a UK resident individual.

An 'interest in possession trust' is a form of trust where the income of the trust belongs to a specific individual. This type of trust pays Income Tax at the basic rate on its income. The trust beneficiary then pays any additional tax if they are a higher rate taxpayer.

A 'discretionary trust' exists where no specific individual is entitled to the trust income. These trusts pay basic rate Income Tax on the first £1,000 of their income and higher rate tax on the remainder. Where income is paid out to a basic rate taxpayer beneficiary, they can reclaim part of the tax paid.

From 6th April 2008, it is proposed that all UK trusts will pay Capital Gains Tax at 18%. Prior to this date, UK trusts pay Capital Gains Tax as if they were a higher rate taxpayer individual.

Where the settlor, or their spouse or minor child, is the beneficiary of a trust, the trust's income and capital gains are treated as belonging directly to the settlor for UK tax purposes. Such a trust is referred to as a 'settlor-interested trust'.

An offshore trust is effectively non-UK resident and may therefore carry significant tax advantages in the right circumstances. Generally, however, it is no longer possible for a UK resident individual to benefit by putting foreign property into an offshore trust of which they or their spouse are a beneficiary as this would be a 'settlor-interested trust' as described above.

Trusts are subject to a different and sometimes complex Inheritance Tax regime in the UK which is covered in detail in the Taxcafe.co.uk guide *'How to Avoid Inheritance Tax'*. Offshore trusts may carry advantages for non-UK domiciled taxpayers, as explained in Section 8.10.

11.3 BUYING FOREIGN PROPERTY THROUGH SIPPS

Under the current UK pension regime, there are no restrictions on the location of property eligible for purchase by a personal pension fund.

As with UK property, however, the foreign property must generally be commercial property (e.g. shops, offices, factories, etc), and not residential. Purpose-built student accommodation will nevertheless still sometimes qualify, as will hotel rooms/apartments purchased under 'leaseback schemes' (see Section 13.9).

Whilst many leaseback schemes allow some personal use by the owner, this is not permitted when the property is owned through a SIPP. To safeguard the position, the leaseback contract should prohibit personal use by the SIPP member and their family.

Wealth Warning

Some foreign countries do not recognise the tax exempt status of a UK SIPP.

Income and gains from foreign properties held within a SIPP may therefore be subject to foreign taxes. As the SIPP is tax exempt in the UK, no double tax relief will be available for these taxes.

Foreign properties held within a SIPP may also be subject to other foreign taxes, such as wealth taxes or inheritance taxes.

Chapter 12

They Do Things Differently There

12.1 THE SAME DIFFERENCE

After over twenty years in the tax advice business, there are few things which still surprise me. One thing which does still amaze me, however, is just how often people still seem to overlook the fact that the UK is not the only country in the world with taxes.

Anyone who lives, works, or invests abroad has a potential exposure to foreign taxes. Not only is property investment no exception to this general rule, it is actually one of the fields with the greatest potential exposure to foreign taxation.

Most of us know just how many taxes the UK Government levies on property owners. Why then, should other countries be any different?

Every Government in the world faces the same basic issue: how to raise revenue to pay for the cost of the country's internal infrastructure and external defence. The way that most countries deal with this issue is the same as the UK: tax!

And, if you are going to need to raise taxes, one of the most obvious things to target is property.

So, with a few exceptions, it is an almost universal truth that whatever country you buy property in, you will face local property taxes.

However, whilst nearly every country has property taxation, the **way** in which they tax the property in their country varies enormously.

So, wherever you go, it's the same problem, only different.

12.2 LOOK BEFORE YOU LEAP

The title of this section is really the key to investing in foreign property successfully. It is essential to get local advice and to understand what you are getting yourself into.

Many people concentrate so hard on avoiding UK taxes that they overlook the fact that foreign taxation can be just as important, or even more so. This will often be to their detriment as an investment which looks attractive before foreign tax is taken into account may provide a pretty poor return after tax, or even a loss!

It's amazing how many people sign up for a foreign property investment during a short trip to the country on the basis of the 'sales talk' from a local salesperson or agent. Would you behave like this in the UK?

Worst of all, local laws frequently provide little or no 'cooling off' period meaning that the most sketchy of preliminary agreements automatically create binding contracts from which it is impossible or, at best, expensive, to escape.

Sales people and real estate agents will rarely tell you anything about foreign taxes or many other important legal issues. Before investing in property abroad, it is essential to seek advice from local professionals, such as lawyers or qualified accountants. Advice should be independent too: don't go to a firm recommended by the people selling the property to you; where do you think their loyalties will lie?

If you're interested in property abroad, look before you leap!

12.3 DANGEROUS ASSUMPTIONS

As explained in Section 12.1, the country in which you intend to buy your property is likely to have its own property taxation regime.

Beyond this, however, assume nothing!

I have worked in the tax profession for over twenty years and during this time I have had my fair share of contact with other country's tax systems. The main thing which I have learned, sometimes painfully, is that you cannot assume anything about another country's tax system.

The tax rates will be different, the tax exemptions will be different, the types of tax may be different, the reliefs, allowances and tax bands will all be different. The tax year will almost certainly be different.

Their rules on residence and domicile will be different and their succession and property laws will all be different.

Someone once said "I don't mind foreigners speaking a different language; I just wish they'd all speak the same one". This brings me to my next point:

Not only is every country's tax system different to the UK, they are all different to each other.

There are, however, similarities and general concepts which apply in many countries. Hence, with the over-riding warning to assume nothing, it is nevertheless still worth us looking at some general principles of international property tax.

12.4 GENERAL PROPERTY TAX PRINCIPLES

In general, most countries will tax non-residents on property in their country. Furthermore, most double taxation agreements do nothing to prevent this.

Foreign property taxes generally fall into the following five categories:

    i)   Tax on property purchases
    ii)   Annual charges
    iii)   Tax on income
    iv)   Tax on property sales
    v)   Tax on death or gifts

It is interesting to note that all but one of the above categories of tax are likely to apply to a foreign holiday home owned by a UK resident. (And, if the property is ever rented out, all five will apply.) This just goes to show that, when it comes to foreign property tax, the investor and the holiday home owner have more in common than you might expect.

We will now look at each of our five categories of property tax in turn. To further illustrate what is meant by each category, I will also list the UK taxes falling into each one. One of those UK taxes is VAT. Since VAT is a European tax, we will look at it further in Chapter 14 rather than include it in the more general discussions below.

Tax on Property Purchases
UK Equivalents: Stamp Duty Land Tax and VAT

Many countries impose a tax charge of some kind when property is purchased, usually based on the purchase consideration paid.

For UK tax purposes, these taxes will be included as part of the property's purchase cost.

Annual Charges
UK Equivalents: Council Tax and Business Rates

Annual charges on property come in many different forms and are often charged by local or regional governments rather than nationally.

There may be an annual charge on property ownership at either a flat rate or linked in some way to the property's value. Additional charges sometimes apply to properties which are not the owner's main residence.

There may also, or alternatively, be an annual charge on property occupation (as in the UK). This again may be at either a flat rate or linked to the property's value.

Another common annual charge is a 'wealth tax'. This is an annual tax based on a person's total wealth. Many countries impose this charge on non-residents based on the net value of the property and other assets which they hold in the country.

Where a UK resident suffers annual charges on occupation or ownership of foreign property these may usually be treated as running costs and can be deducted as an expense from rental income or trading profits for UK tax purposes. As we saw in Chapter 3, however, such costs are only partly deductible where there is some personal use of the property.

The treatment of wealth taxes is less clear and these are often regarded as a personal cost with no deduction available in the UK.

Tax on Income
UK Equivalents: Income Tax, National Insurance, Corporation Tax, VAT and Tax Credit Withdrawal

Most countries will tax profits and income derived from property whether through letting, development or dealing.

Rental income may either be taxed on an accounts basis, based on profits after certain deductible expenses, or as a flat rate on rent received. Where an accounts basis applies, each country will have its own rules regarding what expenses are deductible. Flat rate systems allow for little or no deduction of expenses.

In many cases, the tax on non-resident landlords is a simple flat percentage of rent received and may have to be withheld at source (i.e. a Withholding Tax). Reduced rates of Withholding Tax often apply under double taxation agreements and, as explained in Section 7.6, must be claimed where available.

Profits from property development and dealing are usually taxed on an accounts basis and sometimes also attract additional 'social taxes' like our National Insurance.

For UK tax purposes, double tax relief is usually available for foreign taxes on property income, or they may be claimed as a business expense, as explained in Section 3.7.

Tax on Property Sales
UK Equivalents: Capital Gains Tax and Corporation Tax

Some countries charge tax on the gain arising when a property is sold.

Many countries provide an exemption for the owner's main private residence, although this is not generally available to non-residents. Properties held for longer periods are often also exempt.

Many countries, like the UK, will treat profits derived from property sales by developers and dealers as income.

Double tax relief for foreign tax suffered on capital gains is usually available against UK Capital Gains Tax.

Tax on Death or Gifts
UK Equivalents: Inheritance Tax

I wish I could say that the UK is the only country governed by grave-robbers who tax us when we die, but sadly it isn't. There are many countries which do not have any death taxes but many do.

Generally, where there is a death tax, there will usually be a similar tax on lifetime gifts as an anti-avoidance measure.

Most countries with a death tax will charge it on non-residents in respect of property and other assets within their borders.

Double tax relief for foreign death taxes is available against any UK Inheritance Tax liability arising on the same assets. Double tax relief will also be available for foreign gift taxes if the same gift gives rise to a UK Inheritance Tax liability, although this will be rare unless trusts are involved.

Wealth Warning

Do not assume that there will be an exemption from foreign death or gift taxes in respect of transfers to your spouse or civil partner. This will not always be the case.

Furthermore, it is crucial to be aware that foreign gift taxes may apply to lifetime transfers of property or shares in property (e.g. putting a foreign property into joint ownership with your spouse).

12.5 CORPORATE TAXES

As we saw in Section 10.1, there are a number of reasons why it may make sense to purchase foreign property through a company.

Most countries recognise the concept of companies (unlike other Special Purpose Vehicles, as we shall see in Chapter 13).

Corporate ownership generally does little to change the basic principle that each country usually taxes property located within its borders.

Some countries tax companies in the same way as individuals but many, especially the more developed countries, will have a separate regime for taxing companies owning property in their country.

In some cases, particular types of company may be subject to 'fiscal transparency' and are effectively ignored so that some or all taxes fall directly on the company's shareholders. This concept is explained further in Section 13.8.

Where companies *are* taxed in their own right, the taxes arising will generally fall under the first four of our five categories listed in Section 12.4.

Companies usually pay the same taxes on property purchases as individuals and often pay similar annual charges. Taxes on income and on property sales usually follow similar principles to the taxes on individuals, although the rates of tax applying are often different (as they are in the UK – see Section 10.4).

Companies do not usually pay tax under our fifth category, however, as they do not die and are generally prohibited by law from making gifts. It is therefore in this area that companies are often most effective in avoiding foreign taxes.

Furthermore, foreign death and gift taxes are often avoided on the value of the company shares when the shareholder dies or makes a gift of them. This position often arises because, unlike the underlying property, the shares are not situated in the country concerned.

Using a company to hold foreign property will not generally affect the UK Inheritance Tax position, however.

12.6 AVOIDING EVASION

In the UK, we have a principle that ignorance of the law is no excuse. The same is true in most other countries.

If you buy property in another country, you will almost certainly have responsibilities as a taxpayer there. At the very least, you will probably need to register with the local tax authorities. If you fail to meet your responsibilities as a taxpayer, you will be guilty of tax evasion and that will make you a criminal.

Furthermore, the UK now treats someone who evades tax in another country as a criminal here too.

Practical Pointer

Do not confuse tax evasion with tax avoidance. Tax avoidance is legal; tax evasion is a criminal offence.

As a general rule, if you can save tax but still make a full disclosure of your affairs to the local tax authorities (and to Revenue and Customs in the UK), this will be legal tax avoidance.

Anything which relies on non-disclosure to succeed is likely to be illegal tax evasion.

If in doubt, take local, independent, professional advice (and the same in the UK).

12.7 LOST IN TRANSLATION

When you own foreign property, you will need to deal with the local tax authorities in the country where the property is located. Those local tax authorities will generally write to you in their own language and will often pay no attention to any response made in any other language.

DO NOT ignore correspondence simply because it is written in a foreign language and you do not understand it – it may be extremely important.

Chapter 13

Some Important Concepts

13.1 TAKE NOTHING FOR GRANTED

In Section 12.3, I pointed out that every country's tax system is different and that you should assume nothing.

This same principle extends to many other important concepts which we take for granted here in the UK.

Conversely, there are also some important concepts which have a wide application in many countries overseas.

My aim in this chapter, therefore, is to give you an introduction to some important concepts which apply in many countries and also to point out some of our own concepts which may not always apply.

13.2 RESIDENCE AND DOMICILE

We examined the UK concepts of residence and domicile in Chapters 8 and 9.

Other countries do not apply the same tests although most countries will regard you as resident for tax purposes if you spend more than half of the year there.

As each country has a different test, it is possible to become resident for tax purposes in more than one country. This is referred to as 'dual residence' and can lead to both major problems and tax-saving opportunities. Many double taxation agreements include a clause to determine which country takes precedence in taxing a dual resident.

Most countries do recognise residence as a concept and generally treat residents and non-residents differently. (Remember that, as a UK resident, you will usually be a non-resident in any other country.)

Domicile is not so widely recognised and is irrelevant in many countries.

13.3 PROPERTY LAW

Property law differs from one country to another. In fact, you only need to go as far as Gretna Green to find this out (or to Berwick on Tweed if you're going the other way).

The concept of freehold is not universally recognised and is not always freely transferable when it is.

Joint ownership of property is not always possible.

Most importantly, many countries do not allow non-residents to own land.

13.4 INHERITANCE AND SUCCESSION

Death *is* universal, so all countries have rules to deal with inheritance or succession.

Unlike England and Wales, many countries do not allow individuals to leave their estate to whomever they wish and have statutory rules governing succession rights. These rules often apply to non-residents in respect of property located within the country.

Where a person dies intestate (i.e. without a valid Will), local laws will often govern the distribution of any assets located in a foreign country. It will therefore generally make sense to make a Will in any country where you hold property as well as here in the UK. Legal advice both at home and abroad is essential to ensure that your Wills interact with each other as desired and do not cancel each other out.

In some countries, it remains possible for a UK national to ensure that our own succession laws continue to apply to any property in that country. For those domiciled in most of the UK, this means being able to dispose of your assets as you wish under the terms of your Will. If you are domiciled in Scotland, however, legal rights may apply to your foreign property in the same way as the rest of your estate. See the Taxcafe.co.uk guide *'How to Avoid Inheritance Tax'* for further details.

We will be looking at the rules of succession in a number of countries. To assist readers in better understanding their position, it is worth including a brief definition of some general inheritance terminology.

Absolutely – When assets are left to a person absolutely, this means that they will own those assets outright and have complete freedom to do with them as they wish (subject to normal legal requirements over freely held property).

Life Interest – The right to the use or enjoyment of an asset, or to the income produced by that asset, for the remainder of your life.

Reversionary Interest – The asset will pass to you absolutely on the expiry of another person's life interest.

13.5   MARRIAGE AND CIVIL PARTNERSHIP

I'm pretty sure that every country recognises the concept of marriage. It is probably the next most universally recognised concept after death. Except tax perhaps!

Most countries give special treatment to married couples and often, in particular, to transfers of property between spouses.

It is important to remember that such special treatment will generally only apply to legally married couples.

Civil Partnerships

Since 5th December 2005, the UK has recognised registered civil partnerships between same sex couples and has treated them the same as a married couple for all UK tax purposes.

Civil partnerships are not, however, universally recognised in all countries, although they are spreading more widely and are now recognised in most of Western Europe as well as many other developed countries.

Even where it applies, however, civil partnership status does not bring the same rights in every country.

The terminology also varies. A few countries simply allow same sex marriages. Others use various terms including 'civil partnership', 'civil union' and 'registered partnership'.

In some countries, such as Australia and the USA, the position varies from one part of the country to another.

Some countries also allow opposite sex couples to enter a civil union, thus creating an alternative to marriage for everyone. Again, the rights attached to these civil unions will vary.

The most important point to bear in mind is that not every country will necessarily recognise the legal status of a UK resident couple's registered civil partnership.

13.6 TRUSTS AND NOMINEES

We looked at the UK tax treatment of trusts and nominee companies in Sections 11.2 and 10.2 respectively. These concepts are not universally recognised.

Some countries do not recognise the concept of a trust. Tax arising on foreign property held by a trust may fall on the trustee, or directly on the beneficiary, according to the country's own laws.

A nominee company structure may also be ineffective under a foreign country's local laws, meaning that the company suffers tax on its foreign property income and capital gains. As explained in Section 10.2, this can lead to problems in obtaining double tax relief for the foreign tax.

13.7 PENSION FUNDS

As explained in Section 11.3, some countries do not recognise a pension fund's tax exempt status and local taxes may arise where a UK pension fund invests in foreign property.

Since a pension fund is essentially a form of trust, some countries will not even recognise the pension fund's existence and may tax its foreign property income and capital gains directly on the fund members.

13.8 FISCAL TRANSPARENCY

Many countries, including the UK, recognise the concept of 'fiscal transparency'.

The effect of fiscal transparency is very much like that of a nominee company (see Section 10.2). There is a legal entity, often a special type of company, which is ignored for tax purposes, so that the entity's owners are taxed directly on the income and capital gains received by the entity.

In addition to nominee companies, the UK also treats partnerships and settlor-interested trusts (see Section 11.2) as fiscally transparent.

Unfortunately, however, an entity which is treated as fiscally transparent in another country may not necessarily be treated the same way for UK tax purposes. This again may lead to problems in obtaining double tax relief for foreign taxes paid.

13.9 LEASEBACK SCHEMES

Leaseback schemes originated in France, where they carry significant VAT advantages (see Section 15.4), but have also now been adopted in several other countries. Basically, under a leaseback scheme, the investor buys a hotel room/apartment and leases it back to a hotel operating company for a number of years.

Some leaseback schemes will allow the investor some personal use of the property, albeit restricted.

Chapter 14

The European Union

14.1 BRUSSELS SPROUTS

Beginning with the first six signatories to the Treaty of Rome in 1957, the EU has now grown to include the 27 member states listed in Appendix C.

Each of these countries is now governed by the principles of European Law, whether they like it or not.

Those principles include four 'freedoms of movement' governing goods, persons, services and capital. In other words, every EU citizen should be free to trade, live, work and invest in any country in the EU and should not be discriminated against by local laws.

National taxation law in the UK and other countries often runs contrary to these principles and the European constitution dictates that European Law takes precedence. As a result, year by year, Brussels is sprouting in power as well as territory!

In previous chapters, I have pointed out a number of instances where provisions of UK tax law appear to run contrary to EU law. The UK is by no means unique in this respect.

The key point to remember is that where any EU country's laws appear to discriminate against you as a non-resident then, as an EU citizen, you have the right to demand equal treatment.

This is fine in theory, of course, but 'demanding' these rights may not be so easy in practice. National tax authorities throughout the EU are highly resistant to the idea of being told what to do by the European Court.

Nevertheless, each EU member state is bound by European Law and whilst changes often take years to achieve, some important reforms have been made in recent years.

And it's not just big companies who have achieved success over tax authorities in the European Court, important cases have been won by small companies and even individuals.

As an EU citizen, you have the right to write directly to the European Court and ask them to review any aspect of tax law in any EU country which appears to discriminate against you.

That's some pretty heavy armoury on your side, and they like nothing more than taking national tax authorities down a peg or two.

14.2   VAT

VAT is a European tax and can expect to be encountered in every EU country. VAT rates vary from one country to another, however.

In the UK we are accustomed to the idea that VAT is not payable on the purchase of new residential property.

This, however, is not the case in many other EU countries and VAT often makes a hefty addition to a property's purchase price.

Where VAT is paid on a foreign property purchase and cannot subsequently be recovered, it will form part of the property's purchase price for UK Capital Gains Tax purposes.

Where you have a business registered for VAT in an EU country, you will be able to recover VAT on business expenses including the purchase of business property. Where VAT on a property purchase is recovered, it will therefore no longer form part of the property's purchase price for UK Capital Gains Tax purposes.

14.3   HOLIDAY ACCOMMODATION

The letting of property as holiday accommodation in any country in the EU is likely to be subject to VAT.

Some EU countries, like the UK, have a registration threshold, so that registration for foreign VAT is only necessary if the total annual holiday rental from all of the investor's properties in that country exceeds this limit. Most countries' VAT registration thresholds are considerably lower than ours, however.

Foreign VAT will present an administrative burden and will also result in the effective loss of a major proportion of the gross rents receivable. In Denmark or Sweden, for example, holiday rental income is subject to VAT at 25%, meaning that VAT of £200 would have to be paid out for every £1,000 of gross rental income received.

Remember also that the beneficial rules available for furnished holiday accommodation in the UK are not available when the property is situated abroad. Arguably, this may be contrary to the principles of European law.

14.4   DIVIDEND WITHHOLDING TAXES

Under local domestic tax law in many countries, company dividends are tax-free when received by a resident individual but subject to a Withholding Tax when paid to a non-resident.

The European Court has recently ruled that such withholding taxes are unlawful under EU law when levied on a resident of another EU member state.

If therefore, as a UK resident, you invest in foreign property through a company in another EU country, you should not be liable for any local Withholding Tax under European Law.

Often, however, it does take some time for local domestic law to fall into line with a European Court ruling. Hence, if you are being charged with Withholding Tax in another EU country, the best thing to do is to lodge a protective claim pending the appropriate change to the local law.

14.5 INVESTING IN EUROPE

A large proportion of property investment overseas by UK nationals is made within other EU countries.

This provides the UK resident property investor with the protection of European Law and in the next few chapters we will see several examples of the benefits which this brings.

In Chapters 15 to 18 we will be looking at the four main 'Civil Code' countries of South-Western Europe: France, Spain, Italy and Portugal.

The tax and legal regime in much of Western continental Europe displays a great deal of similarity. This is the work of a certain N. Bonaparte. Whilst his methods may have left something to be desired, it generally seems that the citizens of most of his former empire have been happy to keep a lot of the legal regime which he put in place two centuries ago.

We will therefore see a lot of commonality in the next four chapters, such as the status of the 'Notaire', or 'Notary', who tends to be more of a referee in property transactions, rather than the exclusive agent of one party. UK investors may find this odd but it is considered quite normal in these countries. If in doubt about your rights, however, it always remains sensible to take independent advice.

Another common factor in the 'Civil Code' countries is the fact that a deceased person's children often have legal rights over the estate which can take precedence over the rights of a surviving spouse. Apparently, this is another lasting legacy from Napoleon, who introduced these legal rights to prevent his soldiers from giving everything to the local ladies instead of their own children back home!

Eastern Europe still shows some of the after-effects of half a century of communist rule. In general, this leads to a less well-developed and less sophisticated tax system. It must be remembered that the concept of 'profit' was alien to the communist regimes of these countries less than twenty years ago. (I can well remember a Russian translator once telling me that they had no such word!)

In the Scandinavian North, we tend to find strong socialist principles with resultant high taxation rates but equally high standards of living.

Chapter 15

France

15.1 ENTENTE CORDIALE?

We all know that our closest neighbour across the channel has not always been our closest friend!

Nevertheless, despite the many differences which we have suffered over the centuries, France today stands as one of the most popular locations for UK Residents investing in property overseas. Indeed, UK investment into France represents around 48% of all foreign property investment in the country.

Much of the UK investment in France represents second homes or other holiday homes used predominantly by the investors themselves and their families. In fact, an estimated half a million Britons now own a French holiday home. Over 100,000 Britons have also gone a step further and made France their permanent home.

French property values have increased significantly in recent years, most especially in the South of the country.

Part of the reason behind these increases naturally lies in the level of foreign investment into the country. As in parts of the UK, this sometimes has the unfortunate effect of pricing young locals out of the property market. This, in turn, can lead to a hardening of attitudes towards the 'foreigners' who buy up French property. This manifests itself in the behaviour of both the taxation authorities and the local community and UK investors may find that, as the local pet 'Brit', they do have a few bridges to build in order to gain acceptance into the community.

15.2 THE FRENCH LEGAL SYSTEM

The French legal system is based on a system of codes – 'The Code Civil' which is quite different to the Common Law principles applying in the UK.

For example, the Code Civil, and indeed French culture in general, places far more emphasis on the importance of an individual's children, their natural heirs, than in the UK, where the rights of the spouse usually tend to be paramount. This, as we shall see, causes some unexpected results for the unwary UK investor owning French property.

There is a tendency to blame Napoleon for the whole French Civil Code, although many of the French attitudes to inheritance date back much further and even pre-date Roman Law. The diminutive former Emperor is nevertheless still responsible for much of France's legal system, even today, and let us never forget that he was also indirectly responsible for the introduction of our own Income Tax in the UK in 1799.

Another very significant factor which we need to be aware of is the attitude of the French authorities to foreign investors. This may be summed up as 'when in France you will do as the French do'. In other words, there is a general expectation that foreign investors should be fully subject to French law on their French investments. Despite the existence of a comprehensive UK-France Double Taxation Agreement, this leaves UK investors exposed to the full range of French taxes on any properties which they hold in France.

There are no legal restrictions on the acquisition of French property by non-French residents.

Lawyers in France are known as 'Notaires'. The relationship with one's lawyer is somewhat different in France as the same Notaire will generally act for both the seller and the purchaser in the same property transaction.

An important general point to note about the French legal system is the fact that trusts have no legal status in France. We will explore the consequences of this further in Section 15.18.

France does, however, have its own form of civil partnership, the Pacte Civile de Solidarité, which is available to both same sex and opposite sex couples. As we shall see later in the chapter, a Pacte Civile de Solidarité carries some important rights, but not the same as marriage.

Under European law, it seems reasonable to suggest that a UK registered civil partnership should carry the same rights as a Pacte Civile de Solidarité for French tax and legal purposes. I would, however, suggest taking local advice before relying on this.

15.3 FRENCH PROPERTY TAXES

The French tax year is the calendar year. In general terms, France is a higher tax environment than the UK, with the total tax burden representing 49% of the country's gross domestic product ('GDP'), as opposed to 41% in the UK, or just 32% in the USA.

However, it only takes a ride on the TGV or a visit to a French hospital before most of us begin to think that the French tax system might nevertheless still represent better value for money!

What many UK Residents buying property in France are hoping for of course, is a slice of the French lifestyle, without the full burden of French taxation. Remarkably, most of them are actually able to achieve this seemingly contradictory result!

Nevertheless, at first sight, the array of French taxes applying to property does look somewhat daunting. UK Residents investing in French property may face some or all of the following:

- Registration Tax (*Droits d'Enrigestrement*)
- VAT
- Taxe d'Habitation
- Taxe Fonciere
- Wealth Tax
- Income Tax
- Income Tax on Capital Gains
- Inheritance Tax
- Gift Tax
- Corporate Income Tax
- Corporate Real Estate Tax

Despite this lengthy looking list, most UK Resident investors will find their French tax burden to be smaller than the potential UK tax burden on their French property.

What this means in practice for most UK Residents is that it usually makes more sense to plan their affairs to reduce their UK tax burden rather than their French tax liabilities. (Just as long as this planning doesn't actually produce French tax liabilities in excess of the investor's UK tax bills.)

In addition to its various taxes, France also imposes a system of Social Contributions on its own residents. Fortunately, however, non-French residents are generally exempt from Social Contributions.

Proof seems to be very important to the French tax authorities and it would appear that many practical difficulties arise owing to a taxpayer's inability to prove their claims. Thankfully, this is frequently compensated for by the availability of generous flat rate deductions, where no proof is required to validate a claim.

Nevertheless, where the owner's own particular circumstances warrant a greater deduction than the statutory flat rates, proof will be of vital importance. As a general point, therefore, the importance of retaining all relevant documentation relating to your French property investments cannot be stressed highly enough.

Non-French residents are generally required to file their tax returns at the 'Centre des Impôts des Non-Résidents', 10 rue du Centre, 93 465 Noisy-Le-Grand Cedex.

Enforcement

If the French tax authorities have reason to suspect that all taxes relating to a French property have not been paid in full, they have the power to take a legal charge over the property without any prior warning to the property's owner.

15.4 TAX ON PROPERTY PURCHASES IN FRANCE

The first sale of a new French property less than five years old is subject to the common rate of VAT, 19.6%.

Whilst the VAT is accounted for by the vendor, it is nevertheless inevitably added to the property's purchase price.

VAT can be recovered on the purchase of new residential property in France by undertaking a qualifying 'Bed and Breakfast' activity for at least nine years. This effectively means running the property as a guest house or hotel.

Unfortunately, as a trading activity, the income from the property will be subject to Income Tax, Social Contributions and VAT, as described in Section 15.8.

VAT may also be recovered on hotel room/apartments purchased under 'leaseback' schemes (see Section 13.9). The subsequent lease back to the hotel operator again represents a trading activity, with the same consequences as outlined above, and must continue for at least the requisite nine years. Generally, the owner may use the property personally for up to six weeks each year.

Registration Tax (Droits D'Enrigestrement)

Registration tax at the rate of 5.09% is payable by the purchaser of French property, except in the case of new properties subject to VAT.

Regional registration duties will often also be payable and these can bring the total duty payable on the purchase up to as much as 7.5%.

15.5 ANNUAL CHARGES

A non-French resident owning property in France faces up to four possible annual tax charges:

- Notional Income Tax
- Taxe d'Habitation
- Taxe Fonciere
- Wealth Tax

Wealth Tax is covered in Section 15.6. Before that, however, we will look at the other three potential annual charges.

Notional Income Tax

Some non-French residents owning a private residence in France are subject to an Income Tax charge on three times the property's annual rental value. Fortunately, however, UK resident individuals are exempt from this charge under the UK-France Double Taxation Agreement.

Taxe d'Habitation

Taxe d'Habitation is one of two different forms of local taxation levied on French property and is payable by the **occupier** of any habitable furnished building.

The tax is payable each 1st January by the person 'occupying' the property on that date. Occupation of the property effectively means having it available for your use, so non-French residents must usually pay the tax on any French holiday home.

TV licence fees are collected with Taxe d'Habitation.

Taxe Fonciere (*Taxe Fonciere*)

The other local tax on French property is Taxe Fonciere, which is payable on 1st January each year by the **owner** of the property on that date.

It is common practice in France for the vendor to ask the purchaser to recompense them for the portion of Taxe Fonciere relating to the remainder of the year falling after the date of sale.

Rental leases will often also require the tenant to reimburse the landlord for the Taxe Fonciere.

New property is exempt for a period of two years following completion.

Local Tax Rates

Both Taxe d'Habitation and Taxe Fonciere are based on the '*valeur locative cadastrale*': the rental value according to land records.

The rates of tax are set by the local authorities and therefore vary throughout France. Typically, the total of the two taxes amounts to around 5% of the property's annual market rental value, although rates in Paris tend to be a little lower.

15.6 WEALTH TAX

An investor with total French assets having a net value in excess of €770,000 will be subject to an annual Wealth Tax. Wealth Tax is applied at increasing rates as the total net value of the taxpayer's French assets increases. The provisional Wealth Tax rates for 2008 are as follows:

French estate value:			Rate Applying	Cumulative Tax
Up	to	€ 770,000	0.00%	€ 0
€ 770,000	to	€ 1,240,000	0.55%	€ 2,585
€ 1,240,000	to	€ 2,450,000	0.75%	€ 11,660
€ 2,450,000	to	€ 3,850,000	1.00%	€ 25,660
€ 3,850,000	to	€ 7,360,000	1.30%	€ 71,290
€ 7,360,000	to	€ 16,020,000	1.65%	€ 214,180
Over		€ 16,020,000	1.80%	n/a

The 'Cumulative Tax' column represents the total Wealth Tax payable by an investor with French assets having a total net value equal to the figure at the top end of the relevant band (e.g. total French assets worth €7,360,000 means total Wealth Tax payable of €71,290 for 2008).

Example

John has several properties in France with a total value of €2M. John has no loans outstanding against these properties.

John must pay Wealth Tax as follows:

€770,000 @ 0% =	*€0*
€1,240,000 - €770,000 = €470,000 @ 0.55% =	*€2,585*
€2,000,000 - €1,240,000 = €760,000 @ 0.75% =	*€5,700*
Total Wealth Tax due:	*€8,285*

Loans, mortgages, etc, used to acquire French property are usually deductible in establishing the net value of French assets for Wealth Tax purposes. Loans need not necessarily be taken out in France for this purpose, but it is necessary to prove that the loan was used to finance the French property – this is most easily achieved by securing the loans on the property.

French property may be re-mortgaged with the additional borrowings again being deductible for Wealth Tax purposes. In this case, it will usually be necessary for the additional borrowings to be secured on the French property. Otherwise, it will again be necessary to prove that the borrowings were used to finance the property – e.g. to pay for repairs.

Wealth Tax is assessed on a 'household' basis. In other words, any co-habiting couple are taxed on their combined wealth. When the tax was first introduced it was only married couples who were required to combine their wealth for this purpose. However, this led to a number of couples divorcing for tax purposes, so the law was changed to its current form!

No deduction will be given in the UK in respect of any French Wealth Tax liability.

Trading assets are exempt from Wealth Tax. As explained in Section 15.8, any furnished letting property which is deemed to be a 'trading activity' will be eligible for this exemption.

A 30% discount is also given on the net value of a qualifying principal private residence (i.e. qualifying for French tax purposes – see Section 15.9).

Subject to the above exemptions, French residents are usually subject to Wealth Tax on their worldwide assets.

Under the terms of the new UK-France Double Taxation Agreement signed on 28th January 2004, UK nationals relocating to France are to be exempt from Wealth Tax on non-French assets for their first five years of residence in France. The new Double Taxation Agreement has not yet come into force, however, and may be subject to alteration before it does.

All persons subject to Wealth Tax must declare the value of their assets and pay the tax due by 15th June each year. Where taxpayers fail to do so, the tax may be reassessed and collected up to ten years in arrears.

15.7 RENTAL INCOME

The treatment of rental income from French property is dependent on both the level of gross annual rental income and on whether or not the property is furnished.

Unfurnished Lettings (*Revenus Foncier*)

An individual receiving gross annual rental income of less than €15,000 from unfurnished lettings is eligible for the 'Micro-Fonciers' regime.

Under the 'Micro-Fonciers' regime, a flat rate deduction of 30% of gross rental income is given in respect of expenses.

Furnished Lettings

Furnished lettings are regarded as a commercial activity (i.e. a 'business') under French tax law and are referred to as 'Bénéfices Industriels et Commerciaux' or 'BIC'.

There is, however, a key distinction between whether the letting is a trading activity or an investment activity. In principle, the lettings generally become a trading activity when they represent the taxpayer's principal source of income. We will look at the treatment of such 'professional lettings' in Section 15.8.

Provided that the furnished letting is not a trading activity under French law, an individual receiving gross annual rental income from furnished lettings not exceeding €76,300 is eligible for the 'Micro BIC' regime.

Under the 'Micro BIC' regime, a flat rate deduction of 71% is allowed to cover all expenses, leaving just 29% of the rental income chargeable to tax.

Régime Réel Simplifie

Where an individual's gross annual rental income exceeds the €15,000 or €76,300 threshold (as appropriate), the 'Regime Réel Simplifie' applies and full income and expenditure accounts must be prepared.

Under the 'Regime Réel Simplifie' (i.e. the accounts basis), deductions are allowed for:

- Mortgage interest
- Repairs and maintenance expenses
- Letting agency fees
- Insurance premiums
- Local property taxes

Some improvement expenditure may also be claimed; generally where incurred to modernise the property or to make it more comfortable, but where the structure has not been altered.

Additionally, the taxpayer is allowed a standard deduction equal to 14% of gross rental income.

Landlords eligible for either of the 'Micro' regimes described above may elect instead for the 'Regime Réel Simplifie' to apply to their rental income. Once made, such an election will apply for a minimum of three years.

Such an election will make sense if the actual expenditure exceeds the flat rate deduction available under the appropriate 'Micro' regime and this will most often arise due to mortgage interest.

The accounts basis may also give rise to rental losses. A limited set off against other taxable income in France is allowed for rental losses.

Rental losses from French lettings may also be carried forward for set off against future income from French lettings. Losses from unfurnished lettings may only be set off against future income from unfurnished lettings and any element of the loss arising due to mortgage interest may only be carried forward for a maximum of ten years.

Practical Pointer

UK resident investors will already need to prepare accounts in respect of their French rental income for UK tax purposes. It may therefore make sense to elect for the 'Regime Réel Simplifie' for French tax purposes since detailed accounting records relating to the rental income are going to be required in any case.

French Income Tax Rates

French Income Tax is charged on a progressive basis: i.e. a system of tax bands charged at increasing rates of tax, similar to the system which we have in the UK. Taxable rental income, calculated as described above, is included as part of an individual's total taxable income for French Income Tax purposes.

Non-French residents pay French Income Tax on taxable French income at a minimum rate of 20%. Taxable income in excess of €25,195 but not exceeding €67,546 is taxed at 30% and income over €67,546 is taxed at 40% (at 2007 rates).

Remember that these rates apply only to the taxable element of the income. The minimum effective rate applying to gross rents receivable under the 'Micro BIC' regime, for example, is therefore 5.8% (29% x 20%).

Married couples and civil partners may file joint tax returns for French Income Tax purposes and these can sometimes assist in reducing the overall amount of tax payable where one member of the couple has French taxable income in excess of €25,195.

Double Tax Relief

A UK resident in receipt of French rental income will still need to calculate their rental profit on an actual basis (i.e. deducting actual expenses from the actual gross rent received) for UK Income Tax purposes, regardless of whether they qualify for one of the 'Micro' flat rate deduction regimes in France.

The use of one of the 'Micro' regimes for French Tax purposes does not, however, prevent the French tax arising from being eligible for double tax relief in the UK.

15.8 PROFESSIONAL LETTINGS

As explained in Section 15.7, furnished lettings may sometimes be treated as a trading activity, also known as 'professional lettings'.

It is possible to elect for 'professional lettings' treatment when gross annual rental income from furnished lettings exceeds €23,000 by registering as a professional furnished landlord with the French tax authorities.

Income from qualifying 'Bed and Breakfast' activities and from certain 'leaseback' schemes (see Section 15.4) is also classed as 'professional letting' income. Again, it is necessary to register as a professional furnished landlord.

Care must be taken when registering as a professional furnished landlord since municipal byelaws frequently prohibit the use of residential property in a trading activity.

Professional letting income is subject both to Income Tax, at the rates described in Section 15.7, and to Social Contributions at 11%, even for non-French residents. (Part of the Social Contributions is deductible from the following year's taxable income.)

The 'Micro BIC' regime is not available for professional lettings and full accounts will need to be prepared for French tax purposes.

On the positive side, property used in a professional letting activity is exempt from Wealth Tax as it is regarded as a 'Professional Asset'.

It is important to note, however, that the existence of such a 'Professional Asset' increases the risk of the owner being treated as French tax resident.

VAT on Holiday Lettings, Etc

VAT at the reduced rate of 5.5% is chargeable on income from qualifying 'Bed and Breakfast' activities and 'leaseback' schemes, as well as income from other holiday lettings in France.

15.9 CAPITAL GAINS ON FRENCH PROPERTY

France does not have a separate capital gains tax, but does charge Income Tax on taxable capital gains.

French Income Tax is payable on the taxable capital gain arising on the disposal by any person of property located in France. A UK Resident therefore remains fully liable to French Income Tax on any French property gains. However, the exemptions available on French property gains are quite generous.

The computation of a French property gain starts much as one would expect; we begin with sale proceeds net of any sale costs and then deduct the property's original purchase cost. However, in addition to the purchase cost, the taxpayer may claim an additional flat rate of 7.5% of that cost in respect of acquisition expenses. This claim is available regardless of whether such costs were actually incurred.

For a property owned for five years or more, the taxpayer may also claim a flat rate of 15% in respect of capital improvement expenditure. If actual invoiced expenditure is greater, however, then this may be claimed instead. Actual expenditure may also be claimed where the property has been held for less than five years.

The additional inclusion of the deemed acquisition expenses and the deemed or actual improvement costs produces the 'corrected acquisition price' and deducting this from the net sale proceeds provides the capital gain for French tax purposes.

For properties owned for six years or more, we are then able to claim a form of French taper relief. This relief operates by exempting 10% of the gain for every complete year of ownership after the first five years. Hence, 10% relief is available on a property owned for six years, 20% on a property owned for seven years, and so on until complete exemption is obtained after 15 years of ownership.

Finally, a fixed amount of €1,000 is deducted from any remaining sum to arrive at the taxable capital gain.

Example

In February 2008, Victor buys a house in Brittany for €250,000. He incurs legal and other acquisition costs at the time of the purchase totalling €5,000.

In 2009, Victor makes some improvements to the property at a total cost of €20,000.

In January 2016, Victor sells the property for €500,000 and incurs selling costs of €10,000.

Victor's taxable capital gain is calculated as follows:

	€	€
Selling price net of actual selling costs:		*490,000*
Purchase cost (actual)	*250,000*	
Acquisition expenses (deemed 7.5% of cost, in place of actual spend of €5,000)	*18,750*	
Capital improvements (deemed 15% of cost, in place of actual spend of €20,000)	*37,500*	
Corrected acquisition price		*306,250*
Capital gain		*183,750*
'Taper Relief' – 10% x (whole years of ownership – 5)		
= 10% x (7 – 5) = 20%		
20% x €183,750 =		*36,750*
		147,000
Fixed deduction		*1,000*
Taxable capital gain		*146,000*
French Income Tax on capital gain @ 16%:		*€23,360*

As can be seen from the example, French Income Tax is payable on the resultant capital gain at a fixed rate of 16%. This rate applies to taxable capital gains made on French property by any EU resident or resident of another country which has a double taxation agreement with France. The rate applying to other non-French residents is one third (33.33%).

French residents must also pay Social Contributions at a rate of 11% on any taxable capital gain. Fortunately, any non-French resident person who is a resident of another EU member state is exempt from Social Contributions. Hence, UK residents investing if France should not generally need to pay Social Contributions on any French capital gains (unless they are also French resident – see Section 15.14).

The overall effective rate of French tax suffered by Victor in our example is actually just under 11% (based on his actual purchase and improvement costs). Let us see how this compares with his UK Capital Gains Tax liability on the same sale. For the sake of illustration, we will assume that an exchange rate of €1.50:£1 applies throughout the period of Victor's ownership of the house in Brittany. We will also assume that Victor has no other taxable capital gains in the 2015/16 UK tax year and that the UK's annual Capital Gains Tax exemption for that year is £12,100.

Example Continued

Victor's UK Capital Gains Tax liability is calculated as follows (all amounts have been converted to sterling at €1.50:£1):

	£	£
Selling price net of actual selling costs:		*326,667*
Less:		
Purchase cost (actual)	*166,667*	
Acquisition expenses (actual)	*3,333*	
Improvement costs (actual)	*13,333*	

		183,333

		143,333
Annual exemption		*12,100*

Taxable capital gain in UK		*131,233*
		======

Victor's UK Capital Gains Tax liability at 18% will therefore be £23,622. He will be entitled to double tax relief of £15,573 in respect of his French tax liability of €23,360 but will still be left with a UK tax bill of £8,049.

This example ably demonstrates the fact that, for most UK investors, their French tax liability on French property gains will merely represent an effective prepayment of part of their much larger UK Capital Gains Tax bill.

This fact is further illustrated by the table set out below. This table is based on the following assumptions:

i) A UK resident investor purchases a French property during 2008/9 for €250,000.
ii) The investor's actual acquisition costs are €5,000.
iii) The exchange rate remains €1.50:£1 throughout the investor's ownership of the French property.
iv) The property's value grows at a rate of 7.5% per annum (compound).

v)   Selling expenses amount to 2% of the property's gross sale price.

vi)   There is no actual capital improvement expenditure.

All figures in the table below are given in sterling. Note that our investor's total purchase costs (including the €5,000 acquisition costs) amount to £170,000.

Years of owner-ship	Net Sale Proceeds	French Tax Payable	UK Tax Payable
	£	£	£
1	175,583	0	0
2	188,752	1,427	1,557
3	202,908	3,692	4,034
4	218,127	6,127	6,701
5	234,486	4,744	9,574
6	252,073	6,792	12,667
7	270,978	8,445	15,998
8	291,301	9,652	19,584
9	313,149	10,356	23,445
10	336,635	10,491	27,600
11	361,883	9,987	32,073
12	389,024	8,766	36,868
13	418,201	6,742	42,030
14	449,566	3,820	47,586
15	483,283	0	53,565

An examination of our table soon reveals that the UK Capital Gains Tax always exceeds the French tax payable.

Our UK investor will, of course, be entitled to double tax relief for the French tax paid but, as our table shows, will always be left with some UK Capital Gains Tax to pay.

The biggest difference between the two tax regimes is the fact that the French tax system provides a total exemption after 15 years of ownership whereas the new Capital Gains Tax regime applying in the UK from 6th April 2008 no longer provides any form of relief for long-term ownership and taxes all capital gains at the same rate.

Wealth Warning

Persons making multiple sales of French property or disposing of French property after less than two years of ownership may be reclassified as a *'Merchand de Biens'* (i.e. a property dealer) and would then be subject to Income Tax at the full marginal rates of up to 40% on their French property gains.

Tax Collection and the Fiscal Representative

A non-resident selling French property must have a 'Fiscal Representative' in France. This is usually the Notaire.

As if it wasn't bad enough that your Notaire will very likely also be acting for the purchaser, as the Fiscal Representative, they will also act as the tax collector. In other words, the Notaire will withhold the French Income Tax due on your capital gain from your sale proceeds and account for it directly to the French Government.

Worse still, if you cannot prove your residence in an EU country, or another country with a double taxation agreement with France, on the day of the sale, the Notaire will deduct tax at 33.33% instead of 16% and will also charge interest and penalties on the French Government's behalf.

For this privilege, the Notaire will also retain a fee of around 0.8% to 1% of the sale price.

Exemptions

French residents are exempt from tax on the gain on disposal of their principal private residence (i.e. their main home) under a similar system to our own. This exemption may be obtained after two years of French tax residence.

There is also a blanket exemption from French tax on capital gains where disposal proceeds are less than €15,000.

15.10 INHERITANCE TAX

Prior to 22nd August 2007, French Inheritance Tax posed a serious problem to many UK residents owning property in France.

Thankfully however, following the major reforms introduced with effect from that date by new President Nicolas Sarkozy, French Inheritance Tax is now considerably less of a threat, especially to married couples and civil partners. (But see Section 15.11 for some dangerous pitfalls regarding lifetime transfers.)

Nevertheless, French Inheritance Tax still remains an important factor to be considered when purchasing property in France.

Real French property (i.e. land and buildings) owned by a non-French resident individual, including a UK resident, is liable to French Inheritance Tax. Shares in any French company or Real Estate Investment Company (see Section 15.15) will also form part of the deceased's estate for French Inheritance Tax purposes.

Tax Tip

Loans secured on French property will reduce the value of the estate for Inheritance Tax purposes and thus provide an effective method to reduce the potential liability.

Wealth Warning

It is important to remember that a trust has no legal status in France, meaning that simple trust structures are generally of no use in attempting to avoid French Inheritance Tax (but see Section 15.18 regarding more complex structures).

For deaths occurring on or after 22nd August 2007, inheritances received by the deceased's spouse or Pacte Civile de Solidarité partner are exempt from French Inheritance Tax. Under European Law, the same treatment should also extend to a civil partner in a UK registered civil partnership.

Prior to 22nd August 2007, the position for spouses was the same as for lifetime gifts, as explained in Section 15.11.

In other cases, Inheritance Tax is payable by the beneficiary receiving the inheritance and the rate is dependent on the amount of the inheritance and the beneficiary's relationship to the deceased.

Children and other direct descendants of the deceased are entitled to an 'estate allowance' of €150,000 each. Inheritances in excess of this amount are subject to Inheritance Tax at the following rates:

Excess over Estate Allowance			Rate Applying	Cumulative Tax
Up	to	€ 7,600	5%	€ 380
€ 7,600	to	€ 11,400	10%	€ 760
€ 11,400	to	€ 15,000	15%	€ 1,300
€ 15,000	to	€ 520,000	20%	€ 102,300
€ 520,000	to	€ 850,000	30%	€ 201,300
€ 850,000	to	€ 1,700,000	35%	€ 498,800
Over		€ 1,700,000	40%	n/a

Example

Marcel dies leaving properties in Illiers and Auteuil worth a total of €1,000,000 to his two children Achille and Jeanne equally.

Achille and Jeanne are each entitled to a tax free estate allowance of €150,000, leaving each of them with a taxable inheritance of €350,000.

Each child therefore has an Inheritance Tax bill calculated as follows:

First €15,000, taxed as above:	*€1,300*
Next €335,000 (€350,000 - €15,000):	*€67,000*
Total:	*€68,300*

Siblings are generally entitled to an exemption of just €15,000. The first €23,000 of any excess is taxed at 35% and any further sum at 45%. The exemption for inheritances received by nephews and nieces is just €7,500.

Under certain limited conditions, inheritances received by siblings may be totally exempt but this will usually be of little use to most UK residents.

Inheritances received by persons not related to the deceased, including unmarried partners, are eligible for an exemption of just €1,500, with any excess being taxable at 60%.

Under certain circumstances, however, a 'Pacte Civile de Solidarite' (see Section 15.2) may now provide a suitable means for an unmarried couple to avoid Inheritance Tax.

Holding French property through a UK company may possibly provide a shelter for French Inheritance Tax, although the position here is unclear and such companies carry a number of other disadvantages (see Section 15.15).

The estate of a deceased UK domiciled, or deemed UK domiciled, taxpayer (see Section 8.9) will generally be able to claim double tax relief against its UK Inheritance Tax liability in respect of any French Inheritance Tax suffered by the deceased's beneficiaries.

15.11 GIFT TAX

France also imposes Inheritance Tax on lifetime gifts, generally at the same rates as for inheritances which we looked at in Section 15.10.

The estate allowances of €150,000 for children and other direct descendants, €15,000 for siblings and €7,500 for nephews and nieces also apply to lifetime gifts.

Estate allowances are renewable every six years but any lifetime gifts within six years of death will use up part of the estate allowance available for the inheritance.

The spouse exemption introduced for deaths occurring on or after 22nd August 2007 does not apply to lifetime gifts.

Spouses and Pacte Civile de Solidarité partners (and therefore presumably UK registered civil partners also) are entitled to an estate allowance for lifetime gifts of just €76,000.

Lifetime gifts of French property to spouses or civil partners with a value in excess of €76,000 are subject to Inheritance Tax on the excess as follows:

Excess over Estate Allowance			Rate Applying	Cumulative Tax
Up	to	€ 7,600	5%	€ 380
€ 7,600	to	€ 15,000	10%	€ 1,120
€ 15,000	to	€ 30,000	15%	€ 3,370
€ 30,000	to	€ 520,000	20%	€ 101,370
€ 520,000	to	€ 850,000	30%	€ 200,370
€ 850,000	to	€ 1,700,000	35%	€ 497,870
Over		€ 1,700,000	40%	n/a

Wealth Warning

Despite Monsieur Sarkozy's recent reforms, a lifetime transfer of French property between spouses or civil partners may give rise to a significant French Inheritance Tax liability.

Tax Tip

French Inheritance Tax may be avoided on lifetime transfers between a married couple by using a Universal Community Regime (see Section 15.13).

Some reductions apply to the rates of Inheritance Tax on lifetime gifts made by donors aged under 75.

Double tax relief will seldom be available in respect of French Inheritance Tax payable on a lifetime gift.

15.12 SUCCESSION LAW

A major problem for many UK investors owning French property is the compulsory application of French succession law. Sadly, the major reforms to Inheritance Tax introduced by President Sarkozy on 22nd August 2007 do not affect succession law.

French succession law applies to all immoveable property (*immeubles*) located in France, regardless of the owner's country of residence or domicile. Hence, a UK resident is subject to French succession law on any land and buildings which they own in

France. Such property must therefore be regarded as the owner's 'French estate' for succession or inheritance purposes.

Moveable property (*meubles*), which includes cash, chattels and company shares, owned by a non-French resident, would not be subject to French succession law.

French succession law is based on a fundamental philosophy that inherited property is a family asset. This philosophy overshadows the rights of the deceased, as an individual, to do as they please with their own assets on their death. This restriction of the deceased's individual rights may come as a shock to English and Welsh readers, although it will be more familiar to readers in Scotland.

The Reserve

The Reserve is a part of the deceased's French estate which is protected by law and must be passed to a class of protected heirs (*heritiers reservataires*).

This restriction applies equally to both lifetime gifts and to property passing on death.

Any part of the deceased's French estate not falling into the Reserve represents their free estate (*quotite disponible*) and may be disposed of as the deceased wishes under the terms of their Will.

Just how much of the deceased's French estate falls into the Reserve depends on which family members survive the deceased (or are living at the time of a lifetime gift).

All children of the deceased, including illegitimate and adopted children, rank equally. Grandchildren stand in their parent's places where these have pre-deceased the grandparent whose estate is in question. (Then great-grandchildren, etc, if necessary.)

A child must be alive, or at least conceived, at the date of the deceased's death in order to inherit. Certain classes of persons are disqualified from inheriting, including a child who murdered the deceased parent.

If there is no surviving spouse and the deceased is survived by one child then the Reserve comprises 50% of the deceased's French estate and it passes wholly to that child.

If there is no surviving spouse and the deceased is survived by two children, the Reserve comprises two thirds of the deceased's French estate. One third of the estate passes to each of the deceased's children.

If there is no surviving spouse and the deceased is survived by three or more children, the Reserve comprises 75% of the deceased's French estate and must be divided equally amongst those children.

If the deceased leaves neither a surviving spouse nor any surviving descendants then their entire French estate falls into the Reserve and must be passed to other relatives.

Somewhat bizarrely, this means that a childless person has no freedom to dispose of any part of their French estate as they wish, whereas a person leaving children may dispose freely of at least part of their estate.

An unmarried partner of the deceased has no rights under French law and will therefore not be entitled to any part of the Reserve. Hence, a person leaving no children would generally be unable to pass any part of their French estate to an unmarried partner!

Although a 'Pacte Civile de Solidarite' now provides an Inheritance Tax exemption, it is ignored for French succession law purposes. Partners in a UK registered civil partnership would presumably be in the same position.

The *quotite disponible* may be passed to a surviving unmarried partner where the deceased has also left surviving children but this can only amount to 50% of their French estate at best.

Surviving Spouses

Where the deceased leaves a surviving spouse and one or more children, they may choose one of the following options:

i)   Leave all or part of the *quotite disponible* to their surviving spouse absolutely.
ii)   Leave their surviving spouse up to 25% of their French estate absolutely plus a life interest in the remaining 75%. The reversionary interest over the spouse's life interest passes to the deceased's children.
iii)   Subject to certain conditions, leave their surviving spouse a life interest in their entire French estate, with the reversionary interest passing to their children.

Example

Hugo, who is UK resident and domiciled, owns a house in Provence. He is married to Esmerelda and has three children.

On Hugo's death, the house in Provence will be subject to French succession law. Hugo will nevertheless have a number of choices regarding the house. He could:

i)   *Leave one quarter share in the house to each of his three children as* heritiers reservataires, *thus satisfying the requirement of the Reserve under French law. The remaining quarter share would represent the* quotite disponible *and Hugo would be free to leave this to Esmerelda if he so wishes.*
ii)   *Leave Esmerelda 25% of the house absolutely plus a life interest over the remaining 75%. Each of his children would share equally in the reversionary interest over the portion subject to Esmerelda's life interest.*
iii)   *Subject to various conditions, possibly leave Esmerelda a life interest in the whole house with the reversionary interest passing equally to each of his three children.*

As we can see from the example, the operation of French succession law creates a number of practical difficulties, with the ownership of the French property effectively being 'splintered'. Imagine the problems when Hugo's children also die and are forced to divide their own shares amongst their children!

What concerns most people of course, is the generally poor rights afforded to the surviving spouse and we will consider some of the potential solutions to this dilemma in the next section.

If the deceased leaves a surviving spouse, no children and one or both parents, they must leave a life interest in 25% of their French estate to each surviving parent.

Impact on UK Domiciliaries

A person domiciled, or deemed domiciled in the UK for our own Inheritance Tax purposes (see Section 8.9) will nevertheless remain subject to French succession law on their French estate.

Hence, where French law forces the taxpayer's property to pass to someone other than their spouse or civil partner, UK Inheritance Tax will be payable on those assets. The same assets will also be subject to French Inheritance Tax and the interaction of the two taxes is explained in Section 15.10.

French Residents

For a French resident taxpayer, the French succession rules will generally apply to their entire worldwide estate, although this may not be the case where they are UK domiciled under UK principles.

Wills & Intestacy

Matters may potentially become even worse when the deceased owner of French property dies intestate (i.e. without a valid Will).

Under French intestacy laws, a surviving spouse's rights over the deceased's French estate are limited as follows:

a) Where there are children of the marriage and no other children of the deceased, the surviving spouse may choose between taking 25% of the estate absolutely or a life interest over the entire estate. The surviving spouse may also choose to convert such a life interest into an annuity.

b) Where the deceased has left other children (or grandchildren, etc), the surviving spouse has no choice and may only take 25% of the estate absolutely.
c) Where the deceased leaves no children, but is survived by one or both parents, 25% of the estate must pass to each surviving parent absolutely. The balance of the estate passes to the surviving spouse.
d) Where the deceased leaves no descendants and no surviving parents then the surviving spouse will inherit the entire estate.

A surviving spouse also has the right to occupy the marital home rent free for a period of one year. They may have additional rights over certain business assets if they were a business partner or employee of the deceased.

Nevertheless, it can readily be seen that it is generally advisable to write a Will.

Generally, it makes sense to write a French Will to cover French property, although having multiple Wills can create problems, so professional advice is essential.

A Final Word

French succession law is highly restrictive and extremely complicated. As the French say:

"It's hardly worth going to the trouble of dying. Better to have another glass of burgundy."

15.13 SOLUTIONS TO FRENCH SUCCESSION LAW

There are proposals to reform the current laws of succession to enable children of the deceased to renounce their rights in favour of a surviving spouse. However, a number of practical problems surround these proposals:

i)   Minor children would lack the legal capacity to make a renunciation.

ii)   The renunciation would be entirely at the children's discretion.

iii)   The timing of introduction of this reform is currently unknown.

In the meantime, French succession law will frequently continue to create unwanted consequences. In this section, we will therefore consider the various potential solutions which have been developed to resolve these problems.

Universal Community Regime

Marriage in France creates a binding legal contract. Under the 'Haig Convention' it is possible to alter the terms of that contract and create a 'Universal Community Regime'.

Under the Universal Community Regime, the assets belonging to the married couple are treated as one joint, or 'community', estate for the purposes of French succession law. On the first death, the community assets pass by survivorship to the surviving spouse and are not subject to the general succession law.

A French resident couple must enter the Universal Community Regime at the time of their marriage and it will therefore apply to their entire joint estate.

Non-French residents may, however, use the Universal Community Regime on a 'property by property' basis. This produces the ability for a married couple to create a form of joint ownership of French property which, in effect, is very much like an English joint tenancy.

Example

Jules, who is UK resident and domiciled, has a flat in Paris and a house in Gascony.

Jules and his wife Marie (also UK resident and domiciled) enter a Universal Community Regime in respect of the Paris flat only.

On Jules' death, the Paris flat will pass to Marie by survivorship. The house in Gascony will, however, remain fully subject to the normal rules of French succession law.

At first glance, the Universal Community Regime looks like the perfect solution to the dilemma of French succession law. However, the regime does have a number of drawbacks:

i)   It is a legal contract and could therefore be difficult to undo (e.g. on divorce or separation).
ii)   It cannot over-ride the rights of children from a previous marriage or other relationship.
iii) It is only available to married couples.

A Universal Community Regime can be created by 'notarial declaration'. This is effectively a deed witnessed by a French Notaire (lawyer).

The use of the Universal Community Regime has no effect on a couple's Wealth Tax liability (see Section 15.6).

Using A Company

The shares in a company are moveable property. Hence, if a UK resident owns French property via a company, French succession law should not apply.

This includes the shares in a French 'SCI' (Societe Civile Immobiliere), despite its privileged status for French tax purposes (see Section 15.15).

Investing in French property via a company does, however, have a number of important UK and French tax consequences, as explained in Chapter 10 and Section 15.15 respectively.

Tontine Clauses

A tontine clause inserted into the conveyance on purchase of a French property creates what is, in effect, a joint tenancy by two owners with a built-in survivorship clause. The survivor will then automatically obtain absolute ownership of the entire property on the death of the first of the two joint owners.

Inheritance Tax remains payable on the first death under normal principles regardless of any tontine clause. The use of a tontine clause might also sometimes create a taxable lifetime gift for French Inheritance Tax purposes (see Section 15.11) at the time of purchase.

Nevertheless, a tontine clause may still be useful for a UK resident unmarried couple investing jointly in French property. Where the couple invest equal amounts in the property, no taxable lifetime gift is likely to arise. The tontine clause will overcome the problems of French succession law on the first death and, although French Inheritance Tax will be payable, it probably would have been anyway and can be offset against any UK Inheritance Tax arising on the property at the same time.

A tontine clause might also be useful to a married couple who are unable to use the Universal Community Regime because one or both of them have children from a previous relationship.

A tontine clause may also sometimes be both useful and tax-efficient when included in the constitution of a French company.

15.14 FRENCH TAX RESIDENCE

Under French law, a person may be treated as resident in France for tax purposes if they spend more time in France during a year than they do in any other country. Any person spending 183 days in France in any one year must therefore be French tax resident for that year, but others with a fairly 'nomadic' lifestyle will also be caught by this rule.

French tax residence may also occur:

a) If your main home is located in France,
b) If your 'centre of economic interests' lies in France, or
c) If your immediate family predominantly resides in France.

Tax Tip

In borderline cases, your position may be helped if you correspond with the French tax authorities from your UK address (but still in French, of course).

As can be seen from the previous sections of this chapter, it will generally be disadvantageous for an investor owning French property to become French resident for tax purposes. A French resident is generally subject to French Income Tax on their worldwide income and capital gains, although the UK-France Double Taxation Agreement currently exempts French residents from French taxation on capital gains on a UK property (this exemption is expected to end when the new treaty comes into force).

French residents are also subject to Social Contributions and to French Wealth Tax and Inheritance Tax on their worldwide estate.

The UK-France Double Taxation Agreement provides some protection against deemed French residence, but only where the taxpayer remains UK resident. Generally, however, anyone spending more time in France than in the UK will be at risk of being deemed to be French resident for tax purposes.

Unlike the UK, France has no separate concept of tax domicile. (Rather confusingly, however, the French word for tax residence is 'domicile'.) All French taxes are therefore based on residence rather than domicile, including Inheritance Tax. A person domiciled, but not resident, in the UK might therefore be deemed to be French resident for Inheritance Tax purposes.

When the new UK-France Double Taxation Agreement comes into force, a person resident but not domiciled in the UK may no longer be treated as UK resident for the purposes of French Income Tax on capital gains. This may leave such a person exposed to French tax on worldwide capital gains if they are also French resident under French domestic law.

The rate of French Income Tax payable by a French resident will depend on their worldwide income. This will include income and capital gains made in the UK during the same year, including items which may be exempt under UK tax law. Most importantly, perhaps, the sale of a UK principal private residence, though not directly taxable in France, will nevertheless still push the taxpayer into a higher marginal rate of French income tax.

Tax Tip

If emigrating to France, it will often make sense to dispose of your UK principal private residence before the calendar year of emigration.

15.15 INVESTING IN FRANCE VIA A COMPANY

See Chapter 10 for an examination of the UK tax consequences of foreign property ownership via a company.

French Holiday Homes Owned by Companies

With the exception of an SCI (see below), any company (wherever resident) owning French property which it does not rent out will be assessed for French Corporate Income Tax on three times the property's annual market rental value.

Other than an SCI, therefore, this constitutes a punitive annual charge on the corporate ownership of a French holiday home.

Real Estate Investment Companies

France applies a special tax regime to any company (wherever resident) which is defined as a Real Estate Investment Company, or *Societe a Preponderence Immobiliere*, to give it its proper name.

A Real Estate Investment Company is defined as any company owning French real estate (land and buildings) where the value of its French real estate unconnected with any French business constitutes more than 50% of the company's total assets. It is important to note, however, that furnished lettings do constitute a 'business' for this purpose.

Shares in a Real Estate Investment Company are subject to French Inheritance Tax and may also be subject to Wealth Tax.

There is also a 5% transfer duty on the sale of shares in a Real Estate Investment Company.

UK Companies

Where a UK company owns French property, French Corporate Income Tax at the rate of 33.33% is due on any rental income received (net of qualifying expenses). Neither of the 'Micro' regimes discussed in Section 15.7 will be available.

In addition to the Corporate Income Tax charge on an unrented property, any free use of the property by the company owner (or their relatives) may give rise to a taxable benefit in kind.

The payment of UK Income Tax on any benefit in kind for use of a company-owned French property may over-ride any French tax liability on the same benefit. However, for the reasons explained in Section 10.3, such charges will not always arise in the UK.

As far as capital gains are concerned, there are three major disadvantages to owning French property through a UK company.

Firstly, the rate of tax applying to the taxable capital gain is one third (33.33%) instead of just 16% for a UK resident individual.

Secondly, there is no taper relief given in France in respect of a UK company's taxable capital gain. In fact, the company's allowable purchase cost for the property is actually reduced by 2% for each year of ownership.

Worst of all, the company's shareholders are assessed directly for the tax arising. In the UK, however, the company will generally bear the tax on the capital gain and will not be entitled to any double tax relief for French Income Tax paid by the shareholders, thus giving rise to an effective double tax charge.

Shares in a UK company holding French property will not be subject to French succession law (unless held by a French resident) and may also escape French Inheritance Tax, although this is far from clear.

In summary, however, put simply, a UK company is just not the way to hold French property!

Societe Civile Immobiliere ('SCI')

An SCI is a special purpose French company designed specifically for the ownership of real property (land and buildings). An SCI has 'fiscal transparency' in France. As explained in Section 13.8, this means that the company is ignored for French Income Tax purposes and its income and capital gains are taxed as if they belonged directly to the company's shareholders, exactly as set out in Sections 15.7 to 15.9.

There is no French tax charge in respect of any benefit in kind for the owner of an SCI making private use of French property held through the company. Nor are there any tax charges in respect of unrented property (e.g. a holiday home) held by an SCI.

The value of shares in an SCI is included in the shareholder's French estate for Inheritance Tax purposes, but the shares are regarded as moveable property under French succession law (see Section 15.12). An SCI owned by the taxpayer's children is sometimes used as a method to avoid Inheritance Tax.

Wealth Tax will also be due on the value of shares in an SCI. This is one of the few disadvantages of an SCI as the value of shares in most other companies will not be included in the amount on which the shareholder pays Wealth Tax.

Although 'fiscally transparent' for French tax purposes, an SCI is treated just like any other foreign company for UK tax purposes (see Chapter 10). This can cause some problems in obtaining double tax relief in the UK for French tax paid and may lead to effective double tax charges.

Other French Companies (not SCI's)

The private use by the company's owner or their family of property owned by other French companies gives rise to a taxable benefit in kind for French tax purposes. This is in addition to any Corporate Income Tax charge on unrented property.

French Corporate Income Tax will also be due on any rental profits arising and the company will be ineligible for both of the 'Micro' regimes discussed in Section 15.7.

Corporate Income Tax will be payable at one third (33.33%) on any capital gains made by the company with no taper relief available. However, the additional 2% per annum which is deducted from a UK company's allowable purchase cost does not apply to French companies.

The net value of any shares in a French company will be included in the shareholder's estate for Inheritance Tax purposes. Such shares held by a non-French resident will not, however, be subject to French succession law.

There is also a 5% transfer duty on the sale of shares in a French company.

Other Non-French Companies

Such companies will generally be treated as Real Estate Investment Companies with all of the consequent disadvantages, including a possible annual 3% tax charge on capital value (see Section 15.16). Tax charges on a deemed benefit in kind for private use will usually apply, as will Corporate Income Tax charges on unrented property and the same disadvantageous treatment of French capital gains as applies to UK companies.

The French Inheritance Tax position on shares in such companies is unclear but, if held by a non-French resident, they would at least escape the restrictive French succession laws.

Luxembourg companies have historically been used to avoid French property taxes. This particular 'loophole' ended on 1st January 2008, however, when the new protocol to the France-Luxembourg Double Taxation Agreement came into force.

Danish companies are now being considered as a possible alternative to Luxembourg companies.

These structures are complex and expensive and therefore only worth considering for property purchases worth in excess of €2M.

Capital Gains on Shares

French Income Tax is due on the capital gain arising on the sale of shares in any company owning French property, including an SCI.

As with capital gains on French property (see Section 15.9), the taxable capital gain is reduced by 10% for every complete year of ownership in excess of five years. This reduction does not, however, apply to any company owning property (i.e. land and buildings, whether in France or not) which makes up more than 50% of the company's total net value.

Where the shareholder is UK resident, the tax arising on a sale of shares is generally at the rate of 16% of the taxable capital gain.

The gain arising on the sale of shares in a Real Estate Investment Company is, however, subject to tax at a rate of one third (33.33%).

15.16 CORPORATE REAL ESTATE TAX

An annual tax charge of 3% is levied on the market value of French property owned by any non-exempt Real Estate Investment Company (see Section 15.15).

To claim exemption, the company must provide details of its ultimate owners. The company must also demonstrate that there are no companies in the 'chain of ownership' between the French property and those ultimate owners which are not governed by a suitable double taxation agreement between France and the country of residence of those companies.

In other words, where the ultimate owners attempt to impose an offshore 'tax haven' company within the ownership structure, the annual Corporate Real Estate Tax charge of 3% will be due.

However, a simple structure utilising a UK or French company should be eligible for the exemption.

Wealth Warning

It is vital to remember that the exemption must be claimed on an annual basis – it is not given automatically. Failure to claim will be an expensive mistake!

Unlike Wealth Tax, loans are not deductible in computing this tax, it is based purely on the market value of the French property held by the company.

15.17 COMPANIES HOLDING FRENCH PROPERTY - CONCLUSIONS

In general, there is little reason to suggest holding French property via a company.

The most significant reason for the use of a company will be the dilemmas posed by French succession law (see Section 15.12). However, these can often be resolved through the use of the Universal Community Regime or a Tontine clause.

Where a company is used, a Societe Civile Immobiliere ('SCI') will usually represent the best solution.

A UK company may provide a means to avoid French Inheritance Tax but the other disadvantages which such a company brings will usually make this strategy inadvisable.

15.18 TRUSTS AND FRENCH PROPERTY

A trust has no legal status in France and it is not therefore possible for a trust to directly own French property or shares in a French company.

A trust may, however, own shares in a non-French company which, in turn, owns French property.

This structure will avoid the application of French succession law and may also avoid French Inheritance Tax, although this is a complex area warranting detailed professional advice.

Trust structures also remain useful for non-UK domiciled individuals investing in French property.

Generally speaking, however, assets within a trust are treated as belonging to the trust beneficiaries for the purposes of French Wealth Tax and Inheritance Tax. French Income Tax arising on income or capital gains within a trust is payable by the trustees. It is therefore generally wise to use corporate trustees whenever there is any investment in French property (which will generally need to be made indirectly, through some form of corporate vehicle, in any case).

SIPPS in France

SIPPs are, of course, a type of trust and hence also have no legal status in France and are fully taxable on French income and capital gains. French properties held within a SIPP will also be subject to French Wealth Tax and Inheritance Tax.

Chapter 16

Spain

16.1 A WARM WELCOME

Foreign property investment in Spain is massive. It is estimated that some €10 billion worth of Spanish property has been bought by foreign investors in the last few years and that there are now around one and a half million foreign property owners with Spanish property.

Whilst this inward investment does not come exclusively from the UK, we British do make up a substantial proportion of the foreign investment into Spain, with around a million Spanish properties owned by UK nationals. Furthermore, this staggering figure continues to increase at a rate of around 50,000 to 70,000 properties per year.

Spain vies with France for the title of most popular destination for UK residents buying foreign property and some commentators even suggest that Spain actually accounts for between 40% and 50% of UK investment abroad.

Despite these statistics, the Spanish authorities generally continue to encourage foreign investment in Spain. It seems they appreciate the additional wealth being brought into the country, which has helped to bring one of Western Europe's poorer countries a few decades ago to its current position as the world's ninth largest economy.

The generally warm welcome extended to foreigners investing in Spain has contributed to a booming property market, with prices in Spain increasing by around 30% per annum in the first few years of this century, more than doubling the value of many properties over a five year period.

In fact, over the last 20 years, Spanish property prices have seen the largest increases in the world!

Admittedly, the market has now begun to cool down a little, with an average increase of only around 15% in 2006. Nevertheless, the general expectation is that prices will continue to rise steadily for the foreseeable future.

16.2 HOME FROM HOME?

There is a very sizeable expatriate community of British nationals in Spain. Furthermore, a significant proportion of the property investment by UK residents constitutes holiday homes, easily accessible within a few hours flying time.

A growing number of UK nationals are even becoming Spanish residents, especially after retirement. As we shall see later, this provides some interesting tax planning opportunities.

However, it remains vital to remember that no matter how much Spain may feel like a 'home from home' in the sun, it is nevertheless still a foreign country, with laws very different to our own and to which you and your Spanish property will be subject.

For example, it is very common in Spain for property to be part of a community and to be subject to the internal rules of that community. These internal rules are backed up by national legislation in the form of the 'horizontal law' which governs the rights of communities to enforce both certain statutory rules and their own internal ones.

Communities will charge the property owners within their community for their share of the cost of upkeep of common areas, such as pools, garages, corridors, hallways, etc. In larger private developments this may even extend to street lighting and roadways.

Thanks to the horizontal law, communities can enforce the collection of community charges and other internal rules, such as a ban on pets, for example. In extreme cases, the community may even be able to evict badly behaved property owners!

16.3 THE SPANISH TAX & LEGAL REGIME

The Spanish Tax Agency is known as the Hacienda and the Spanish tax year is the calendar year. Every Spanish taxpayer has a tax identification number: 'Numero Identification de Extranjero' or 'NIE' for short. UK residents must obtain an NIE as soon as they acquire any Spanish property.

It is probably well known that the Spanish attitude to tax evasion has historically been somewhat more relaxed than here in the UK. There has in the past perhaps even been a general attitude that tax evasion was a taxpayer's right.

Be under no illusion; that has all changed. The Spanish tax regime has undergone substantial modernisation in recent years, with a strong focus on anti-avoidance. Hacienda, for its part, is now just as keen to track down and punish illegal tax evasion as any other tax authority in Western Europe.

So, however much you may hear about what someone else got away with a few years ago, my advice to you today is, when in Spain, respect the Spanish tax laws. (That does not mean that there isn't a whole raft of legitimate tax planning to be considered, as we shall see in the sections which follow.)

Spain does still have a four year statute of limitation on the collection of back taxes (based on the original due date for the tax). However, anyone deliberately trying to make use of this for fraudulent tax evasion faces substantial fines, surcharges and late payment interest!

Spanish tax law is not the exclusive domain of the national government in Madrid. Spain has 17 autonomous regions (15 on the mainland plus the Canary Islands and the Balearic Islands) and the two enclaves of Ceuta and Melilla on the North African coast. Many of these autonomous regions have exercised their power to vary the tax regime applying in their territory, particularly in the case of Inheritance Tax. We will look at some of these regional tax variations in Section 16.18.

Spanish Income Tax actually comes in two different varieties. Spanish residents pay 'IRPF' (Impuesto sobre la Renta de las personas fisicas) on their worldwide income, whereas non-Spanish residents pay 'IRNR' (Impuesto sobre la Renta de no residentes) on Spanish-source income only. To save space, however, I will refer to both of these as simply 'Spanish Income Tax' for the rest of this chapter.

There are no legal restrictions on the acquisition of Spanish property by non-Spanish resident purchasers.

In 2005, Spain recognised marriages between same sex partners. In principle, this should give married same sex couples the same rights as any other married couple.

This is not to be confused with a 'parejo de hecho', under which an unmarried couple (of either the same or opposite sex) can register their partnership. This does not usually confer any of the rights applying to married couples for taxation purposes, although it does affect inheritance rights and Inheritance Tax in some regions (see Section 16.18).

Under European law, it seems reasonable to suggest that a UK registered civil partnership should be recognised for Spanish legal and tax purposes. I would, however, suggest taking local advice before relying on this.

Joint ownership of property is recognised in Spain and each joint owner will generally be subject to the appropriate Spanish taxes on their share of the property.

Under Spanish law, it is very difficult to remortgage a property without selling it, leading to practical problems or unnecessary tax bills for investors.

There is a double taxation agreement between Spain and the UK which covers most of each country's national taxes, although it does not cover Inheritance Tax. When it comes to Spanish property owned by UK residents, however, the treaty has little impact since it allows Spain to tax such property.

16.4 VALOR CATASTRAL

An unfortunate legacy from Spain's past attitude to taxation is the fact that, even today, there is effectively a two tier system of property values in Spain.

There is the property's actual, or market, value which a purchaser would be willing to pay to buy it and then there is the officially declared value for tax purposes: the 'Valor Catastral'.

Whenever a Spanish property is transferred from one person's ownership to another, its market value must be registered with the 'Catastro', one of Spain's two property registration systems. It is this registered value which becomes the Valor Catastral.

The odd quirk in this system (which has led to the problems which we shall soon see) is that it is the property's **value** which must be registered with the Catastro, not necessarily the actual **price** paid.

As we shall see in the following sections, the Valor Catastral is used for a number of Spanish tax purposes. The temptation therefore exists to declare a lower value to the Catastro than the price actually paid.

Historically, purchasers have declared some extremely low values to the Catastro; often with more than a little encouragement from the seller. Even today, there are still some properties with a Valor Catastral as low as 25% of their true market value.

However, whilst a low Valor Catastral might save some taxation at the time of a property's purchase, it has quite detrimental consequences when the owner comes to sell the property. We will explore this point further in Section 16.10.

In recent years, Hacienda has been working to narrow the historic gap between the true market value of Spanish property and the Valor Catastral. Some sharp increases have been implemented since 1994 and Hacienda will now reject any artificially low values declared on a property transfer. If a value is rejected, Hacienda will raise assessments for the additional tax due.

Wealth Warning

Additional taxes assessed in this way will generally fall on the purchaser.

Hacienda maintains tables of property values and will advise purchasers of an acceptable value for the Catastro if requested.

Under the current situation, it is advisable for a purchaser to declare either the value suggested by Hacienda or the real price actually paid.

16.5 SPANISH PROPERTY PITFALLS

Before we get on to taxation, it is worth giving some consideration to some of the other legal and practical issues facing a UK resident buying property in Spain.

As explained in Section 16.2, the 'horizontal law' gives a great deal of power to any community in which a property is located. Community charges are not strictly a tax but they are backed by the force of law and should therefore be taken into account whenever a Spanish property lies within a community.

Annual community charges for a small flat might be around €400. At the other end of the scale, the charge for a luxury villa could be ten times as much.

Where property within a community is being purchased with the intention of renting it out, it will be vital to ensure that this is permitted by the community's own internal rules.

16.6 SPANISH PROPERTY TAXES

Spain imposes a number of national, regional and local taxes on UK nationals owning Spanish property, either directly or indirectly, including:

- Property Transfer Tax ('ITP')
- Document Fees
- VAT ('IVA')
- Imputed Income Tax
- Wealth Tax ('Patrimonio Tax')
- Municipal Real Estate Tax ('IBI')
- Income Tax on rental income
- Income Tax on capital gains
- Plus Valia Tax
- Inheritance Tax
- Corporation Tax
- Corporate Real Estate Tax

Following the above sequence, these can broadly be described as three taxes on property purchases; three annual taxes on ownership; one on rental income; two on property sales; one on death and two on corporate ownership.

As we can see, therefore, there is a formidable list of Spanish taxation to be considered when buying a property in Spain.

16.7 TAXES ON PROPERTY PURCHASES IN SPAIN

The purchase of a new Spanish property is generally subject to IVA (Spanish VAT) at 7%.

Other property purchases are subject to Property Transfer Tax (Impuesto de Transmisiones Patrimoniales) at 6%.

All property purchases are also subject to a Document Fee (akin to Stamp Duty) of 0.5%.

Plus Valia Tax may also be payable on a property purchase (see Section 16.11).

Practical Pointer

Property Transfer Tax, Document Fees and Plus Valia Tax are all charges on the property rather than specifically on the vendor or the purchaser.

It is usual for the purchaser to pay the Property Transfer Tax and the Document Fee and the vendor to pay the Plus Valia Tax but this is not required by law (although Spanish consumer regulations state that this should be the normal practice).

Any taxes not paid by the vendor, however, will inevitably fall on the purchaser as the new owner of the property. It is not unknown for a vendor to disappear, leaving the purchaser to foot the bill!

In view of this inherent risk, many purchase contracts now require the purchaser to meet all the taxes and other expenses arising. This means that the purchaser knows where they stand and a suitable reduction in the purchase price can be negotiated to take account of the extra costs arising.

16.8 ANNUAL TAXES

As we saw in Section 16.6, Spain imposes three annual taxes on property. We will now look at each of these in turn.

Imputed Income Tax (Impuesto de la Renta)

Spain imposes an imputed Income Tax charge on any property other than the owner's principal private residence.

Unlike the position for UK Capital Gains Tax purposes, which we explored in Section 5.6, the view taken in Spain is that a non-resident cannot have a principal private residence in Spain.

Hence, any non-Spanish resident with a Spanish property will be subject to the imputed Income Tax charge on that property.

The charge works by treating a percentage of the property's Valor Catastral as notional income. The amount of notional income is calculated as 2% of the Valor Catastral in most cases, or 1.1% where the Valor Catastral has been revised since 1994.

Non-residents then pay Income Tax on this notional income at the rate of 24%, resulting in an annual charge equal to either 0.264% or 0.48% of the property's Valor Catastral.

Where a Spanish resident is taxable on a property other than their principal private residence, they pay the imputed Income Tax at their usual marginal tax rate (see Section 16.15).

Wealth Tax (Patrimonio Tax)

Non-Spanish residents are subject to Spanish Wealth Tax on the net value of all their Spanish capital assets.

The full name of this Wealth Tax is 'Impuesto Extraordinario sobre el Patrimonio', although it is generally known simply as 'Patrimonio Tax'.

Patrimonio Tax was introduced as a temporary ('Extraordinario') measure in 1978 to enable the Spanish government to force many of its citizens to bring their hidden wealth out into the open.

Almost thirty years later, this 'temporary' tax continues, although both major political parties have promised to abolish it if elected in the March 2008 General Election.

For Spanish property, the tax is based on the current market value of the property determined by Hacienda and not on the Valor Catastral.

Household contents are generally exempt from Patrimonio Tax but this does not extend to valuable antiques, works of art, etc.

Mortgages against Spanish property may be deducted from the value of the owner's Spanish assets before calculating the tax due. Business debts may also be deducted.

A simple way for a UK resident to avoid Patrimonio Tax is to mortgage their Spanish property and invest the borrowed funds outside Spain. In view of the difficulty in re-mortgaging Spanish property, this is best done at the time of purchase.

A Spanish resident must pay Patrimonio Tax on the total net value of their worldwide assets but is exempt on the first €108,182 of assets generally plus the first €150,253 of value of a principal private residence. Both of these exemptions apply on a 'per person' basis.

Patrimonio Tax Rates

The current Patrimonio Tax rates are as follows:

Spanish estate value:			Rate Applying	Cumulative Tax
Up	to	€ 167,129	0.20%	€ 334
€ 167,129	to	€ 334,253	0.30%	€ 836
€ 334,253	to	€ 668,500	0.50%	€ 2,507
€ 668,500	to	€ 1,337,000	0.90%	€ 8,523
€ 1,337,000	to	€ 2,673,999	1.30%	€ 25,904
€ 2,673,999	to	€ 5,347,998	1.70%	€ 71,362
€ 5,347,998	to	€ 10,695,996	2.10%	€ 183,670
Over		€ 10,695,996	2.50%	n/a

The 'Cumulative Tax' column represents the total Patrimonio Tax payable by an investor with Spanish assets having a total net value equal to the figure at the top of the relevant band (e.g. total Spanish assets worth €5,347,998 means total Patrimonio Tax payable of €71,362 per annum).

Tax Tip

Patrimionio Tax is charged on a 'per person' basis. Any couple buying a Spanish property for more than €167,129 (net of any mortgage) can therefore save tax simply by holding the property jointly.

Municipal Real Estate Tax

The municipal real estate tax, 'Impuesto sobre Bienes Inmeubles', or 'IBI' for short, is a local municipal tax, rather like council tax. The tax is payable annually and is based on the property's Valor Catastral.

The rate at which IBI is payable varies widely from town to town. The annual charge for a typical property could fall anywhere between €60 and €3,000.

You must present a receipt for the current year's IBI before you can sell a Spanish property.

Summary of Annual Taxes

As we have seen, the purchase of a Spanish property makes the owner liable for three annual taxes based, one way or another, on the property's capital value and payable regardless of whether the property is held as an investment or as a holiday home.

Example

Don buys a small villa in Murcia for €500,000. He pays €300,000 of the purchase price in cash and takes out a mortgage secured on the property for the remaining €200,000.

Before the purchase, Hacienda had advised Don that €480,000 would be an acceptable value for the property and Don duly declares this value to the Catastro.

The local municipal real estate tax (IBI) is charged at the rate of 0.4%
of Valor Catastral.

Don's annual tax cost on the property is as follows:

Imputed Income Tax based on Valor Catastral	
€480,000 x 2% x 24% =	*€2,304*
Patrimonio Tax based on actual value less mortgage	
€500,000 - €200,000 = €300,000	
First €167,129 @ 0.2%	*€334*
Remaining €132,871 @ 0.3%	*€399*
Local municipal real estate tax	
€480,000 x 0.4% =	*€1,920*
Total annual tax cost:	*€4,957*

Typical Costs

It is not possible to produce a definitive formula for total annual
tax costs as there are too many variable factors. However, the
typical total cost of the three annual Spanish property taxes can
generally be expected to amount to around 1% of the property's
purchase price.

Community charges will often also need to be paid in addition to
these tax charges (see Section 16.5).

No Relief!

There are no equivalent taxes in the UK to the Imputed Income
Tax charge or Patrimonio Tax. Our equivalent to municipal real
estate tax is council tax, but this will not be payable on a Spanish
property. Hence, no double tax relief is available for any of these
tax costs.

And No Escape!

Where a non-Spanish resident owes any unpaid Patrimonio Tax or
imputed Income Tax at the date of sale of a Spanish property,

Hacienda will collect any amounts due within the previous four years from the 3% deposit withheld by the purchaser (see Section 16.10).

And you can't even sell the property if you haven't paid your IBI!

16.9 RENTAL INCOME

Non-Spanish residents are generally liable for Spanish Income Tax at a flat rate of 24% (25% before 1st January 2007) on the gross rents received from Spanish rental property with no deduction available for mortgage interest, nor usually for other expenses. This will very often produce a Spanish tax liability well in excess of any UK liability on the same income. Whilst, as explained in Chapter 7, Spanish tax may be deducted from any UK tax liability on the same income, no refund is available where the Spanish tax exceeds the UK liability.

A profitable Spanish investment property may easily produce an after tax loss. Imagine a property with gross annual rents of €15,000, but annual mortgage interest of €10,000 and other costs of €2,000. In the UK we would see this as a profit before tax of €3,000, yielding a maximum tax charge (at 40%) of €1,200.

In Spain, however, the tax based on gross rents will remain €3,600 (€15,000 at 24%), giving an overall after tax loss of €600 (€3,000 - €3,600).

The Spanish tax is well in excess of the UK tax payable on the same income, leaving nothing to pay in the UK. (See Section 3.7 for advice on the best way to treat the Spanish tax in these circumstances.)

Nevertheless, the investor has ended up with a net loss of €600 on an otherwise profitable property!

Tax Tip

A good way to reduce the Spanish Income Tax on rental income is to pass on as many costs as possible to the tenant. This may be done through the rental agreement and can include IBI (see Section 16.8) and community charges (see Section 16.5).

It is important to clearly stipulate the charges payable by the tenant within the rental agreement as, under Spanish law, both IBI and community charges are the owner's liability.

Example

Laurie decides to rent out his villa in Valencia. The market rent for the villa would be €12,000 per year. This would give Laurie a Spanish Income Tax liability of €2,880 (24%).

However, Laurie negotiates with Rosie, the prospective tenant, that he will reduce the rent to €7,800 per year if she pays the IBI and community charges totalling €4,000.

This will reduce Laurie's Spanish Income Tax liability to €1,872 (€7,800 at 24%), leaving him with net income after tax of €5,928 (€7,800 - €1,872).

If Laurie had charged the full market rent and paid the IBI and community charges himself, he would have been left with just €5,120 (€12,000 - €2,880 - €4,000).

Hence, by simply altering the terms of his rental agreement with Rosie, Laurie is €808 a year better off.

Rosie will be happy too, as she is also better off by €200 a year (Laurie reduced the rent by €200 more than the actual cost of the IBI and community charges as an incentive for Rosie to accept the terms of the rental agreement).

Holiday Lettings

Short-term holiday lettings made on a regular basis are regarded as a business. This business must be legally registered as a tourist letting operation and will be subject to inspection to ensure that it meets the relevant standards. The lettings will also be subject to IVA (Spanish VAT) at 16%.

Holiday letting income continues to be subject to Spanish Income Tax at 24%. However, where a property is registered as a tourist letting operation, maintenance costs may be claimed as an allowable deduction from gross rents for Spanish Income Tax purposes. Furthermore, the maintenance costs themselves are effectively reduced since the property owner will be able to reclaim any IVA incurred.

Comparing Holiday Lets and Residential Lets

At this point, it is worth giving some thought to the comparative merits of short-term holiday lets or longer leases. We will start with an example designed to illustrate the different tax consequences of each type of letting for a UK resident owner of Spanish property.

For the sake of illustration, we will stick to Euros for all of the calculations in this example. In reality, of course, the UK tax calculations would need to be carried out in sterling.

Example

Miguel owns 'Cervantes', a villa in Alcala de Henares a few miles outside Madrid. The property will command roughly the same rental income of around €50,000 a year in total whether Miguel rents it out for short-term holiday lets or under a twelve month lease.

Miguel estimates that the annual maintenance costs for Cervantes will amount to around €17,000, including IVA of €2,000.

His estimated tax position for the two possible types of letting may be compared as follows:

	Holiday Lettings €	Twelve Month Lease €
Gross rental income	*50,000*	*50,000*
IVA included in holiday letting income		
16/116 x €50,000	*6,897*	*n/a*
	---------	---------
Rent receivable	*43,103*	*50,000*
Maintenance costs	*15,000(1)*	*17,000*
	---------	---------
Rental profit before tax	*28,103*	*33,000*
Income tax payable at 24%	*6,745*	*12,000(2)*
	---------	---------
Net profit after tax	*21,358*	*21,000*
	=====	=====

Notes

1. *If Miguel rents Cervantes out for short-term holiday lets, he will be able to reclaim the IVA of €2,000 on his maintenance costs, thus reducing his effective cost to €15,000.*
2. *If Miguel lets the property out under a long lease (i.e. not a short-term holiday let), he will pay Income Tax at 24% on his gross rental income of €50,000.*

In this particular example, we can see that Miguel would be just slightly better off overall after taking all Spanish taxes into account if he were to rent Cervantes out for short-term holiday lets. However, as Miguel is a UK resident, this is not the end of the story, as he will also pay UK Income Tax on his rental profits.

Assuming that Miguel is a higher rate taxpayer, his UK tax liability would be calculated as follows:

	Holiday Lettings	*Twelve Month Lease*
	€	*€*
Rental profit before tax	*28,103*	*33,000*
	=====	=====
UK Income Tax thereon at 40%	*11,241*	*13,200*
Less double tax relief for Spanish Income Tax suffered:	*6,745*	*12,000*
UK tax payable:	*4,496*	*1,200*
	=====	=====

After accounting for UK Income Tax, Miguel would be left with an after tax profit of €16,862 (€21,077 - €4,496) if he rented the property as a short-term holiday let or €19,800 (€21,000 - €1,200) if he rented it out under a longer lease.

At this stage, the longer let appears preferable and this is mainly due to the fact that almost 14% of Miguel's gross rental income would be lost in IVA if he rented the property as a short-term holiday let.

In many cases, however, the UK tax position will be altered by the existence of additional deductible expenditure, such as mortgage interest.

Example Continued

In addition to his maintenance costs, Miguel also pays mortgage interest of €10,000 a year on Cervantes.

This does not alter his Spanish tax calculations in any way. His UK tax position, however, is now as follows:

	Holiday Lettings €	Twelve Month Lease €
Rental profit before tax and interest	28,103	33,000
Less mortgage interest	10,000	10,000
Rental profit for UK tax purposes	18,103	23,000
UK Income Tax thereon at 40%	7,241	9,200
Less double tax relief for Spanish Income Tax suffered:	6,745	9,200
UK tax payable:	496	Nil

Remember that double tax relief cannot exceed the amount of UK tax payable. In this case, this means that Miguel cannot obtain full relief for the Spanish Income Tax suffered on a long lease of the property.

We now see that Miguel's final after tax profit from short term holiday lets would be €10,862 (€21,358 - €10,000 - €496) compared with €11,000 (€21,000 - €10,000) for a longer let.

In practice, there is no simple answer to the question of which type of letting will yield the better result. Each case will need to be decided on its own merits. However, my goal with the example above has been to demonstrate the principles involved.

In reality, it is perhaps unlikely that a property would yield the same gross rental income and incur the same running costs under both types of letting. The disparity in both income and expenditure would need to be taken into account and would naturally have an impact on the outcome.

In some cases, there may not even be any choice. Furthermore, the substantial rights to which sitting tenants under a longer lease are entitled in Spain may well outweigh any tax considerations in practice.

Spanish Resident Landlords

Spanish-resident landlords (see Section 16.15) enjoy a much better tax regime on their rental income.

Firstly, they are able to deduct a wide range of expenses from their rental income, regardless of the type of letting involved.

Secondly, there is a statutory 50% reduction in rental income for tax purposes for resident landlords. This measure was introduced to stimulate the rental market in Spain. The restriction of this relief to resident landlords may be contrary to European law (see Section 14.1), but no-one has yet been brave (or foolish) enough to challenge the authorities on this.

Spanish residents do, however, pay Income Tax on rental income at their usual marginal rate (see Section 16.15), rather than the flat rate of 24% applying to non-residents, and this will often be higher.

Combating Tax Evasion

Tenants of rented properties in Spain are required to provide their landlord's name and NIE (see Section 16.3) when filing their own tax declarations.

In this way, Hacienda is able to identify any undeclared rental income.

16.10 CAPITAL GAINS ON SPANISH PROPERTY

There is no separate Capital Gains Tax in Spain but Income Tax is charged on taxable capital gains.

Following a reprimand from the EU, the rate of Spanish Income Tax payable by non-Spanish residents on the sale of a Spanish property was reduced from 35% to 18% with effect from 1st January 2007. All individuals, both resident and non-resident alike, now pay the same rate of tax on capital gains in Spain.

The amount of gain subject to tax depends on when the property was acquired.

Property acquired before 1st January 1987 is only subject to tax on the proportion of the gain arising after 20th January 2006 calculated on a time-apportionment basis.

Where the property was acquired between 1987 and 1994, part of the gain arising before 20th January 2006 is also taxable. The taxable element of the pre-20th January 2006 gain is one ninth for each year after 1986 that the property was purchased. For example, a purchase during 1990 was made four years after 1986, meaning that four ninths of the pre-20th January 2006 gain is taxable.

For property acquired after 31st December 1994, the gain is fully taxable.

As in the UK, both purchase costs and selling expenses may be deducted when calculating the amount of capital gain arising. Allowable purchase costs include the Document Fees and IVA or Property Transfer Tax paid on the purchase, as well as notary fees, lawyer's fees and property registration fees.

Critically, however, the deduction for the cost of the property itself is the Valor Catastral declared at the time of the purchase and not the actual price paid. Hence, where an artificially low value was originally declared, this now comes home to haunt the vendor!

An official 'inflation corrector' factor ('coeficiente de actualizacion') is applied to the allowable purchase costs to compensate for the effects of inflation. The coefficient is roughly equal to a compound rate of 2% per annum for recent years, but is reduced for costs incurred in 1994 or earlier due to the other reliefs also available.

The actual coefficients applying in the case of a sale during 2007 and estimated coefficients for 2008 are as follows:

Purchase Date	Coeficiente de Actualizacion 2007	Coeficiente de Actualizacion 2008 (Estimated)
1994 and earlier	1.2162	1.2406
1995	1.2849	1.3106
1996	1.2410	1.2659
1997	1.2162	1.2406
1998	1.1926	1.2164
1999	1.1712	1.1946
2000	1.1486	1.1716
2001	1.1261	1.1486
2002	1.1040	1.1261
2003	1.0824	1.1041
2004	1.0612	1.0824
2005	1.0404	1.0612
2006	1.0200	1.0404
2007	1.0000	1.0200

Example

On 20th January 2008, Camilo sold a house in the village of Cela in Galicia for €182,406, net of selling expenses.

Camilo had bought the house exactly 17 years earlier, on 20th January 1991, for the equivalent of €30,000. The value declared to the Catastro at that time was, however, equivalent to just €8,000.

Camilo also incurred various purchase costs totalling the equivalent of €2,000, bringing his total allowable costs for the Cela house to €10,000.

As these costs were incurred before 31st December 1994, they are multiplied by a factor of 1.2406 (see table above) to give Camilo an adjusted cost of €12,406.

Camilo's capital gain is thus €170,000 (€182,406 - €12,406).

Camilo sold the property two years after 20th January 2006 and held it for 17 years in total, hence his 'post-20/1/2006' gain is 2/17^{ths} of the total gain. He bought the property five years after 1986 – hence five ninths of his 'pre-20/1/2006' gain is taxable.

The taxable element of Camilo's gain is therefore as follows:

Post-20/1/2006 element: 2/17 x €170,000 =   *€20,000*
Pre-20/1/2006 element: 15/17 x €170,000 x 5/9 =   *€83,333*

Taxable gain: *€103,333*

Camilo will therefore be liable for Spanish Income Tax at 18% on a gain of €103,333, i.e. €18,600.

The allocation of the gain to the pre- and post 20th January 2006 periods should, in practice, be calculated in exact days rather than years (which I have used here merely for the sake of illustration).

It is worth noting that if Camilo had declared the true purchase price of €30,000 to the Catastro in 1991, his Income Tax liability on the sale would have been reduced by €2,986 to €15,614. For anyone purchasing Spanish property now, the additional tax cost arising on the property's sale as a result of an under-declaration to the Catastro (if it were accepted) is likely to be far greater!

Withholding Tax

A purchaser buying a Spanish property from a non-Spanish resident must withhold 3% of the purchase price and place it on deposit with Hacienda as a down-payment against the vendor's Spanish tax liability on the sale. Prior to 1st January 2007, the required withholding was 5%.

The non-Spanish resident vendor is required to account for any balance of Spanish tax due, or claim a refund, as appropriate, within 30 days of the sale using Form 212. Refunds are meant to be made within 90 days of the receipt of Form 212, but in practice may take up to a year.

Capital Losses

Capital losses may be set off against capital gains arising in the same year and the following four years.

16.11 PLUS VALIA TAX

An additional local municipal tax, 'Plus Valia Tax', is payable on the sale of a property. This tax is based on the increase in the value of the land comprised in the property during the vendor's ownership. Rates vary tremendously and work out at between 10% and 40% of the average annual increase in the land's value.

Spanish property purchasers beware! Plus Valia Tax is a charge on the property itself and may be paid by either the vendor or the purchaser – the local authority does not care which. If not paid by the vendor, the tax will fall on the purchaser.

However, a purchaser paying Plus Valia Tax may claim it as an additional purchase cost in their own capital gains calculation when they eventually sell the property.

16.12 INHERITANCE TAX

Spanish Inheritance Tax is payable on Spanish property owned by non-Spanish residents. The tax applies on both lifetime gifts and transfers on death.

Spanish Inheritance Tax is paid by each beneficiary and not by the estate as a whole. The rate applying varies from 7.65% to 81.6% and depends on the beneficiary's relationship with the deceased (or lifetime donor), the amount of the legacy or gift, and the amount of pre-existing wealth already held by the beneficiary before receipt.

Pre-existing wealth is calculated under the same rules as are used for Patrimonio Tax (see Section 16.8) but earlier gifts from the same donor may be excluded (as these will have been taxed previously). Where the beneficiary is a non-Spanish resident, only their Spanish assets (if any) need to be taken into account.

Beneficiaries are divided into four classes in order to determine the amount of Inheritance Tax payable, as follows:

Class I: Children and other descendants of the transferor aged under 21.

Class II: Spouses, children and other descendants aged 21 or more, parents and remoter ancestors.

Class III: Siblings, aunts, uncles, nephews, nieces and certain other relatives by marriage such as son-in-laws, daughter-in-laws and step-children.

Class IV: Anyone else. This generally includes unmarried partners, but see Section 16.18 for some regional variations.

Beneficiaries in Class I are each entitled to an exemption of €15,957 plus an additional €3,991 for every year they are below the age of 21, up to a maximum exemption of €47,859 for children aged 13 or less.

Those in Class II, *including spouses*, receive an exemption of just €15,957 each.

Class III beneficiaries are each entitled to an exemption of €7,993.

For transfers or legacies left to anyone else (i.e. Class IV) there is no exemption at all and the first Euro attracts Inheritance Tax at an effective rate of at least 15.3%.

Illegitimate children fall into Class IV in respect of transfers from their father but can be brought into Class I or II by adoption.

For beneficiaries falling into Class I or Class II and with pre-existing wealth (see above) of no more than €402,678, the rate of Inheritance Tax applying to any amount in excess of any available exemption is as follows:

Spanish estate value:			Rate Applying	Cumulative Tax
Up	to	€ 7,993	7.65%	€ 611
€ 7,993	to	€ 15,981	8.50%	€ 1,290
€ 15,981	to	€ 23,968	9.35%	€ 2,037
€ 23,968	to	€ 31,956	10.20%	€ 2,852
€ 31,956	to	€ 39,943	11.05%	€ 3,735
€ 39,943	to	€ 47,931	11.90%	€ 4,685
€ 47,931	to	€ 55,918	12.75%	€ 5,704
€ 55,918	to	€ 63,906	13.60%	€ 6,790
€ 63,906	to	€ 71,893	14.45%	€ 7,944
€ 71,893	to	€ 79,881	15.30%	€ 9,166
€ 79,881	to	€ 119,758	16.15%	€ 15,606
€ 119,758	to	€ 159,635	18.70%	€ 23,063
€ 159,635	to	€ 239,389	21.25%	€ 40,011
€ 239,389	to	€ 398,778	25.50%	€ 80,655
€ 398,778	to	€ 797,555	29.75%	€ 199,291
Over		€ 797,555	34.00%	n/a

Example

Manuel dies leaving his Spanish property, Villa Araña, to his wife Maria. The property is worth €500,000 and Maria has no pre-existing Spanish assets.

After deducting her exemption of €15,957, Maria has a taxable inheritance of €484,043. From the above table, we see that the first €398,778 of this gives rise to an Inheritance Tax charge of €80,655. The remaining €85,265 is taxed at 29.75%, giving rise to a further charge of €25,366. Maria's total Inheritance Tax bill is thus €106,021.

Where the beneficiary falls into Class III or Class IV, or has pre-existing wealth of more than €402,678, the tax is worked out using the above rates but is then also increased by a multiplication factor as follows:

Pre-existing Wealth			Multiplier for Beneficiaries in:		
			Class I & II	Class III	Class IV
Up	to	€ 402,678	n/a	1.5882	2.0000
€ 402,678	to	€ 2,007,380	1.0500	1.6676	2.1000
€ 2,007,380	to	€ 4,020,770	1.1000	1.7471	2.2000
Over		€ 4,020,770	1.2000	1.9059	2.4000

Example Revised

As before, Manuel leaves his Spanish property to Maria, but let us now assume that the couple were not married.

As a Class IV beneficiary, Maria is not entitled to any exemption and the entire €500,000 value of Villa Araña is therefore subject to Spanish Inheritance Tax. The tax is now calculated as follows:

First €398,778, as per table above:	*€80,655*
Remaining €101,222 @ 29.75%:	*€30,114*

Sub-Total	*€110,769*
Multiplier	*x 2.0000*
Total tax due	*€221,538*

Furthermore, if Maria had any pre-existing assets in Spain, the tax could be as high as €265,845.

The value used for Inheritance Tax calculations on Spanish property is usually the current market value of the property. It is usual to include a further 3% on top of the net value of the estate to cover personal possessions unless it can be proved that a lower value is appropriate.

Hacienda takes a statutory lien (a type of charge) over property passing on death or by way of lifetime gift until the Inheritance Tax arising has been paid. This makes it impossible to borrow against the property to pay the tax, leading to severe practical difficulties for many people.

Spanish residents are entitled to an additional exemption on 95% of the value of their main residence when they have lived there for at least three years.

The property must pass to a spouse or child of the deceased who is also Spanish resident and there is a limit of €120,202 to the exemption. The recipient must retain the property for at least ten years or the tax which has been avoided will become due.

The same exemption is also available to siblings aged over 65 who have lived in the property for at least two years.

Inheritance Tax on lifetime gifts is generally greater than that arising on death as many of the exemptions set out above are not available. The tax must also be paid much quicker – after 30 days as opposed to six months for transfers on death.

Many of Spain's autonomous regions have used their authority to vary the national Inheritance Tax rates set out above. We will take a closer look at these regional variations in Section 16.18.

16.13 PLANNING FOR SPANISH INHERITANCE TAX

Spanish Inheritance Tax poses a significant potential problem for UK residents investing in Spain, especially couples.

Take the case of a UK resident couple who jointly own a Spanish property valued at €1m.

When one of the couple dies, the property will pass to the survivor. As jointly owned property is deemed to be held 50/50 in Spain, this means that the survivor has an inheritance of €500,000.

If the couple were married, the Inheritance Tax arising will be between €106,021 and €127,225. If not, it could be as much as €265,845 (see Section 16.12 for further details).

A simple way for a UK resident to avoid Spanish Inheritance Tax, however, is to mortgage their Spanish property and invest the borrowed funds outside Spain. In view of the difficulty in re-mortgaging Spanish property, this is best done at the time of purchase.

In this way, only the equity value of the property will be subject to Inheritance Tax in Spain, thus substantially reducing the bill.

Taking up residence in Spain will provide a substantial exemption in respect of your main home after three years, with further benefits following after five years in some regions. Spanish residents are, however, subject to Inheritance Tax on their worldwide estate, so this strategy is not always beneficial.

Non-Spanish resident individuals can avoid Spanish Inheritance Tax by holding Spanish property through a non-Spanish resident company. A Spanish resident company may also provide a reduction in the amount of Inheritance Tax arising and can also provide exemption from Inheritance Tax on lifetime transfers.

Another common method used to reduce Spanish Inheritance Tax is a 'usufruct'. This is something similar to a life interest in the property.

Care must be taken over any lifetime transfers of Spanish property as these can lead to substantial Inheritance Tax liabilities.

16.14 SUCCESSION LAW

The legal position regarding the application of Spanish succession law to UK residents is somewhat unclear.

Spanish law states that foreign nationals owning property in Spain should be subject to their own succession laws. English and Scottish law, however, both state that the law of the country in which the property is located should prevail.

So, Spain says our law should apply and our laws say Spanish law should apply. (This reminds me of when, as a boy, each of my parents would tell me to ask the other if I could have something. In the end, of course, I realised that I could simply tell each of them that the other had said yes!)

Thankfully, this deadlock is broken by the fact that Spain interprets its own rules to mean that a national of a country whose laws permit the free disposal of assets on death may apply that principle to their Spanish property if they make a valid Will.

In practice, therefore, a UK national's Will is generally honoured for Spanish succession law and the UK national may dispose of their property freely under the terms of their Will. (Technically, a person domiciled in Scotland does not have the right of free disposal, but this does not seem to have been noticed in Spain.)

There does, however, remain the danger that a person who might benefit under the Spanish laws of succession could challenge a UK national's Will and force a change to the disposition of the deceased's Spanish assets.

Where a UK national dies intestate (i.e. without a valid Will), Spanish succession law will apply to their Spanish property.

Where Spanish succession law does apply, it provides as follows:

- A surviving spouse retains all assets which they owned personally before marriage and half of the assets acquired by the couple during their marriage. These assets do not pass into the deceased's estate.
- The deceased's estate is divided into thirds:
  i) The surviving spouse has a life interest in one third. On their death, this share must pass to the deceased's children but can be divided amongst them in any proportion under the terms of the deceased's Will.
  ii) One third passes immediately to all of the deceased's children in equal shares.
  iii) The deceased may dispose freely of the remaining third under their Will.
- If the deceased has no surviving children, their parents are entitled to one third of the estate (if still alive). This increases to a half if there is no surviving spouse.

Illegitimate children have no rights in their father's estate and are excluded from the shares passing to children set out above.

16.15 SPANISH TAX RESIDENCE

An individual will become tax resident in Spain if they:

i) Spend more than 183 days in the country during a calendar year, or
ii) Have their 'centre of vital interest' in Spain. This effectively means that their main professional, business or other economic activity is in Spain.

A married person will also generally be regarded as resident in Spain if their spouse and dependent minor children have their permanent home there.

Under certain conditions, a person who moves to Spain to take up residence there may elect to be taxed as either a resident or non-resident for the year of the move and the following five years. The main rules are that the individual must not have been resident in Spain during the previous ten years and must be working for a Spanish business.

Being tax resident in Spain carries both advantages and disadvantages. The main disadvantage is that Spanish taxes will apply to all of the individual's worldwide income, gains and wealth. The main advantages spring from the various tax exemptions on the individual's main home in Spain.

Hence, residence in Spain is generally advantageous if your Spanish home is your main asset. This is particularly useful for UK nationals retiring to Spain (but see Section 16.14 regarding the application of Spanish succession law).

On the other hand, if most of your wealth is held outside Spain, Spanish residence would generally be disadvantageous.

Spanish residents are entitled to an Income Tax personal allowance of €5,151 for 2008. This is increased to €6,069 at age 65 and €6,273 at age 75.

Additional allowances are also given for minor children, elderly relatives living with the taxpayer, disabled people and maternity. Further allowances are also given in respect of employment income.

Remaining income after deducting all available allowances is taxed at the following rates (for 2008):

Income after allowances			Rate Applying	Cumulative Tax
Up	to	€ 17,707	24.00%	€ 4,250
€ 17,707	to	€ 33,007	28.00%	€ 8,534
€ 33,007	to	€ 53,407	37.00%	€ 16,082
Over		€ 53,407	43.00%	n/a

Approximately one third of the Income Tax paid by Spanish residents is allocated to the regional Government. Some regions have varied this element of the tax (see Section 16.18).

Spanish residents also pay social security contributions on employment income.

16.16 INVESTING IN SPAIN VIA A COMPANY

Spanish Resident Companies

A company is generally regarded as Spanish resident if:

i)   It is incorporated under Spanish law,
ii)   Its registered office is in Spain, or
iii)   Its place of effective management is in Spain.

A UK registered company might be regarded as resident in Spain under heading (iii) and the UK-Spain Double Taxation Agreement would generally permit this.

Companies registered in a 'tax haven' (i.e. a low or nil tax jurisdiction) are also regarded as Spanish resident if most of their assets or business is located in Spain.

Spanish resident companies pay Corporate Income Tax at 25% on the first €120,000 of annual profit and 30% thereafter. (The main rate of Spanish Corporate Income Tax was reduced from 32.5% to 30% with effect from 1st January 2008.)

These rates apply to both income and capital gains which are simply added together for Corporate Income Tax purposes.

Spanish Corporate Income Tax must be paid in three instalments, on 20th April, 20th October and 20th December during the year to which the tax relates. Any remaining balance is payable when the annual return is filed. Any excess payment is also refunded at this time.

A Spanish property-holding company is called a Sociedades Patrimoniales. Prior to 1st January 2007, these companies enjoyed a special tax regime in Spain but they are now taxed at the same rates as any other Spanish resident company.

Shares in a Spanish resident company will be subject to Wealth Tax and Inheritance Tax in Spain.

Dividends

Dividends paid to non-resident shareholders by a Spanish resident company are subject to withholding tax at 18%.

Spanish residents are exempt from Income Tax on their first €1,000 of Spanish dividend income.

Non-Resident Companies

Shares in non-Spanish resident companies are exempt from Spanish Wealth Tax and Inheritance Tax.

Non-Spanish resident companies are subject to Spanish Income Tax on rental income and capital gains from Spanish properties at the same rates as non-Spanish resident individuals (see Sections 16.9 and 16.10 respectively).

A non-Spanish resident company owning Spanish property is subject to an annual Special Tax at 3% of the Valor Catastral of the property.

This charge does not apply if both the company and its ultimate owners reside in a country which has a normal double taxation agreement with Spain. To claim exemption, the ultimate owner's details must be disclosed to Hacienda together with certification proving that the company pays tax in its own country.

Partial exemption is given where the ultimate ownership vests in more than one individual and one or more of the ultimate owners qualifies for exemption.

UK residents owning Spanish property via a UK company will therefore be able to claim exemption from the Special Tax. The tax would apply, however, if an offshore company (e.g. in the Channel Islands) were used.

Share Sales

Spanish Income Tax at 18% will be due on the capital gain arising on a sale of shares in a Spanish resident company. The same tax is also due on any element of the gain on sale of shares in a non-

Spanish resident company which relates to Spanish property owned by the company.

The taxable capital gain is calculated under the same principles as set out in Section 16.10 except that the 'coeficiente de actualizacion' does not apply.

16.17 TAX COMPLIANCE IN SPAIN

Any non-Spanish resident owning two or more Spanish properties must appoint an official tax representative in Spain known as a 'representante fiscal'. This does not need to be a professional tax agent (although it is generally advisable) but could be any Spanish resident.

Failure to appoint a representante fiscal, when required to do so, incurs a fine of up to €6,000.

It is important to note that each registered title is treated as a separate property. Hence, for example, a person with a house and a garage which has a separately registered title is regarded as having two properties, with all of the resultant additional compliance obligations.

Any non-Spanish resident selling property in Spain must use a legal representative in Spain.

Spanish Tax Forms

A UK resident owning Spanish property will need to use some or all of the following forms.

Form 210
This form is used to declare the Imputed Income Tax liability and must be submitted between 1st May and 20th June in the calendar year after the year to which the charge relates.

Non-Spanish residents must also use the same form to declare any rental income from Spanish property. Strictly, a Form 210 should be submitted within 30 days of each rental receipt but it is possible to apply to file quarterly instead.

Form 212

Non-Spanish residents use this form to report capital gains on Spanish property (see Section 16.10).

Form 213

Non-Spanish resident companies must use this form to either pay the Special Tax at 3% or to claim exemption where available. See Section 16.16 for further details.

Form 214

A non-resident with just one Spanish property can declare their Patrimonio Tax on Form 214. This form can be submitted at any time during the year.

Form 714

The more complex Form 714 must be used to declare Patrimonio Tax where more than one Spanish property is owned.

16.18 REGIONAL VARIATIONS

As explained in Section 16.3, many of Spain's autonomous regions have passed legislation to vary the tax or legal regime within their territory.

As a general rule, most of these variations will apply to property which is located within the relevant region. Some Inheritance Tax variations, however, also require the deceased (or transferor), the beneficiary, or both, to be tax resident in the region.

Tax residence in Spanish regions is usually attained after living in the region for five consecutive years.

Some of the variations which may affect UK resident property investors are set out below.

Andalusia

Document Fees on new property purchases are at 1%.
Property Transfer Tax is at 7%.
The Inheritance Tax exemption for close family members who are tax resident in Andalusia is €125,000 in some cases. The exemption for main residences (see Section 16.12) is increased to 99.99% if the property is also the beneficiary's main residence.

Unmarried couples in a registered 'parejo de hecho' are treated as spouses for Inheritance Tax purposes.

Undeveloped rural land can be commandeered by a private developer designated as an 'urbanising agent', with minimal levels of compensation for the owner of the land. There is more protection for the land owner here than in Valencia where this problem has been quite severe.

Aragon

Inheritance Tax rates vary from national scale.

Rules of succession apply to only half of the estate rather than two thirds.

Balearic Islands

Inheritance Tax rates vary from national scale.

Additional Inheritance Tax relief is available for spouses and close relations who are tax resident in Spain and in the region.

Basque Country

A separate Income Tax system applies.

Inheritance Tax rates vary from national scale.

Additional Inheritance Tax relief is available for spouses and close relations who are tax resident in Spain and in the region.

Canary Islands

IVA does not apply. The territory has its own form of VAT, known as IGIC.

Cantabria

Additional Inheritance Tax relief is available for spouses and close relations who are tax resident in Spain and in the region.

Castilla y León

Additional Inheritance Tax relief is available for spouses and close relations who are tax resident in Spain and in the region.

Catalonia

Inheritance Tax rates vary from national scale. Estates not exceeding €600,000 in value may be fully exempt.

La Rioja

Additional Inheritance Tax relief is available for spouses and close relations who are tax resident in Spain and in the region.

Madrid
Inheritance Tax rates vary from national scale.

Additional Inheritance Tax relief is available for spouses and close relations who are tax resident in Spain and in the region. Unmarried couples in a registered 'parejo de hecho' are treated as spouses for Inheritance Tax purposes.

Murcia
Additional Inheritance Tax relief is available for spouses and close relations who are tax resident in Spain and in the region.

Navarre
A separate Income Tax system applies.

Inheritance Tax rates vary from national scale.

Additional Inheritance Tax relief is available for spouses and close relations who are tax resident in Spain and in the region.

Valencia
Inheritance Tax rates vary from national scale.

Additional Inheritance Tax relief is available for spouses and close relations who are tax resident in Spain and in the region.

Undeveloped rural land can be commandeered by a private developer designated as an 'urbanising agent', with minimal levels of compensation for the owner of the land. These rules have been badly exploited by property developers in Valencia and the EU has recently intervened to demand a change in this law.

Enclaves of Ceuta and Melilla
IVA does not apply.

In addition to those noted above, many other regions also apply Property Transfer Tax at 7%.

Chapter 17

Italy

17.1 LA DOLCE VITA

Italy is a very popular destination for UK residents buying property abroad. The property market in Italy has been pretty stable, especially when compared with the UK and some other countries.

Italians generally prefer newer property and tend to keep the same home for life. This leaves a lot of investment potential in older properties. Property speculation is frowned upon, however, with high tax charges applying to property sold after less than five years.

Non-refundable deposits of between 10% and 50% are common on Italian property purchases.

17.2 THE ITALIAN TAX REGIME

Non-resident purchasers must obtain an Italian fiscal code number before they can complete the purchase deed ('Rogito') or obtain a mortgage.

Italy's tax year is the calendar year.

An official value is assigned to Italian property for tax purposes. This is called the 'Cadastral Value'.

Historically, the Cadastral Value has been subject to a great deal of manipulation and fraudulent under-declaration. Typical values have been a quarter to a third of the property's real value.

As a result, the purchase deed registered with the Italian authorities must now include both the real purchase price and the Cadastral Value.

The Cadastral Value is subject to a statutory inflationary increase each year.

17.3   TAXES ON PROPERTY PURCHASES IN ITALY

Non-residents buying Italian property must pay Registration Tax at the rate of 7%. In addition, most purchasers will also pay Mortgage Tax of 2% and Cadastral Tax of 1%, bringing the total purchase taxes up to 10% of the actual purchase price.

Italian residents buying their main home pay Registration Tax at the reduced rate of 3% plus a fixed charge of €336 in respect of the other purchase taxes.

Italian VAT (IVA) at 10% is payable on the purchase of new properties. The other purchase taxes are, however, reduced to €168 each, giving a total fixed charge of €504.

The IVA rate is generally reduced to 4% for Italian residents buying their main home.

Local taxes ranging from 0.4% to 0.8% of the Cadastral Value may also be payable.

Certain types of purchase contract must be registered for which there is an additional charge of 0.5%.

17.4 ANNUAL CHARGES

Properties not rented out (e.g. your own holiday home) are subject to a tax on notional rental. This is usually no more than 1% of the property's value per annum.

All owners of Italian property pay a local Community Tax at rates varying between 0.4% and 0.7% of the property's Cadastral Value.

An additional local tax, the 'TARSU', is levied to cover the cost of waste collection. This is usually paid by the occupier but the owner of a holiday letting property will need to pay it.

In Venice, there are further charges to contribute towards the cost of keeping the city above sea level!

17.5 RENTAL INCOME

Non-Italian residents receiving Italian rental income are subject to Italian Income Tax on that income at the normal Italian Income Tax rates. Expenses, such as mortgage interest, are deductible from rental income in a similar way to the UK's system.

Italy has a system of progressive Income Tax rates. The rates applying for 2007 are as follows:

Income			Rate	Cumulative Tax
Up	to	€ 15,000	23%	€ 3,450
€ 15,000	to	€ 28,000	27%	€ 6,960
€ 28,000	to	€ 55,000	38%	€ 17,220
€ 55,000	to	€ 75,000	41%	€ 25,420
Over		€ 75,000	43%	n/a

Regional surcharges of between 0.9% and 1.4% and local municipal surcharges of up to 0.5% may also apply.

Registration Tax and Stamp Duty are charged on leases every six months.

Holiday letting income is subject to IVA (Italian VAT) at 20%.

17.6 CAPITAL GAINS ON ITALIAN PROPERTY

The gain on a property sold within five years of purchase is subject to Income Tax at the rates described above. After five years of ownership, however, any gain is exempt from all Italian taxes.

Exemptions also apply to main residences and inherited property.

17.7 INHERITANCE TAX

Inheritance Tax was abolished in Italy in 2001 but sadly it was re-introduced in November 2006. Nevertheless, the tax is still considerably less of a burden in Italy than in many other countries, with rates as low as 4%.

Italian Inheritance Tax applies to both transfers on death and lifetime gifts.

The rate of tax applying is dependent on the beneficiary's relationship with the deceased or lifetime donor.

For transfers made to a spouse, child or other direct descendant, parent or remoter ancestor, there is an exemption of €1,000,000, after which any excess is taxed at 4%.

Transfers to siblings benefit from a €100,000 exemption with any excess taxed at 6%.

There is no exemption for other transfers, but the rates applying are just 6% for transfers to most other relatives, or 8% in other cases.

For non-Italian residents, Italian Inheritance Tax applies to property and other assets located in Italy.

17.8 SUCCESSION LAW

The application of Italian succession law to UK nationals owning property in Italy seems to be a bit of a 'grey area'.

It seems that property in Italy will normally be subject to the terms of a UK national's Will but Italian law will prevail where there is an Italian heir.

If there is no valid Will, Italian succession law will apply to property in Italy.

Under Italian succession law, the deceased's spouse, children and surviving parents have prior rights over 25% to 40% of the estate, depending on the circumstances.

17.9 ITALIAN TAX RESIDENCE

An individual is considered resident in Italy for tax purposes if, for the greater part of the year (i.e. 183 days or more), they:

i)   Are present in Italy,
ii)   Have their habitual place of abode in Italy, or
iii)   Have their centre of business interests in Italy.

Italian residents are subject to Italian Income Tax on their worldwide income and capital gains and to Italian Inheritance Tax on their worldwide estate.

17.10 COMPANIES AND TRUSTS

Italian resident companies pay Corporate Income Tax. The rate of Corporate Income Tax was reduced from 33% to 27.5% with effect from 1st January 2008.

Companies carrying on commercial activities in Italy are also subject to a local regional tax (IRAP) of 3.9%.

An interest in possession trust is treated as 'fiscally transparent' for Italian tax purposes (see Sections 11.2 and 13.8 for explanations of these terms).

Other trusts are generally treated as a company but funds may be distributed to beneficiaries without any further tax charge arising.

Italian Inheritance Tax will apply to the transfer of Italian assets into a trust.

Chapter 18

Portugal

18.1 OUR OLDEST ALLY

Portugal is Britain's oldest ally and it is perhaps for this reason that UK nationals are generally welcome; although there is also a general dislike of immigrants.

I have heard it said that "Portugal is the new Spain". In other words, many UK property buyers looking for the lifestyle which Spain offered twenty years ago are now choosing Portugal instead.

The Algarve, in particular, has been a popular destination for UK resident investors for many years but the 'Spanish overflow', as one might call it, is resulting in a great deal of UK investment in other parts of the country.

As in many other 'Civil Law' countries, in Portugal the Notary acts for both the vendor and the purchaser on the same transaction.

There are effectively two property markets in Portugal: one for the locals and one for foreign investors. Prices in the local market tend to be around 30% lower.

Land and buildings usually have separate legal titles in Portugal.

Portugal only recognises absolute ownership of property so concepts such as trusts and nominees do not apply (except in Madeira). Joint ownership is recognised however. Timeshares and leasebacks are also recognised.

There are no restrictions on the purchase of Portuguese property by non-residents.

18.2 THE PORTUGUESE TAX REGIME

Non-Portuguese residents must obtain a 'Número Fiscal de Contibuinte' (i.e. a Portuguese tax reference number) before purchasing Portuguese property.

The Portuguese tax office is the 'Finanças' and the tax year is a calendar year.

Like other countries in Southern Europe, Portugal has a historic problem with under-declarations of property prices. The price must be declared in the 'Escritura de Compra e Venda' (the deed of conveyance). Major under-declarations are now punished with fines of up to €12,000.

A non-Portuguese resident who owns property in Portugal must have a 'Fiscal Representative' in the country. The Fiscal Representative must be resident in Portugal but does not need to be a lawyer or other professional and could simply be a friend.

18.3 TAXES ON PROPERTY PURCHASES IN PORTUGAL

Property Transfer Tax (IMT) is payable on purchases of Portuguese property at rates varying from 0% to 15%. The tax must be paid before completion of the purchase.

Residential property is subject to IMT at a series of increasing rate bands as the price of the property increases. A system of allowances smooths the transition between each rate band and the next.

The rates of IMT on residential property which is not being purchased as the buyer's main residence are as follows:

Price of Property			Rate	Allowance	Tax Due	
					Minimum	Maximum
Up	to	€ 85,500	1%	€ 0	€ 0	€ 855
€ 85,500	to	€ 117,200	2%	€ 855	€ 855	€ 1,489
€ 117,200	to	€ 159,800	5%	€ 4,371	€ 1,489	€ 3,619
€ 159,800	to	€ 266,400	7%	€ 7,567	€ 3,619	€ 11,081
€ 266,400	to	€ 511,000	8%	€ 10,231	€ 11,081	€ 30,649
Over		€ 511,000	6%	n/a	€ 30,660	n/a

The 'Minimum' column indicates the tax due on a property purchased for the price at the bottom of the rate band and the 'Maximum' column indicates the tax due on a property purchased for the price at the top of the rate band. As we can see, the allowance system ensures that there is no sudden 'step up' in the amount of tax due at any stage (unlike the Stamp Duty Land Tax system in the UK!).

To demonstrate how this system works, let's look at a short example.

Example

Jose is buying a holiday home in Portugal for €200,000. The amount of IMT payable is calculated as follows:

€200,000 @ 7%:	*€14,000*
Less allowance:	*€7,567*
Amount to pay:	*€6,433*

Property purchased as the buyer's main residence is subject to a lower rate of IMT than other residential property and is exempt from the tax where the purchase price does not exceed €85,500.

IMT is payable at flat rates of 6.5% and 5% on commercial property and rural land respectively.

Where the purchaser is resident in a 'tax haven', the rate of IMT is increased to 15%. This should not affect UK residents unless an offshore company structure is being used.

New builds are exempt from IMT but Portuguese VAT (IVA) at the rate of 21% will be incurred on the construction costs.

Stamp Duty (Imposto de Selo) at the rate of 0.8% is also payable on all property purchases.

18.4 ANNUAL CHARGES

Municipal Property Tax (IMI) is payable annually at rates varying from 0.2% to 0.8% of the property's registered value by the registered owner of the property on 31st December the previous year.

The rate increases to 5% where the property owner is resident in a 'tax haven'. Again, this should not usually affect UK residents.

Main residences may be exempt for a period of up to six years.

Unpaid IMI is subject to a system of fines but is often allowed to accumulate over a number of years. The unpaid amount becomes a charge on the property so it is vital to ensure that the vendor has paid the tax before completing a purchase.

Further local municipal taxes may sometimes apply.

18.5 RENTAL INCOME

Non-Portuguese residents are subject to Portuguese Income Tax at a flat rate of 15% on rental income received from Portuguese property.

Deductions are allowed for certain expenses, including repairs and maintenance costs, insurance and local taxes but not for mortgage interest.

Holiday lettings in Portugal will also be subject to Portuguese VAT (IVA) at 21%.

18.6 CAPITAL GAINS ON PORTUGUESE PROPERTY

At present, non-Portuguese residents are subject to a flat rate of tax at 25% on capital gains arising on disposals of Portuguese property.

Portuguese residents, however, are exempt from tax on 50% of any capital gains on property and also receive further relief for inflation in respect of property held for at least two years. The remaining non-exempt gain is treated as additional income and taxed at the normal Income Tax rates for Portuguese residents (see Section 18.9).

In late 2007, the European Court of Justice held that the Portuguese tax regime in respect of capital gains discriminated unfairly against non-Portuguese residents and was therefore in breach of European Law (see Section 14.1). We can therefore expect amendments to the Portuguese tax system in this area soon.

Portuguese residents are exempt from tax on capital gains arising on the sale of their main residence as long as they reinvest the sale proceeds in a new home within two years. At present, the new home must be in Portugal but this rule has also recently been challenged successfully in the European Court of Justice.

Capital gains on property or other assets purchased before 1st January 1989 are exempt.

Capital gains are calculated on the basis of the declared purchase price in the 'Escritura de Compra e Venda' (see Section 18.2). Any under-declaration in the original purchase price will therefore result in additional tax at the time of the property's sale.

Capital losses on property sales may be carried forward for set off against future capital gains for up to five years.

A further local municipal tax, 'Mais Valia', may also be payable on property sales. This tax is based on the increase in value of the property and depends on when the property was built.

18.7 INHERITANCE AND LIFETIME GIFTS

Portugal abolished Inheritance Tax in 2004 but does still apply a Transfer Tax to lifetime gifts and transfers on death at the rate of 10% on the value of the property transferred.

The Transfer Tax applies to transfers of Portuguese property owned by non-Portuguese residents.

Transfers to spouses, children, other direct descendants and parents are, however, exempt from this tax.

18.8 SUCCESSION LAW

Portuguese succession law will generally apply to any property in Portugal.

Under Portuguese law, the deceased's spouse, children and surviving parents (if any) have rights to a fixed quota of the deceased's estate known as the 'legitima'. The beneficiaries may waive their rights if they wish.

If the deceased's Will conflicts with the legal rights under Portuguese law, it is rendered invalid and the Portuguese intestacy rules will apply to the deceased's Portuguese property. It is therefore generally recommended that any owner of Portuguese property should make a Portuguese Will.

18.9 PORTUGUESE TAX RESIDENCE

An individual is generally regarded as resident in Portugal for tax purposes if:

i)   They are present in Portugal for 183 days or more in the year,

ii)   They visit the country for any period during the year and have a place of abode in Portugal at 31st December which they intend to occupy as their permanent residence, or

iii)   They visit the country for any period during the year and their centre of economic interests is in Portugal.

Portuguese residents pay Income Tax at rates between 10.5% and 42% depending on the level of their income, with the top rate applying to income over €61,260 in 2007.

18.10 COMPANIES IN PORTUGAL

Corporation Tax is levied at a standard rate of 25% on Portuguese resident companies. Local municipal surcharges of up to 2.5% may also apply.

A Portuguese resident company will pay Corporation Tax on net rental profits meaning that tax relief can be obtained for mortgage interest and other expenses for which relief is denied for a non-resident individual.

Capital gains realised by Portuguese resident companies are taxed at the company's usual Corporation Tax rate. Half of the capital gain arising on the sale of property held by a Portuguese resident company for more than a year may be exempt if the sale proceeds are reinvested in new property.

A 16% Transfer Tax applies to transfers of Portuguese properties by some non-resident companies resident in 'tax havens'.

18.11 MADEIRA AND THE AZORES

The island territories of Madeira and the Azores form part of Portugal.

A lower rate of IVA applies in Madeira and the Azores. This lower rate will apply to new property construction and holiday letting income in these territories.

Unlike the rest of Portugal, trusts are recognised in Madeira.

Companies based in Madeira or the Azores may benefit from a reduced rate of Corporation Tax between 17.5% and 22.5%.

Chapter 19

Cyprus

19.1 A DIVIDED ISLAND

When buying property in Cyprus it is very important to ensure that you know what country you are investing in. This is because, politically speaking, there is not one Cyprus but two!

Since 1974, the island has been divided into the Republic of Cyprus in the South and the Turkish Republic of Northern Cyprus in the North.

The South is a member of the EU, the United Nations and the British Commonwealth. The North is not generally recognised by the international community, with only Turkey recognising it as a sovereign state.

So, before you snap up that fabulous deal in Famagusta, make sure you know which side of the line your investment is on!

My last word of warning about the North of Cyprus is to watch out which kind of property title you are buying. There are both Greek and Turkish property titles in Northern Cyprus so you could easily find that someone else already owns your property!

For the rest of this chapter, we will concentrate purely on the South of the island: the Republic of Cyprus, which we will refer to simply as 'Cyprus'.

19.2 THE CYPRIOT LEGAL AND TAX REGIME

Cyprus was under British rule before obtaining independence in 1960, so the legal system is still based largely on the English legal system and will be quite familiar to most UK resident investors.

Non-Cypriot residents may purchase one property in Cyprus or a piece of land of up to 4,012 square metres in area. This law is under review but no firm proposals for change have yet emerged. Until then, any investor wishing to acquire two or more properties in Cyprus will need to use a company incorporated in Cyprus.

Foreign nationals also need to seek approval from the Council of Ministers to buy Cypriot property.

On 1st January 2008, Cyprus adopted the Euro as its currency in place of the Cyprus Pound. The conversion factor used was one Euro to 0.585274 Cyprus Pounds. The various tax bands and allowances quoted in this chapter have been calculated using this conversion factor.

The tax year in Cyprus is the calendar year.

The country has one of the lowest levels of taxation in Europe and the standard rate of Corporation Tax is the lowest in the EU.

Cyprus recognises trusts and Cyprus International Trusts are, in fact, a recognised international tax planning device. These trusts are, however, designed to assist investors with property outside Cyprus.

19.3 TAXES ON PROPERTY PURCHASES IN CYPRUS

Stamp Duty is charged at 0.15% on first €170,860 and 0.2% thereafter.

Property Transfer Fees are also payable when the purchaser receives the title deeds. The rates applying are:

Property Price			Fee	Cumulative Fee
Up	to	€ 85,430	3%	€ 2,563
€ 85,430	to	€ 170,860	5%	€ 6,834
Over		€ 170,860	8%	n/a

Fees are charged at the above rates on the amounts falling within the relevant bands. The 'Cumulative Fee' represents the total amount payable on a property purchased for the price at the top of the relevant band.

Property Transfer Fees are calculated on an individual basis so savings can be made by buying property jointly.

Example

Ann is buying a house in Limassol for €300,000. The Property Transfer Fees on her purchase will therefore be as follows:

First €170,860, as per table above: €6,834
Remaining €129,140 (€300,000 - €170,860) at 8%: €10,331

Total Fees: €17,165

Later, however, Ann and her husband Deryck decide to buy the property jointly. Each of them is therefore treated as making a purchase for just €150,000 and each person's Property Transfer Fees will therefore be as follows:

First €85,430 at 3%: €2,563
Remaining €64,570 (€150,000 - €85,430) at 5%: €3,228

Total Fees (each): €5,791

Taken together, the couple will thus incur total Property Transfer Fees of €11,582 (2 x €5,791), thus providing a saving of €5,583 compared with the Fees which Ann would pay if she bought the property in her sole name.

Typically, it takes around two years after completion for a buyer to receive their title deeds. It is quite legitimate to sell the property on during this period, thus avoiding any Property Transfer Fees.

New property is subject to VAT at 15% unless the application for planning permission for the construction was filed before 1st May 2004. A reduced rate of 5% applies to first-time buyers.

A mortgage registration fee of approximately 1% of the value of the loan will also apply where property is purchased subject to a mortgage.

19.4 ANNUAL CHARGES

Real Estate Tax is an annual municipal tax based on the hypothetical market value of properties in Cyprus on 1st January

1980. The property is valued at 1980 rates (even if it had not been built at that time) and the tax is charged at the following rates:

Taxable Value			Rate	Cumulative Tax
Up	to	€ 170,860	Nil	€ 0
€ 170,860	to	€ 427,150	0.25%	€ 641
€ 427,150	to	€ 854,301	0.35%	€ 2,136
Over		€ 854,301	0.40%	n/a

The tax is charged at the above rates on the amounts falling within the relevant bands. For example, in the case of a property with a 1980 value of €200,000, the tax is just 0.25% of €29,140 (€200,000 - €170,860), or €73. The 'Cumulative Tax' column indicates the tax payable on a property with a value at the top of each band.

Taking almost thirty years' worth of inflation into account, it seems likely that most property will not attract any Real Estate Tax.

Further annual local authority taxes ranging from 0.1% to 0.5% will generally also apply.

19.5 RENTAL INCOME

Non-Cypriot residents are subject to Cypriot Income Tax on rental income from properties in Cyprus.

Rental income is subject to a flat rate deduction of 20%. Interest paid on borrowings to purchase letting property is also deductible.

Any remaining balance is taxed at the general Cypriot Income Tax rates which are as follows:

Income			Rate	Cumulative Tax
Up	to	€ 17,086	0%	€ 0
€ 17,086	to	€ 25,629	20%	€ 1,709
€ 25,629	to	€ 34,172	25%	€ 3,844
Over		€ 34,172	30%	n/a

Example

Stylianou receives rental income of €50,000 from a villa in Paphos, on which he pays mortgage interest of €12,000.

Stylianou is entitled to deduct 20% from his gross rental income, leaving €40,000, from which he can also deduct his mortgage interest of €12,000. The remaining sum of €28,000 is then taxed as follows:

First €25,629, as per table:	*€1,709*
Remaining €2,371 (€28,000 - €25,629) at 25%:	*€1,593*
Total Income Tax due:	*€3,302*

Rental losses on property in Cyprus can be carried forward indefinitely for set off against future rental income in Cyprus.

Furnished holiday lettings in Cyprus are subject to VAT at the standard rate of 15%. Owners must register for VAT if their gross annual rental income exceeds €15,377.

19.6 CAPITAL GAINS ON PROPERTY IN CYPRUS

Cyprus does not charge Capital Gains Tax on all capital gains but does charge it on immoveable property (i.e. land and buildings) in Cyprus. This extends to capital gains on shares in companies which hold property in Cyprus.

The Capital Gains Tax rate is 20% and relief is provided for inflation. The first €17,086 of capital gain is exempt. This is a lifetime exemption which may be used only once.

A further lifetime exemption of €85,340 is available against capital gains on properties occupied as the owner's main residence for a period of at least five years prior to sale.

The total cumulative lifetime exemption available to any individual is limited to a maximum of €85,340.

Gains accruing prior to 1st January 1980 are exempt and this is achieved by substituting the property's value at that date in place of its cost in the capital gains calculation.

Capital losses may be carried forward indefinitely for set off against future capital gains.

19.7 INHERITANCE AND GIFTS

Inheritance Tax was abolished in Cyprus on 1st January 2000.

Property Transfer Fees apply to lifetime gifts of property between family members at the following rates:

Parents to Children:	4%
Between Spouses:	8%
Other relatives:	8%

However, the value of the property used for this purpose is the title deed value which is based on values in 1920.

19.8 TAX RESIDENCE IN CYPRUS

An individual is regarded as resident in Cyprus for tax purposes if they spend 183 or more days in the country during the year.

Cyprus tax residents are subject to Cypriot taxes on their worldwide income and capital gains.

Residents must also pay an additional 'Defence Contribution', which is levied at varying percentages on different types of income. In the case of rental income, the tax is charged at the rate of 3% after a statutory deduction of 25%.

Cypriot residents are exempt from tax on the first €3,417 per annum of overseas pension income and may elect to be taxed at a special rate of 5% on any excess.

19.9 COMPANIES IN CYPRUS

The standard Corporation Tax rate in Cyprus is just 10%, which, along with Bulgaria, is the lowest in the EU. Cypriot Corporation Tax is payable by any company which is registered in Cyprus or whose management and control is exercised in Cyprus.

Companies pay tax on capital gains at the same 20% rate as individuals.

Dividends

There is no Income Tax charge on dividends in Cyprus but Cypriot residents are subject to the Defence Contribution on dividend income at the rate of 15%. Where it applies, the tax is withheld at source.

Chapter 20

Bulgaria

20.1 NEW KID ON THE BLOCK

Along with its neighbour Romania, Bulgaria is the newest member of the EU, having joined on 1st January 2007.

As with all new EU members, the country inevitably has to undergo a period of transition, as its laws are aligned with the requirements of European law.

Investors buying property in Bulgaria may not yet enjoy the full protection of European law, therefore, as it is usual for the European Court of Justice to allow new member states a 'grace period' before expecting them to be fully compliant.

Nevertheless, as Bulgaria takes its place in the European community, its attraction as a destination for UK property buyers is steadily growing.

Bulgaria became a democracy in 1990 and has since joined both NATO and the EU. It has a respectable economic growth rate and property prices are now seeing rapid growth as investors from the UK and other EU countries bring extra money into the market.

Nevertheless, there is still some 'catching up' to do and prices remain considerably lower than in other EU countries.

The unit of currency in Bulgaria is the Lev (лв). The exchange rate at 31st December 2007 was 2.66519 Levs to the UK pound.

20.2 THE BULGARIAN TAX AND LEGAL REGIME

Non-Bulgarian nationals may buy buildings, leasehold property or construction rights in Bulgaria but may not usually buy land personally.

Buying an apartment is therefore straightforward enough, but buying freehold property in Bulgaria is rather more complex.

A popular solution to this problem is to use a Bulgarian registered company to buy the property. This is best done through a Bulgarian lawyer and costs around £500 to set up. The company must have a minimum share capital of at least 5,000 Levs and this must be deposited in a company bank account in Bulgaria.

There will be further ongoing costs to run the company which will need to continue to be administered locally.

Given some of the complexities involved in using a company, it is worth remembering that you only need the Bulgarian company to buy the land. You can still buy the buildings personally.

The taxation of Bulgarian companies is covered in Section 20.10.

Prior permission from the Ministry of Finance may sometimes be required before non-Bulgarian nationals can buy property.

The Bulgarian government guarantees full repatriation of a non-Bulgarian investor's property profits. A certificate proving payment of all Bulgarian taxes due must first be presented to the bank making the funds transfer however.

Following the country's accession to the EU on 1st January 2007, it is anticipated that the constitution will soon be changed to allow foreign investors to buy land in Bulgaria but the necessary changes may not come into force until as late as 2014. In the meantime, nationals of other EU countries who take up permanent residence in Bulgaria are permitted to own land.

It is important to be aware that mortgages on Bulgarian property are not personal liabilities but transfer with the property.

The Bulgarian tax year is the calendar year.

Non-Bulgarian residents must obtain a Bulgarian tax identification number within seven days of purchasing a Bulgarian property. This number is also required to open a Bulgarian bank account.

Bulgaria is another country where under-declarations of property prices are common. This can lead to additional tax on the property's disposal. Furthermore, this practice may not be legal, so local advice is essential.

20.3 TAXES ON PROPERTY PURCHASES IN BULGARIA

A Transfer Tax similar to Stamp Duty is payable on the purchase of Bulgarian property at the rate of 2% of the declared purchase price. This is paid to the local authority in the area where the property is located.

National Registration Tax at 0.1% is also payable.

VAT at 20% is due on the purchase of new property under five years old.

Total purchase costs, including notary fees, agent's commission and all taxes can amount to more than 25% of the purchase price.

20.4 ANNUAL CHARGES

An annual Real Estate Tax of 0.15% of the property's official value is payable.

Local Municipal Tax is also payable at rates varying from around 0.2% to 0.8%.

20.5 RENTAL INCOME

Non-Bulgarian residents are generally subject to Withholding Tax at a flat rate of 10% on gross Bulgarian rental income with no deduction for expenses.

The rental of property for residential use is generally exempt from VAT. Commercial property rentals may be subject to VAT at 20% if annual rental income exceeds the VAT registration threshold of 50,000 Levs.

Accommodation provided as part of a tour package may be subject to VAT at the reduced rate of 7%.

20.6 CAPITAL GAINS ON BULGARIAN PROPERTY

EU citizens are exempt from tax on any capital gain when they sell only one Bulgarian property in the year, or no more than two properties which have both been held for at least five years.

As a result, UK residents should generally be exempt from local tax on capital gains on sales of Bulgarian property provided that they time their disposals carefully.

Property used as the owner's main residence for at least three years prior to sale is also exempt.

Where a property is purchased from a non-Bulgarian resident vendor, the purchaser is required to withhold 10% of the sale price and pay it over to the authorities. The vendor will then need to reclaim the excess tax paid. The authorities will, however, retain any monies relating to other unpaid taxes.

Any taxable capital gain which does arise is treated as additional income and taxed at 10%, (i.e. the same rate as the rental income from the property).

The taxable gain is based on the purchase price originally declared for tax purposes.

Relief for inflation is given by adjusting the purchase price in the capital gain calculation.

A flat deduction of 10% of the gain is given in respect of allowable expenses.

Relief is not generally available for capital losses.

20.7 INHERITANCE AND GIFTS

Bulgarian Inheritance Tax applies to Bulgarian property owned by non-Bulgarian residents. Where the tax is payable, the liability falls on the beneficiary.

In 2005, Bulgaria abolished Inheritance Tax for transfers arising on death to spouses, children and other direct descendants.

Inheritance Tax still applies, however, to other transfers on death in excess of 250,000 Levs in value in total. The rate applying is 0.7% for transfers to siblings, nephews and nieces and 5% in all other cases.

Lifetime gifts of property to spouses, children, other direct descendants and parents are also exempt from tax.

A Donation Tax applies to other lifetime gifts. The rate applying is again 0.7% for gifts to siblings, nephews and nieces and 5% in all other cases.

20.8 SUCCESSION LAW

Non-Bulgarian nationals are subject to Bulgaria's 'forced heirship' rules in respect of property located in Bulgaria. Unlike some other countries, it appears that these rules cannot be avoided by holding property through an offshore company or other entity.

Married couples are deemed to jointly own all property acquired during the marriage, regardless of whose name it is held in. Hence, when one member of the couple dies, half of the assets of the marriage located in Bulgaria will fall into the deceased's estate for the purposes of Bulgarian inheritance law, including a half share in any Bulgarian property held in the name of the surviving spouse (unless they held it before marriage).

The forced heirship rules apply to a reserved proportion of the deceased's Bulgarian estate. The size of that proportion depends on the exact circumstances. Remember, however, that half of the assets of the marriage will already be deemed to belong to a surviving spouse.

The reserved proportion is dealt with as follows:

- Where the deceased leaves a surviving spouse and children, the spouse is entitled to half of the reserved proportion and the children share the other half equally. The size of the reserved proportion depends on the number of children, as follows:
  - One child: two thirds
  - Two children: three quarters
  - Three or more children: five sixths

- Where the deceased leaves children or other descendants but no surviving spouse, the reserved proportion is shared equally between the descendants, as follows:
  - One descendant: half
  - Two or more descendants: two thirds

- Where the deceased leaves a surviving spouse but no descendants, the spouse is entitled to a reserved proportion of half of the estate, but this is reduced to a third if the deceased has surviving parents, who are then also entitled to a third of the estate.

- Surviving parents of the deceased are also entitled to a reserved proportion of one third where there is no surviving spouse or descendants.

Additional claims may sometimes be made by individuals who lived with and cared for the deceased or who contributed to the value of the deceased's estate.

As things stand, these complex rules would appear to be simply unavoidable in respect of Bulgarian property.

The remaining 'free estate' which does not fall within the reserved proportion as set out above can be dealt with as the deceased wishes under the terms of their Will.

If the deceased dies intestate (without a valid Will), the Bulgarian laws of intestacy will apply to any property held in Bulgaria. These rules are even more complex but, broadly speaking, apply similar rules to those set out above to the deceased's entire Bulgarian estate rather than just a reserved proportion.

In the absence of any other heirs, the deceased's property may pass to the state, so it is a good idea to write a Will which is accepted as legally valid in Bulgaria.

20.9 BULGARIAN TAX RESIDENCE

An individual is considered resident in Bulgaria for tax purposes if they spend 183 or more days in the country in a year.

An individual may also be Bulgarian tax resident if their main residence is in Bulgaria or if their 'centre of vital interests' (family, business, etc) is in Bulgaria.

On 1ˢᵗ January 2008, Bulgaria underwent a major tax reform and Bulgarian residents now pay Income Tax on their worldwide income and capital gains at a single flat rate of 10%, except for business income which is taxed at 15%.

It is not clear which of the two new rates will apply to rental income received by Bulgarian residents and this may also depend on the nature of the property being rented (e.g. furnished holiday lettings are likely to be regarded as a business).

Previously, the country had a system of progressive Income Tax rates ranging from 20% to 24% with an exemption on the first 2,400 Levs.

20.10 COMPANIES INVESTING IN BULGARIAN PROPERTY

Bulgarian companies receiving rental income from property in Bulgaria are subject to tax on gross rents less various tax-deductible property expenses including:

- Repairs and maintenance
- Management charges
- Renovation costs
- Local taxes
- Interest on loans used to acquire the property (but see Section 20.11)

Statutory depreciation at the rate of 4% per annum on buildings (not land) may also be deductible but not in the case of an investment property. This deduction may be available, however, where the property is used for furnished holiday lettings.

Further statutory depreciation at the rate of 15% may be available on the cost of furniture.

A Municipal Tax at the rate of 10% is payable on the rental profit derived as above. This Municipal Tax then forms a deductible expense when calculating the company's Corporation Tax bill.

The standard rate of Corporation Tax in Bulgaria was reduced from 15% to 10% on 1st January 2007. The overall effective tax rate on rental profits received by a Bulgarian company is thus now 19% (Municipal Tax at 10% plus Corporation Tax at 10% on the remaining 90%).

Capital gains received by a Bulgarian company are treated as additional income and taxed in the same way as outlined above.

Losses may be carried forward for set off against future profits arising within the next five years.

Non-Bulgarian companies will be subject to the same tax regime as a Bulgarian company if they are considered to be carrying on a business in Bulgaria.

Otherwise, a non-Bulgarian company is taxed on Bulgarian rental income and capital gains at the same rates as a non-Bulgarian resident individual (see Sections 20.5 and 20.6 respectively).

Bulgarian companies are required to deduct Withholding Tax at 5% from dividends (reduced from 7% with effect from 1st January 2008).

There is no benefit in kind charge in Bulgaria for any private use of a holiday home owned through a Bulgarian company.

20.11 FINANCING A BULGARIAN COMPANY

Any loan from a non-Bulgarian resident individual or company to a Bulgarian company must be registered with the Bulgarian National Bank. This would apply, for example, if a UK resident individual set up a Bulgarian company to buy property in Bulgaria and lent the purchase monies to the company.

If the amount of the loan to the Bulgarian company exceeds the amount of the company's share capital, limitations may apply to how much of the loan interest the company may deduct for Corporation Tax purposes.

Interest payments made by a Bulgarian company are also subject to Withholding Tax at 10%.

If the loan is not denominated in Bulgarian Levs, it must be revalued at the end of each month. The exchange differences arising are treated as taxable income or deductible expenses, as appropriate. No revaluation is required in the month of the loan's repayment.

Chapter 21

Dubai

21.1 EASTERN PROMISE

Dubai is one of the most popular destinations outside Europe for UK nationals investing in foreign property.

Dubai is not strictly a country as such but is one of the seven autonomous states of the United Arab Emirates (UAE).

The UAE itself is also a member of the Gulf Co-operation Council (GCC) along with Bahrain, Kuwait, Oman, Qatar and Saudi Arabia. GCC nationals are generally afforded the same rights in the UAE as UAE nationals, including the property rights covered in Section 21.2 below.

The unit of currency in the UAE is the dirham (AED). The exchange rate at 31st December 2007 was 7.33852 dirhams to the UK pound.

Country or not, Dubai has undergone a phenomenal amount of development in recent years and a significant proportion of this development has ended up in the hands of foreign investors.

Dubai is a land of extraordinary contrast: 80% of its land area comprises uninhabited desert but the city of Dubai is bristling with fabulous new developments.

These developments present a very different kind of investment to a Spanish villa or a French farmhouse.

Modern Dubai is certainly a land of opportunity but the phrase 'buyer beware' has seldom been more apt. Before rushing in to this 'land of dreams' remember that this is an Islamic country ruled by a hereditary monarchy which declined to join the British Commonwealth when it gained its independence in 1971.

21.2 DUBAI PROPERTY LAW

Dubai recognises several different forms of property title. In addition to freeholds, Dubai recognises long leases of up to 99 years duration, rights of usufruct and rights of musataha. The right of usufruct is very similar to a lease and gives the holder the right to use a property.

The right of musataha is the right to use and exploit land and includes the right to build on that land. This right is often granted through a 'Ground Development Lease'.

Each building is covered by one single title deed so that apartments within a larger building are subject to a contractual commonhold title only.

It has only been since 2002 that non-UAE nationals have been allowed to purchase freehold property in specially selected areas in Dubai.

Furthermore, it took another four years before the law governing the ownership of freehold property was finally enacted. Even now, there is still a major technical problem with this law.

Under the Dubai Property Law of 2006, non-UAE nationals are allowed to own freehold property, long leases and other rights in property in 23 'designated areas' of Dubai. The law stated that the designated areas would be shown on the maps attached to the published regulations.

Unfortunately, however, when the regulations were published, no maps were attached!

The regulations do still specify the 23 designated areas by their plot numbers but this still leaves a great deal of room for some very expensive errors!

Subject to these concerns, foreign individuals and companies should now be able to purchase freehold property or other property rights in the designated areas set out in the Dubai Property Law.

Leases granted to non-UAE nationals outside the designated areas are 'unregistered leases'. These leases still have legal validity in

Dubai but are regarded as a personal contractual right rather than a property title. In practice, this should make little difference but legal advice is called for.

Any freehold title outside the designated areas which is purported to be owned by a foreigner is, however, void. This includes any arrangements where foreigners attempt to acquire freehold property through a UAE national nominee.

Private companies with foreign shareholders are considered to be foreign companies even if registered in Dubai. Hence, unlike many other countries, it is not possible for foreign investors to use a Dubai registered company to bypass Dubai property law.

In summary, therefore, the best way for a non-UAE national to acquire any property outside the areas set aside for foreign investment under the Dubai Property Law is to take a long lease. Although such a lease would be unregistered, it would still carry contractual rights which, to all intents and purposes, are as good as ownership (for 99 years anyway).

Many changes have been made to the Property Register in Dubai as a result of the provisions of the Dubai Property Law of 2006. It would therefore be sensible for existing owners of property in Dubai to check their title with the Register.

Escalating rent increases led to the introduction of statutory rent control in Dubai in 2005. Rent increases are now capped at 7% per annum.

In general terms, Dubai's property laws are very new and the infrastructure required to implement and enforce those laws is still evolving. Anyone investing in Dubai will need local advice to help them keep abreast of the changes.

21.3 TAXATION IN DUBAI

Many people regard Dubai as being 'tax-free'. This is not strictly accurate as Dubai does have some taxes, albeit quite small.

A Registration Tax of 1.5% of the purchase price is payable to the Dubai Land Department when a property purchase is registered. A 10 dirham 'Knowledge Fee' is added to this (about £1.50).

The Dubai Land Department will increase the Registration Tax to the appropriate level if it feels that a property has been undervalued for any reason.

Where property is purchased subject to a mortgage, a further charge of 0.25% of the value of the loan up to a limit of 1.5m dirhams (i.e. a maximum fee of 3,750 dirhams) is also payable.

Developers in Dubai may charge a transfer fee of anywhere between 1% and 7% of the purchase price. This is the fee to register the transfer in the developer's own records. In truth, this is actually just an additional charge by the developer but it is dressed up to look like a tax.

An annual Residential Tax of 5% of a property's rental value is payable by the occupier.

A similar 5% tax also applies to 'hotel services' and might therefore extend to furnished holiday lettings in some cases.

The Dubai Land Department will charge another fee of 0.5% when a property is sold.

The country's 'tax-free' reputation is not entirely undeserved, however, as there is no Income Tax on rental income, no Capital Gains Tax and no Inheritance Tax. Furthermore, most companies do not pay any Corporation Tax if operating within one of the 'Free Zones' (see Section 21.7).

21.4 LAND DEPARTMENT FEES

In addition to the main fees on purchase and sale already detailed in the previous section, the Dubai Land Department also charges fees for many other services, including:

- Valuations (up to 15,000 dirhams)
- Issuing title deeds (up to 5,000 dirhams)
- Public auctions (1% of auction value up to a maximum of 30,000 dirhams)

A 'mustaha' (see Section 21.2) must also be registered for a fee of 1% of the contract value. The transfer of a 'mustaha' incurs a fee of 0.25% of the debt up to a limit of 1.5m dirhams.

Conversion of a long leasehold to a freehold (where permitted – see Section 21.2) is subject to a fee of 1.75% of the contract price.

Fees are also payable to the Dubai Land Department whenever you want to do just about anything with land in Dubai and most things seem to need to be registered. Local advice is essential here.

21.5 INHERITANCE, GIFTS AND OTHER TRANSFERS

Dubai has no Inheritance Tax but the recipient of inherited or gifted property must register their title with the Dubai Land Department, for which there is a registration fee of 0.125% of the property's value.

In the case of lifetime gifts, the transferor will also have to pay an additional fee of 1%.

Separating or dividing land titles gives rise to a fee of 1% of the value of the separated or divided share.

21.6 SUCCESSION LAW

Property in Dubai held by UAE nationals is subject to Sharia'h law and hence, on the owner's death, must pass to their surviving spouse and children in pre-determined proportions.

However, under a new Federal law brought into force throughout the UAE in late 2005, it appears that property held by non-UAE nationals can be passed according to the laws of their own country. For UK nationals, this generally means being free to dispose of any property in Dubai under the terms of your Will (see Section 13.4).

Unfortunately, the new Federal law is not entirely clear but it is believed that the Dubai Land Department does support the view that foreigners may dispose of their property under the laws of their own country.

The risk that Sharia'h law might apply, however, is greatly increased if the owner should die intestate (without a valid Will).

21.7 FREE ZONES

Further economic incentives apply in Dubai's 'free zones', including the Jebel Ali Free Zone and the Dubai International Financial Centre.

The special status of these zones is principally aimed at businesses investing in Dubai. The benefits available in the free zones are not always permanent. The special treatment afforded to investors in the Jebel Ali zone is given for an initial period of 15 years, with a further 15 year extension sometimes being available on application.

Appendix A

Top 20 Destination Countries: Quick Guide

Country	DTA (1)	Political (2)	Currency (3)	Exch Rate (4)
France	ICG/IHT	EU/NATO	Euro	1.475
Spain	ICG	EU/NATO	Euro	1.475
Bulgaria	ICG	EU/NATO	Lev	2.90279
USA	ICG/IHT	NATO	Dollar	1.8932
Italy	ICG/IHT	EU/NATO	Euro	1.475
Ireland	ICG/IHT	EU	Euro	1.475
Cyprus (5)	ICG	EU/CW	Pound	0.8508
Portugal	ICG	EU/NATO	Euro	1.475
Australia	ICG	CW	Dollar	2.4739
Turkey	ICG	NATO	Lira	2.7546
Dubai	None	-	Dirham	6.9571
Canada	ICG	CW/NATO	Dollar	2.1567
New Zealand	ICG	CW	Dollar	2.8853
South Africa	ICG/IHT	CW	Rand	13.341
Germany	ICG	EU/NATO	Euro	1.475
Greece	ICG	EU/NATO	Euro	1.475
Romania	ICG	EU/NATO	Leu	5.1239
Morocco	ICG	-	Dirham	16.3655
Croatia	ICG	-	Kuna	10.82698
India	ICG/IHT	CW	Rupee	85.6028

Notes

1. The 'DTA' column indicates whether country has a Double Taxation Agreement with the UK. 'ICG' denotes agreements covering income and capital gains and 'IHT' denotes agreements covering Inheritance Tax.
2. The 'Political' column indicates members of the European Union, 'EU', Commonwealth countries, 'CW', and NATO allies.
3. The country's official currency is listed here. In some cases, however, the US Dollar or the Euro have effectively become an unofficial currency and may be used for many property and other transactions.
4. The 'Exch Rate' column provides the average exchange rate for the year ended 31st March 2007.
5. Cyprus converted to the Euro on 1 January 2008.

Appendix B

UK Tax Rates and Allowances: 2006/2007 to 2008/2009

	Rates	Bands, allowances, etc.		
		2006/2007	2007/2008	2008/2009
		£	£	£
Income Tax				
Personal allowance		5,035	5,225	5,435
Starting rate band	10%	2,150	2,230	n/a (3)
Basic rate band (2)	20%	31,150	32,370	35,700(1)
Higher rate:	40%			
Normal higher rate threshold:		38,335	39,825	41,135(1)
National Insurance Contributions				
Class 1 – Primary	11%	) On earnings between earnings threshold and		
Class 4	8%	) upper earnings limit.		
Earnings threshold		5,035	5,225	5,435
Upper earnings limit		33,540	34,840	40,040
Class 1 – Secondary	12.8%	- On earnings above earnings threshold.		
Class 1 & Class 4	1%	- On earnings above upper earnings limit.		
Class 2 – per week		2.10	2.20	2.30
Small earnings exception		4,465	4,635	4,825
Class 3 – per week		7.55	7.80	8.10
Pension Contributions				
Annual allowance		215,000	225,000	235,000
Lifetime allowance		1.5M	1.6M	1.65M
Capital Gains Tax				
Annual exemption:				
Individuals		8,800	9,200	9,500 (1)
Trusts		4,400	4,600	4,750 (1)
Inheritance Tax				
Nil Rate Band		285,000	300,000	312,000
Annual Exemption		3,000	3,000	3,000
Pensioners, etc.				
Age allowance: 65-74		7,280	7,550	9,030
Age allowance: 75 and over		7,420	7,690	9,180
MCA: born before 6/4/1935		6,065	6,285	6,535
MCA: 75 and over		6,135	6,365	6,625
MCA minimum (4)		2,350	2,440	2,540
Income limit		20,100	20,900	21,800
Blind Person's Allowance		1,660	1,730	1,800

Notes

1. Estimated on the basis of an assumed inflationary increase of 3%.
2. Basic rate Income Tax on income other than interest, dividends and other savings income is 22% until 5 April 2008. The rate applying to dividends will remain 10% (see Section 10.10).
3. From 6 April 2008, the starting rate band will only apply to interest and other savings income.
4. The Married Couples Allowance, 'MCA', is given at a rate of 10%.

The European Union &
The European Economic Area

The European Union

The 27 member states of the European Union are:

Austria	admitted 1ˢᵗ January 1995
Belgium	founding member
Bulgaria	admitted 1ˢᵗ January 2007
Cyprus	admitted 1ˢᵗ May 2004
Czech Republic	admitted 1ˢᵗ May 2004
Denmark	admitted 1ˢᵗ January 1973
Estonia	admitted 1ˢᵗ May 2004
Finland	admitted 1ˢᵗ January 1995
France	founding member
Germany	founding member
Greece	admitted 1ˢᵗ January 1981
Hungary	admitted 1ˢᵗ May 2004
Irish Republic	admitted 1ˢᵗ January 1973
Italy	founding member
Latvia	admitted 1ˢᵗ May 2004
Lithuania	admitted 1ˢᵗ May 2004
Luxembourg	founding member
Malta	admitted 1ˢᵗ May 2004
Netherlands	founding member
Poland	admitted 1ˢᵗ May 2004
Portugal	admitted 1ˢᵗ January 1986
Romania	admitted 1ˢᵗ January 2007
Slovakia	admitted 1ˢᵗ May 2004
Slovenia	admitted 1ˢᵗ May 2004
Spain	admitted 1ˢᵗ January 1986
Sweden	admitted 1ˢᵗ January 1995
United Kingdom	admitted 1ˢᵗ January 1973

Any rights which citizens of countries admitted on 1ˢᵗ May 2004 or 1ˢᵗ January 2007 have under UK tax law commence on the date that their country was admitted to membership.

The European Economic Area comprises the 27 member states of the European Union plus:
    Iceland
    Liechtenstein
    Norway

Tax Return Supplements

Supplement	Download Document
Employment	www.hmrc.gov.uk/forms/sa101.pdf
Self-Employment	www.hmrc.gov.uk/forms/sa103.pdf
Partnership	www.hmrc.gov.uk/forms/sa104.pdf
Land & Property	www.hmrc.gov.uk/forms/sa105.pdf
Foreign	www.hmrc.gov.uk/forms/sa106.pdf
Trust Income	www.hmrc.gov.uk/forms/sa107.pdf
Capital Gains	www.hmrc.gov.uk/forms/sa108.pdf
Non-Residence	www.hmrc.gov.uk/forms/sa109.pdf

Alternatively, forms may also be obtained by calling the Revenue & Customs orderline: 0845 9000 404.

Specialist Tax Offices

Where relevant, forms P85 or DOM 1 should be sent to:

Revenue & Customs
Financial Intermediaries and Claims Office*
St John's House
Merton Road
Bootle
Merseyside
England
L69 9BB

(Tel: +44 151 472 6196)

* Also known as 'FICO'

Pay Less Tax!

...with help from Taxcafe's unique tax guides and software

How to Avoid Property Tax
By Carl Bayley BSc ACA

How to Avoid Property Tax is widely regarded as *the* tax bible for property investors. This unique and bestselling guide is jam packed with ideas that will save you thousands in income tax and capital gains tax.

"A valuable guide to the tax issues facing buy-to-let investors" - *THE INDEPENDENT*

Using a Property Company to Save Tax
By Carl Bayley

Currently a 'hot topic' for the serious property investor, this guide shows how you can significantly boost your after-tax returns by setting up your own property company and explains ALL the tax consequences of property company ownership.

"An excellent tax resource....informative and clearly written" **The Letting Update Journal**

Tax-Free Property Investments
By Nick Braun PhD

This guide shows you how to double your investment returns using a variety of powerful tax shelters. You'll discover how to buy property at a 40% discount, paid for by the taxman, never pay tax on your property profits again and invest tax free in overseas property.

Property Capital Gains Tax Calculator
By Carl Bayley

This powerful piece of software will calculate in seconds the capital gains tax payable when you sell a property and help you cut the tax bill. It provides tax planning tips based on your personal circumstances and a concise summary and detailed breakdown of all calculations.

Non-Resident & Offshore Tax Planning
By Lee Hadnum LLB ACA CTA

By becoming non-resident or moving your assets offshore it is possible to cut your tax bill to zero. This guide explains what you have to do and all the traps to avoid. Also contains detailed info on using offshore trusts and companies.

"The ultimate guide to legal tax avoidance" **Shelter Offshore**

288

The World's Best Tax Havens
By Lee Hadnum

This book provides a fascinating insight into the glamorous world of tax havens and how you can use them to cut your taxes to zero and safeguard your financial freedom.

How to Avoid Inheritance Tax
By Carl Bayley

Making sure you adequately plan for inheritance tax could save you literally hundreds of thousands of pounds. *How to Avoid Inheritance Tax* is a unique guide which will tell you all you need to know about sheltering your family's money from the taxman. This guide is essential reading for parents, grandparents and adult children.

"Useful source of Inheritance Tax information" **What Investment Magazine**

Using a Company to Save Tax
By Lee Hadnum

By running your business through a limited company you stand to save tens of thousands of pounds in tax and national insurance every year. This tax guide tells you everything you need to know about the tax benefits of incorporation.

Salary versus Dividends
By Carl Bayley

This unique guide is essential reading for anyone running their business as a limited company. After reading it, you will know the most tax efficient way in which to extract funds from your company, and save thousands in tax!

Selling Your Business
By Lee Hadnum

This guide tells you everything you need to know about paying less tax and maximizing your profits when you sell your business. It is essential reading for anyone selling a company or sole trader business.

How to Avoid Tax on Stock Market Profits
By Lee Hadnum

This tax guide can only be described as THE definitive tax-saving resource for stock market investors and traders.

Anyone who owns shares, unit trusts, ISAs, corporate bonds or other financial assets should read it as it contains a huge amount of unique tax planning information.

How to Profit from Off-Plan Property
By Alyssa and David Savage

This property investment guide tells you everything you need to know about investing in off-plan and new-build property. It contains a fascinating insight into how you can make big money from off-plan property... and avoid all the pitfalls along the way.

How to Build a £4 Million Property Portfolio:
Lifetime Lessons of a Student Landlord
By Tony Bayliss

Tony Bayliss is one of the UK's most successful student property investors. In *How to Build a £4 Million Property Portfolio* he reveals all his secrets – how he picks the best and most profitable student properties; how he markets his properties (ensuring they are rented out months in advance), and how he enjoys capital growth of 12% pa, year in year out.

Disclaimer

1. Please note that this Tax Guide is intended as general guidance only for individual readers and does NOT constitute accountancy, tax, investment or other professional advice. Neither Taxcafe UK Limited nor the author can accept any responsibility or liability for loss which may arise from reliance on information contained in this Tax Guide.

2. Please note that tax legislation, the law and practices by government and regulatory authorities (e.g. Revenue & Customs) are constantly changing. We therefore recommend that for accountancy, tax, investment or other professional advice, you consult a suitably qualified accountant, tax specialist, independent financial adviser, or other professional adviser. Please also note that your personal circumstances may vary from the general examples given in this Tax Guide and your professional adviser will be able to give specific advice based on your personal circumstances.

3. This Tax Guide covers taxation applying to UK residents only. Please note that references to the 'UK' do not include the Channel Islands or the Isle of Man. The tax position of non-UK residents is beyond the scope of this Tax Guide.

4. Whilst in an effort to be helpful, this Tax Guide may refer to general guidance on matters other than the taxation of UK residents, neither Taxcafe UK Limited nor the author are expert in these matters. Neither Taxcafe UK Limited nor the author can accept any responsibility or liability for loss which may arise from reliance on such information contained in this Tax Guide.

5. Please note that Taxcafe UK Limited has relied wholly on the expertise of the author in the preparation of the content of this Tax Guide. The author is not an employee of Taxcafe UK Limited but has been selected by Taxcafe UK Limited using reasonable care and skill to write the content of this Tax Guide.

6. All persons described in the examples in this guide are entirely fictional characters created specifically for the purposes of this guide. Any similarities to actual persons, living or dead, or to fictional characters created by any other author, are entirely coincidental.

Printed in the United Kingdom
by Lightning Source UK Ltd.
126974UK00002BA/1-9/P